PREFACE

With his four-year term as governor of Georgia rapidly drawing to a close, Jimmy Carter met with reporters at the National Press Club in Washington, D.C. and formally announced his candidacy for president of the United States. By his own assessment his gubernatorial administration had been highly controversial, aggressive, and combative. He was proud of it. In the weeks and months of hard campaigning that lay ahead, he planned to publicize his record of accomplishment in the Georgia statehouse as one means of establishing his credentials for the presidency. Indeed, he took such pride in his gubernatorial record and was so confident it could withstand even the closest scrutiny that he made his gubernatorial papers available to scholars and other interested researchers immediately upon the conclusion of his governorship.

On the last day of his term, officials at the Georgia Department of Archives and History received a phone call from Carter's office informing them that they could pick up the Governor's papers for transfer to the archives. Archives' officials immediately dispatched two staff members to take care of the matter. On arriving at the Governor's office, the archivists witnessed a confusing scene as members of Carter's office staff completed the last minute chores associated with vacating the gubernatorial office. Meanwhile, newly elected Governor George Busbee and his staff were working to organize the office to suit their purposes. When ushered into a room stacked high with sturdy cardboard boxes containing several hundred linear feet of Jimmy Carter's gubernatorial papers, the young men from the archives immediately recognized the inadequacy of the small truck they had brought with them and put in a call for a larger vehicle and more manpower. According to the terms of the agreement previously reached with the Governor, officials at the archives promised to make the papers available to the public as quickly as possible with no restrictions on access.[1]

Although the papers contained material potentially embarrassing to a presidential candidate, especially if taken out of context, Carter suffered no bad publicity from his unprecedented disclosure. Several reporters did visit the archives during the campaign, but few spent more than a few hours examining the collection. Arranged in the order in which they had been received from the Governor's office, the unprocessed papers simply proved too large and difficult to be used for the purposes of reporters facing daily deadlines. More surprisingly, none of the authors who wrote about Carter after the election used the Carter papers. Since the 1976 elections well over thirty books have appeared on Jimmy Carter, but none treats the critical period of his governorship in any depth nor shows any evidence that the authors consulted the Carter papers, the single most important source of information on their subject.[2]

More than anything else, it was the availability of those papers that led me into a study of Jimmy Carter's governorship. Yet, as so often happens, the combination of accident and circumstance had much more to do with the initiation of this project than conscious decision.

During the winter of 1977, I offered students several options for a group research project in a seminar on quantitative analysis in historical research. They ultimately chose to do a roll-call analysis of legislative voting on Carter's state government reorganization bill. The results of that analysis proved so intriguing that the following quarter students in a political history seminar continued the study, building on the quantitative analysis through a qualitative study of the politics of state government reorganization. Preparations for the seminar took me to the state archives and the Carter gubernatorial papers. It took only a few hours to recognize the unusually substantive character of the collection and the insights it offered into the political character and leadership style of Jimmy Carter. Ultimately, the unprecedented opportunity of examining the pre-presidential papers of an incumbent president proved an irresistible temptation.

I approached the research with as much objectivity as possible given the nature of the project. My family and I had arrived in Atlanta during the late summer of 1970 just as the bitter Democratic primary election contest between Jimmy Carter and former Georgia Governor Carl Sanders came to a conclusion. Although ineligible to vote, my sympathies in that election, like that of most of my academic colleagues, rested with the former governor. Sanders, however, ran a poor second in the first primary and lost the runoff election by an even larger margin. Disenfranchisement relieved me of any necessity of making a choice in the general election between Carter and his Republican opponent, Hal Suit, an attractive former television news commentator who had conducted a vigorous and generally constructive campaign.

Carter's four years in the governorship did little to gladden the hearts of state employees or, more specifically, University System personnel. Twice during a period of rampant inflation, he clamped a virtual freeze on the salaries of state employees. But for a chance coincidence, my attitude toward the Governor undoubtedly would have reflected the same general cynicism exhibited by so many of my academic colleagues, who were glad to be done with Jimmy Carter by 1975. In January 1972, the Governor's son, Chip, enrolled in my undergraduate methods and historiography class. Chip Carter divided his time during the quarter between his course work, lobbying for his father's reorganization plan on Georgia's capitol hill, and attempting (successfully) to convince his instructor to assign him an incomplete for the quarter. Several long talks with the younger Carter convinced me there was more to his father than I previously had recognized. Thereafter, I began to observe and study that aggressive and unorthodox politician more closely and, ultimately, more sympathetically.

Still, I was not yet ready to jump on the Carter bandwagon when he announced his presidential candidacy shortly before the end of his gubernatorial term. Having previously been involved in Democratic Farmer-Labor politics in Minnesota, I had acquired a favorable impression of Senator Walter Mondale, and, when he announced his candidacy, I resolved to support him. Chicken dinners, Holiday Inns, and depressingly low recognition levels in national polls, however, soon drove the Minnesota senator out of the race. Of the remaining candidates only Carter, Henry Jackson, and Morris Udall appeared to be serious contenders. A process of elimination left only Carter. Too much of the old cold war warrior still haunted Henry Jackson, and Morris Udall's too self-conscious liberalism seemed a bit contrived and, after the McGovern debacle, politically unrealistic. My enthusiasm for Carter grew appreciably when he selected Mondale as his running mate.

Thus, I approached my study of Carter's governorship with a sympathetic view of the subject but with no great personal stake in the outcome of the research. For some months after finishing classes, I walked the several blocks from the Georgia State campus to the state archives. The journey took me through the state capitol grounds and past the illustriously inscribed statues of Tom Watson, Eugene Talmadge, and Richard Russell. Gradually, I began adding lines to the inscriptions: disillusioned racist, demagogic racist, patrician racist. Increasingly, I speculated about where Carter fit into that pantheon of Georgia political heroes. While exhibiting some of the qualities and characteristics of each man, Carter differed in many other ways; most significantly, he did not share their racial views. Georgians still maintain that Richard Russell, but for his southern origins, would have been the first Georgia native to be elected president of the United States. What they obviously fail to realize—and what Jimmy Carter proved—is that it was not Russell's southern roots that disqualified him for the presidential office but his unacceptable position on the race issue. While Carter's racial liberalism most obviously separated him from his predecessors in Georgia politics, closer observation revealed other important differences. Carter not only practiced a new style of southern politics but also exhibited a mode of political leadership that transcended sectional divisions or identity.

How, then, did this unorthodox politician come to the pinnacle of political power in Georgia? Certainly, his early ambitions did not include a career in politics. An appointment to the United States Naval Academy and the pursuit of a naval career represented the earliest and only childhood ambition of the future governor. He pursued that goal with a single-minded dedication that would later mark his political career. After matriculating for a year at Georgia Southwestern College in nearby Americus, he enrolled in the naval ROTC program at the Georgia Institute of Technology before receiving the cherished appointment to Annapolis. He did well academically at the naval academy, graduating in the upper 10 percent of his 1946 graduating class. While mastering the required engineering curriculum, he also continued to pursue an earlier interest in literature, theology, philosophy, art, and music. No doubt he was as unusual a cadet as he would later be a politician.

After graduation, the newly commissioned naval officer married Rosalynn Smith, a hometown girl, and then fulfilled his required two years of surface duty before being accepted into the submarine service, where he served during the remaining five years of his naval career. For a short time during that period, he came under the much publicized influence of Admiral Hyman Rickover. By Carter's own assessment, Rickover had a profound effect upon him. It would appear, however, that the admiral's character more than the quality of his mind most impressed the young naval officer. Rickover's tenacity, self-discipline, boldness in response to challenge, and capacity for hard work so inspired Carter that he later used Rickover's response to his proud declaration that he had stood fifty-ninth in a graduating class of 820 as the title for his autobiography: Why not the best? The death of his father in 1953 ended Carter's promising naval career. He returned to Plains and began to manage family business affairs in a manner that increasingly characterized his own behavior as much as that of his former naval mentor.

The family peanut business, however, could not long contain his interest and energies, and he gradually became more involved in local community affairs and eventually regional and state activities. He served on the Sumter County Library Board, the school board, and the hospital authority board, and as state president of the Certified Seed Organization, a Lions International district governor, chairman of the district planning commission, and later president of the Georgia Planning Association, which he had helped to organize. Of those positions, his service on the Sumter County School Board had the greatest immediate impact. Confronted with all the pressures generated by the U.S. Supreme Court's 1954 segregation ruling, the school board had to cope with the explosive issue of integration. While certainly no integrationist at the time, his determination to improve educational opportunities for blacks as well as whites, and his later refusal to join a white citizens' council in resisting integration drew criticism from friends and relatives alike. Reflecting both a genuine desire to improve the quality of education and an early propensity for reorganizing existing institutions, Carter led a drive to consolidate the Sumter County and Americus school systems. Critics, including his cousin Hugh Carter, viewed the proposal as the first step in the eventual integration of local schools and rejected it at the polls. Prior to the referendum vote, Carter had vigorously campaigned throughout the county for the school merger plan. While disappointed with the outcome, Carter found his first taste of campaigning satisfying and soon announced his candidacy for the same state Senate seat his father had once held. He approached the campaign with the same hard-driving intensity he would employ in future political contests. After the ballots had been tallied, it became obvious that Carter had been counted out of the nomination by a local county political boss. With the assistance of John Pennington, an *Atlanta Journal* investigative reporter, and Charles Kirbo, a young Atlanta attorney, he successfully challenged the election returns and eventually won his seat in the Georgia Senate.[3]

During his two Senate terms, Carter devoted much of his time to educational reform. He secured the chairmanship of the standing Senate Committee on Education and from that position labored successfully to update and revise the Minimum Foundation Program for Education first inaugurated in 1949. He also served on the agriculture and appropriations committees. By the end of his first term, his colleagues already recognized him as one of the five most effective legislators in the Georgia Senate.[4]

In 1966 he decided to challenge his long-time rival, Howard "Bo" Callaway, the incumbent congressman from his Southwest Georgia district. Callaway, the first Georgia Republican elected to Congress in 100 years, had slipped into office two years earlier in the wake of Barry Goldwater's popular presidential candidacy in the area. A natural rivalry had developed between the two men. Callaway had graduated from West Point while Carter studied at Annapolis. They were both young, talented, and ambitious; and they represented rival political parties. Moreover, while serving on the State Board of Regents, Callaway had attempted to sabotage the Plains senator's effort to secure four-year status for Southwest Georgia College in Americus. When Callaway dropped out of the congressional race to run for governor, Carter, in one of the few impulsive acts of his political career, forfeited an almost sure seat in the House of Representatives to enter the gubernatorial sweepstakes. Having geared himself for a contest with Callaway, Carter was determined to have it.[5]

Although he was not well known throughout the state and had entered the race relatively late, Carter conducted a vigorous campaign and came within a few thousand votes of capturing a place in the Democratic primary runoff election. He ran moderately well among all categories of voters; but, campaigning as a moderate progressive, he proved especially attractive to college-aged youths. Hamilton Jordan, a political science major at the University of Georgia, joined the campaign organization after Carter's appearance on the Georgia campus. Another young political activist, Jody Powell, also joined the campaign, serving as the candidate's chauffeur and confidant. Meanwhile, Carter issued his "Blueprint for a Greater Georgia," an elaborate campaign platform itemizing sixty-five programs that he promised to initiate if elected.

Ellis Arnall, a former governor who captured much of the urban and liberal vote, ran first in the Democratic primary and was followed by Lester Maddox, the conservative, segregationist candidate. Maddox's unexpected victory in the Democratic primary runoff greatly enhanced Bo Callaway's candidacy, although Arnall's decision to permit his supporters to conduct a write-in campaign on his behalf during the general election qualified the Republican candidate's advantage. Ultimately, Arnall siphoned off enough anti-Maddox votes to deprive Callaway of a majority. As a consequence, under the Georgia constitution the election was thrown into the Democratic-dominated General Assembly which denied Callaway his victory and installed Lester Maddox in the governor's mansion.

Bitterly disappointed by his defeat in the primary, Carter fell into a deep depression that finally ended with his born-again religious experience. A short time later he initiated a four-year campaign for the 1970 gubernatorial nomination that took him through virtually every village and hamlet in Georgia. Carl Sanders, a popular former governor who had announced his own candidacy for the Democratic nomination, was the major obstacle to Carter's hopes. Sanders had established a solid record during his gubernatorial term and quickly became the favorite of urban and liberal voters as well as most Democratic party leaders. With the moderate left preempted, Carter pitched his campaign to the Maddox-Wallace voters to whom Sanders had little appeal. Nevertheless, Carter's platform, if any of his supporters had bothered to read it, bore a striking resemblance to the same moderately liberal reform program he had advanced four years earlier. Surprising most political forecasters, Carter ran well ahead of Sanders in the first primary. Although he failed to win the 50 percent of the vote that was needed to secure the nomination outright, he easily defeated Sanders in the runoff and then crushed his Republican opponent, Hal Suit, in the general election.

Although the new governor was not a typical southern politician, he was clearly the product of the southern culture in which he was reared. The son of a wealthy small-town landowner and businessman, he inherited a sense of noblesse oblige that was traditional among the southern elite. However, that sense of paternalism, which had its roots in the ante-bellum South, was altered and refined by the historical progression of the South from an agriculturally based, rural society toward social and economic modernity, a progression that had been retarded for many years but had accelerated by the third quarter of the twentieth century. Whether as a cadet at the naval academy, an engineer in the United States Navy, a community leader and activist, a state senator, or as governor of Georgia, Carter felt a responsibility to use the influence, resources, and talents he possessed to contribute to the improvement of the society in which he lived. Thus the idealism that Carter espoused owed little to political ideology or social theory; rather it sprang from a sense of social ethics derived from culture and tradition and fed by religious conviction and an inbred sense of history. These same sources greatly influenced the character of Carter's social vision. He had little patience with utopian visions built upon a romantic conception of the perfectibility of man and the society in which he lived. Carter's vision was more limited and practical. He evidenced more concern with reforming society as it already existed than with fundamentally reconstructing it.

In the days following the election, Carter publicized a long list of specific reforms he planned to institute during his term in office.

The most distinctive feature of the reforms he proposed was that few of them involved the expenditure of large sums of money. Instead, the reforms were designed to get greater value from funds already appropriated, or to reallocate spending for existing programs. Carter was a fiscal conservative strongly committed to a liberal social agenda. This peculiar combination of commitments became the trademark of the reform program Carter advanced. Although he did not reduce state government spending but rather increased it substantially even when measured in constant dollars, he did seek ways of fulfilling his social commitments without increasing taxes. The educational and environmental reforms he advocated were expensive, but he never hesitated to spend money on them. The effort to force government agencies to justify every dollar in their budgetary appropriation through zero-based budgeting typified his approach to fiscal management. Moreover, many of the reforms he advocated, such as judicial reform, consumer protection, tax reform, welfare reform, and, above all, the reorganization of state government, did not involve the expenditure of vast amounts of new money. Rather, they were designed to save money that could be spent more productively in other areas.

Carter's reform agenda created complex political problems. No natural constituency automatically mobilized behind the type of management reforms that Carter proposed. Coalitions of support had to be built, and public opinion had to be mobilized behind them. The type of reforms Carter advocated and the manner in which he went about building support for his programs produced much of the distinctiveness in his unorthodox style of political leadership.

Using state government reorganization as a case study, the Carter gubernatorial papers provide numerous insights into Governor Jimmy Carter's political character and legislative leadership style. Even before his inauguration, Carter had identified government reorganization as the major priority of his governorship. The proposal dominated two of the four regular General Assembly sessions during his term of office, and in his presidential campaign he emphasized the reform as an example of his administrative ability. Reorganization also provides a valuable case study because it is so typical of the type of reform that attracted him, the manner in which he developed reform programs, and the way he went about gaining legislative approval of his proposals. Finally, it holds a special attraction to the researcher because of the thorough documentation contained in the Carter papers.

This is not a study of the successes and failures of reorganization. While that is an important issue, it does not bear directly on the questions posed in this monograph. It is the politics and character of the reorganization effort and how it reflects upon Carter's political style that is of paramount concern.

The introduction surveys Governor Jimmy Carter's political character and social commitments. Chapters 1 and 2 contain a discussion of the legislative obstacles to reorganization and the manner in which the reorganization study was conducted and the plan developed. Part II consists of three chapters describing Carter's effort to build support for his program among three vital constituencies: Georgia citizens, the state bureaucracy, and the General Assembly. Part III comprises a legislative history of the reorganization bill derived from both qualitative and quantitative research techniques. In the concluding chapter Carter's often volatile legislative relations and his style of legislative leadership are described and analyzed.

It should be emphasized that this is exclusively a study of the political character and legislative style Carter exhibited while Governor of Georgia. Although obvious parallels exist between his governorship and his presidency, those parallels must be drawn by the reader. This is done with the full recognition that it is Carter's presidency that invests his activities as Governor with special historical significance.

PRELUDE
TO THE
PRESIDENCY

INTRODUCTION

THE TEMPERAMENTAL PRAGMATISM OF JIMMY CARTER

> I am a Southerner and an American. I am a farmer, an
> engineer, a father and husband, a Christian, a poli-
> tician and former governor, a planner, a businessman,
> a nuclear physicist, a naval officer, a canoeist, and
> among other things, a lover of Bob Dylan's songs and
> Dylan Thomas' poetry.
>
> Jimmy Carter, *Why Not The Best?*

"Jimmy Who?" Georgia voters first asked the question in 1966
upon learning of the gubernatorial candidacy of a relatively ob-
scure state senator from Plains. Initially something of an epithet,
the query had certain positive attributes, especially for a candidate attempting to project a down-home populist image. Moreover, it positioned Carter in the role of an underdog, a useful label
for a politician running on an antiestablishment platform. Carter
campaign managers, who had had the question imposed on them
in 1966, actively promoted it in later campaigns.

As Jimmy Carter became better known, the question gradually
changed from "Jimmy Who?" to "Jimmy What?" Despite increased name recognition and public visibility, questions concerning his stand on a variety of public issues and his position on the
liberal to conservative continuum still perplexed political observers.
Indeed, after four years in office, most Georgians, including newspaper reporters who had closely observed his administration, still
had difficulties pinning an accurate ideological label on the Governor. He not only refused to embrace but even seemed diligently
to avoid espousing either the conventional liberal or conservative

litany endorsed by so many political candidates and public office-holders.

The ambitious south Georgia politician, however, appeared unconcerned about the ambiguity surrounding his ideological convictions. Although widely read and deeply interested in broad philosophical questions, he devoted little time to speculating about the wisdom of alternative political philosophies and found no particular merit in ideological purity. When asked during the 1966 gubernatorial campaign whether he would consider himself a conservative, moderate, liberal, or middle-of-the-roader, Carter exhibited his impatience with such labeling. "I believe," he said, "I'm more complicated than that."[1] Nevertheless, when pressed by political exigencies to be more specific, he inevitably described himself as a conservative, a safe and relatively meaningless label in the context of Georgia politics, especially when used by a racial liberal.

Although, as Governor, Carter did hold remarkably conservative views in a number of important respects, he also was a populist, a business progressive, a social gospeler, a technocrat, and a modern liberal. Rather than providing some clue to his basic ideological convictions, a survey of the people with whom he associated and the personalities that influenced and impressed him only further confuses the issue. How does one come to grips with a political figure who found so much to admire in such varied figures as Admiral Hyman Rickover and Bob Dylan? Reinhold Niebuhr and Richard B. Russell? Sören Kierkegaard and Willie Nelson? And, indeed, Lillian and James Earl Carter?[2] While evidently finding in these diverse personalities traits worthy of his attention and emulation, Carter also discovered useful qualities in the variety of ideologies contending for acceptance in the American political milieu.

In retrospect, it is apparent that there existed an internal logic and coherence approaching eclecticism in Carter's process of picking and choosing from a great variety of extant ideas, concepts, and examples; yet, the process was practical rather than theoretical. Born and bred in the provincial environment of the rural South, Carter acquired a conservative outlook and an impatience with theoretical abstractions later tempered or, in some cases, nurtured by his education at the Georgia Institute of Technology and the naval academy and his experiences as a career naval officer, a small-town businessman and community activist, and a local and state elected official. Practicality and experience became the crucial determinants of Carter's eclecticism. Although these are important tenets of American pragmatism, he was no more a philosophical pragmatist than a philosophical eclecticist. His pragmatism was not the product of considered thought but rather the philosophical and psychological temperament of a vigorous and reflective mind drawing upon experience, both personal and historical, in quest of a practical understanding of contemporary society.

It is unrealistic to assume that political activists, especially those achieving some measure of success, devote much time or energy to theorizing on the higher plane of speculative thought. They are, after all, politicians and not philosophers. Nevertheless, while they are not inclined toward intellectual or philosophical introspection, they do function on the basis of a more or less rationally evolved set of principles, conceptions, and convictions, which might be termed the politicians' "political temperament."

In Jimmy Carter, more than anything else, that temperament was pragmatic. To be sure, he did not consciously employ a pragmatic train of thought nor did he practice a pragmatic style of politics. He simply tended to think like a pragmatist. He manifested that tendency in his self-perception as a realist, planner, pluralist, educator, scientist, and something of an empiricist, in his rejection of determinism and adversion to theoretical abstractions, and in his belief in a generational flow of knowledge. Above all, Carter's reliance upon observation and experience pointed to a pragmatic cast of mind. On the first page of his autobiography, Carter describes the book "as a kind of summing up of my opinions about our nation—based on my own observations and experiences."[3] This emphasis on observation and experience appears repeatedly in his writings, his speeches, and in his correspondence.[4]

Carter's pragmatic temperament greatly influenced his evolving political philosophy. None of the prevailing political philosophies fully stood the test of his practical empiricism, but he found elements in most that were worthy of consideration. As a consequence, the political character Carter exhibited and the social commitments he espoused during his governorship represented a remarkable mixture of conservative caution, progressivism, liberal idealism, and populist suspicion. Of these, Carter's conservative instincts, reinforced by religious convictions, appeared most fundamental in his philosophical make-up.[5]

In his study of American conservatism, Clinton Rossiter identifies the basic principles of the American conservative tradition. Rossiter's enumeration provides a convenient means of separating those conservative elements of Carter's political character from his more liberal convictions. Carter seems to have subscribed to precisely half of Rossiter's twenty-two conservative principles while equivocating on or rejecting the remainder. Those he generally endorsed were:

The duties of man—service, effort, obedience, cultivation of virtue, self-restraint—as the price of rights.

The indispensability and sanctity of inherited institutions, values, symbols, and rituals, that is, of tradition.

The essential role of religious feeling in man and organized religion in society.

The fallibility and limited reach of human reason.

The civilizing, disciplining, conserving mission of education.

The mystery, grandeur, and tragedy of history, man's surest guide to wisdom and virtue.

The existence of immutable principles of universal justice.

The primacy of the organic community.

Reverence, contentment, prudence, patriotism, self-discipline, the performance of duty—the marks of the good man.

Order, unity, equity, stability, continuity, security, harmony, the confinement of change—the marks of the good society.

Dignity, authority, legitimacy, justice, constitutionalism, hierarchy, the recognition of limits—the marks of a good government

Those to which Carter partially subscribed:

The desirability of diffusing and balancing power—social, economic, cultural, and especially political.

The rights of man as something earned rather than given.

The prime importance of private property for liberty, order, and progress.

Those rejected:

The mixed and immutable nature of man, in which wickedness, unreason, and the urge to violence lurk always behind the curtain of civilized behavior.

The natural inequality of men in most qualities of mind, body, and spirit.

The superiority of liberty to equality in the hierarchy of human values and social purposes.

The inevitability and necessity of social classes, and consequent folly and futility of most attempts at leveling.

The need for a ruling and serving aristocracy.

The fallibility and potential tyranny of majority rule.

The uncertainty of progress—and the related certainty that prescription, not purposeful reform, is the mainspring of such progress as a society may achieve.

The absolute necessity of conservatism—as temperament, mood, philosophy, and tradition—to the existence of civilization.[6]

A survey of those principles to which he subscribed suggests that at an immediate and personal level Carter had conservative instincts. This inclination appeared most clearly in those areas related to such personal qualities as effort, self-discipline, duty, patriotism, and self-restraint. Undoubtedly Carter's experience at the naval academy and his association with and admiration of Hyman Rickover reinforced his fundamentally conservative mentality, which in turn conditioned his view of the characteristics of a good society—order, stability, continuity, harmony—and of a good government—dignity, legitimacy, justice, recognition of limits. Yet Carter's personal conservatism did not translate into a broadly conservative social or political outlook. He rejected the conservative's pessimistic view of progress, democracy, and man and his potentialities. In this respect he exhibited the liberal's faith in man's capacity to control his own destiny and to create a more just and equitable society.

Carter's religious faith helped to meld a conservative mentality and a liberal social outlook into a practical political philosophy. Because of this, a study of the theologians who impressed and influenced Carter provides a valuable guide to the content of his political character and the nature of his social commitments. Among those theologians, none was more important than Reinhold Niebuhr. Given Carter's own cast of mind, it is not surprising that Niebuhr, who introduced a note of pragmatism and existentialism to neo-orthodox Christian theology, should have appealed to him. Indeed, William Gunter, a Carter appointee to the Georgia Supreme Court and fellow student of theological literature, described a compilation of Niebuhr's writings on politics as Carter's "political Bible."[7] Clearly, there were two dimensions to Carter's religious thought—a personal or theoretical dimension that related to his personal relationship with God and with his fellow man, and a social or applied dimension concerned more with social ethics and the continuous struggle of competing forces within society. It is the latter dimension that must be of primary interest to the student of Carter's political behavior, and it was to this dimension that Niebuhr spoke most directly.[8]

Religion, in Carter's view, served an important social function. The Bible, just as the writings of the historian or the poet, represented human experience. Moreover, education and organized religion were vital to the transmission of that wisdom to contemporary society. Human experience, especially as revealed in the Bible, helped to link Carter's conservative pessimism, grounded in man's dismal past, and his liberal optimism that man could cope with the past. It was, perhaps, in this context that he found Niebuhr's maxim that "the sad duty of politics is to establish justice in a sinful world" so appealing.[9]

Despite the fundamentalist character of his formal religious affiliation, Carter appeared uncomfortable with the concept of unquestioning faith.[10] He believed that religion represented the search for truth and that the Bible was an important instrument in that quest. Along with whatever spiritual needs it fulfilled, religion served Carter in a practical way. It provided a source of comfort, joy, understanding, hope, and, above all, the psychological security that accompanied the perception of a meaningful and rational existence.[11]

The influence of history and religion as well as his liberal optimism were reflected in Carter's response to a column by James Reston concerning the question of values and purpose in American society.

I had read Reston's column wherein he merely raises a question. There are truths and standards which never change and about which I try to talk on occasion. They arise from a restudy of the tortuous historical development of our nation—from birth through populism and the New Deal, Viet Nam, etc. and from a restudy of the Bible.

Our people are simply hungry for something finer than they have. Most of the highest ideals are, unfortunately, much more apparent in retrospect to most of us.

A quotation from Tillich sticks in my mind. "Religion is the *search* for the truth about man's existence, and his relationship with God." Maybe our search will be fruitful.[12]

History, like religion, offered information on human experience and thus contributed to human understanding. Carter's interest in history fostered his convictions concerning the unity of the past, present, and future and the obligation each generation owed succeeding generations. This, in turn, fueled an interest in reform and nurtured a commitment to the conservation of natural and human resources. Carter's devotion to history, however, also reinforced more conservative inclinations toward patriotism and a reverence for tradition, especially as represented by inherited customs, symbols, values, and institutions.

Carter exhibited his interest in history in a variety of ways. As a voracious reader, his subject matter was often historical. He had a great interest in his family background and that of the state and region in which he lived. He initiated the effort to produce a new history of Georgia which Kenneth Coleman and a group of historians at the University of Georgia brought to fruition. Carter took a personal interest in the project, encouraging the authors and urging them to avoid any tendency toward parochialism. Upon seeing an early draft of the manuscript, he expressed both pride and satisfaction with the outcome.[13] The Governor also exhibited a sensitivity to the need for developing and preserving the sources of historical inquiry. He urged staff members to write memoranda for the record and, most significantly, as already noted, made his gubernatorial papers available to scholars immediately upon the conclusion of his governorship.[14]

As the foregoing suggests, education was vital to Carter's conception of the good society. He believed educational deficiencies had retarded the economic and social development of his state and region and consequently made educational reform a major priority of his governorship. Carter's interest in education had been greatly stimulated by his service on the Sumter County School Board and by his two terms in the Georgia Senate during which he served as chairman of the Senate Education Committee. He also served on a special study commission which reviewed and updated the state's Minimum Foundation Program for Education in an effort to equalize educational opportunity. Carter's educational goals and objectives centered upon quality, equity, and accessibility.[15] He opposed a tuition increase voted by the Board of Regents of the University System and frowned upon private financing of college dormitories, believing it would increase the costs of higher education.[16] He considered his Early Childhood Development Act, which committed Georgia to the development of a state-wide kindergarten program, one of the most important accomplishments of his administration.[17] While refusing to reappoint to the state Board of Regents an influential segregationist who had served several terms, he appointed the first black Georgian to the board.[18]

The Governor's dedication to conservation ranked next to his commitment to education. He worked closely with an influential private environmentalist organization, the Georgia Conservancy, to preserve the state's natural heritage. He took a special interest in the state's rivers and streams as well as the Georgia coastline and the sea islands. Also interested in historic preservation, he established the Georgia Heritage Trust to inventory and recommend additions to the state's historical site program and closely followed its activities.[19]

In Carter's view the Army Corps of Engineers and private land developers represented the two greatest threats to the Georgia environment. A conviction that he had been consistently misled about the merits of proposed projects influenced his view of the Corps of Engineers, and his observation of development on the Chattahoochee River conditioned Carter's attitude toward private land developers. In a letter about the future of the Chattahoochee, the Governor clearly revealed his own attitude:

I share your concern about the river. A look at the disgusting and destructive developments which have stripped the banks and filled the river with mud has destroyed my confidence in private owners' ability to protect it. One in ten who does not share your feeling can ruin the area, and are doing so. Public law with broad prohibitions against excessive development would help you and me in what we both want.[20]

While dedicated to the preservation of private property, when private exploitation threatened the public interest, Carter did not hesitate to recommend public control.

One of the more complex aspects of Carter's practical political philosophy involved his attitude toward change. He approached change with the conservative's caution but often exhibited the liberal's impatience to get on with it. Those conservative elements in his nature, reinforced by a sense of historical continuity, dictated a skepticism and reserve regarding change but also a recognition of the necessity of change to preserve. His education, particularly in science and engineering, created within him a sense that change should be rationally conceived, orderly, and planned. During his governorship Carter introduced few innovative, new programs. He had little interest in short-term experimentalism in either social programs or governmental policies. Rather, he preferred long-term, planned solutions. Exhibiting little enthusiasm for treating symptoms, he sought cures. While the changes he promoted tended to be less immediate and dramatic, they were often more far-reaching and more comprehensive than those of quixotic reformers.

Carter's commitment to planning greatly influenced his attitude toward change. His interest in planning became apparent shortly after resigning his naval commission and returning to Georgia in the mid-1950s. At that time, he helped to organize the West Central Georgia Planning Commission and, for several years, served as chairman of it. Reflecting upon that experience, Carter later recalled:

We tried to assess what our rural counties and people possessed in natural and human resources, what we would like to be in years to come, and the alternative courses of action open to us. We learned as planners to assume the roles of servants and not masters, and we also learned to combine practical implementation plans with theoretical concepts of planning.[21]

A few years later he helped to organize and became the first president of the Georgia Planning Association, which sought to accomplish on the state level what the west central commission had attempted regionally. Hoping to sensitize Georgians to the importance of long-term planning, Carter launched a "Goals for Georgia" program shortly after becoming Governor. Fifty-one public meetings were held throughout the state during which participants established goals in such areas as mental and physical health, tax equalization, education, prison reform, transportation, criminal justice, preservation of historic sites and natural areas, environmental quality, and industrial development.[22]

Carter evidenced his interest in rationality and order in the decision-making process in other ways. When confronted with a perplexing public issue about which he had doubts, he often appointed a study commission and agreed to abide by its recommendations regardless of his own predispositions. Power, he felt, bred responsibility. Thus, the members of such commissions needed to know their decisions would be considered. Two of the more complex issues in which he utilized commissions in this manner were an Atlanta freeway already under construction and a proposed dam on the Flint River.

The freeway, designed to connect Stone Mountain, Georgia, and the downtown Atlanta area, would have cut through many historic public parks in the area, disrupted or destroyed residential housing, and divided older neighborhoods. Carter initially favored construction, believing it would relieve the congested traffic flow between the central city and the suburban areas east of Atlanta. But when a study commission concluded that the highway would do more harm than good, he accepted its recommendation, killed the project, and resisted pressures to reopen the issue.[23]

A similar situation occurred regarding a proposed Army Corps of Engineers' dam at Sprewell Bluff on the Flint River, Georgia's only remaining wild river. Again Carter originally favored construction, but public controversy led to the appointment of a commission to study the matter. The commission recommended against construction, and the Governor implemented the recommendation. In this case, he did so with considerable enthusiasm because of his conviction that the Corps of Engineers had misled, manipulated, and deceived him and the people of Georgia concerning the project's merits.[24]

Carter's interest in planning and his conservative emphasis on orderly, measured change, preferably in response to a growing public consensus, all reduced his receptivity to experimental, short-term innovation. In his attitude toward change, however, he once again revealed the pragmatic temperament that influenced his social and political commitments. When the logical product of his own observation and reasoning dictated fundamental change immediately implemented, he did not shrink from that conclusion even when facing considerable opposition and hostility. Carter's response to the civil rights movement, the greatest promoter of fundamental social change in modern southern history, provided the most dramatic example of this attitude. Against the wishes of friends, neighbors, and even some family members, he resolutely refused to join efforts to obstruct civil rights advances and instead became involved in promoting them. He did this with almost benign faith that those who initially opposed him would eventually support him when they better understood the issues.[25]

An organic sense of community also greatly influenced his attitude toward change and reform. The ultimate test of any program or proposal depended upon its potential consequences for the public as a whole. In Carter's view reforms designed to promote simple justice always should serve the public interest; however, most public issues did not lend themselves to such a simple moral equation. More often proposals to satisfy the legitimate concerns of one group involved sacrifices by other groups. In these situations, Carter sought a middle course that would do the least violence to the public interest while providing some measure of relief to the groups with legitimate grievances. The Governor found little merit in solving one problem by creating another or in providing justice for one group by sacrificing the rights of other groups. Rather than treating manifestations of the problem, he assumed that attacking the problem at its source would create little or no conflict between the special interests of the group and the general interests of the community.

Carter's response to two of the most volatile issues of his governorship—property tax relief and civil rights—illustrates his efforts to harmonize special and public interests. The movement for property tax relief permeated the political atmosphere during Carter's four-year term. While believing property owners had a legitimate basis for complaint, he resolutely rejected the proposal to lower property taxes by increasing sales taxes. "There are many public officials in this state panting for the opportunity to load the poor with more sales tax and take off from the rich their property tax burden," he declared. "I favor the income tax option."[26] Along similar lines, he told the delegates attending the annual convention of the Georgia AFL-CIO:

Anybody who says he is going to lower your property taxes fifty dollars a year and then raises what you pay in sales tax by a hundred dollars a year with a one-cent increase is not your friend. I am not a party to that sort of con game. I never have been, and I never will be.[27]

In another instance when the chairman of the House Appropriations Committee proposed slashing the state education budget to provide money for property tax relief, Carter protested to the Speaker of the House: "There are some things more important than a tax reduction."[28]

Carter had more difficulty reconciling the demands for justice by black Georgians with the corresponding loss of individual rights other citizens would suffer if the demands were met. Two of the most volatile issues of this kind during his administration involved school integration through mandatory busing of school children and affirmative action in employment. In both instances Carter supported the principle involved but had reservations about the specific solutions proposed by civil rights activists. He considered mandatory school busing a threat to public education. While supporting state-assisted voluntary busing programs, he felt the ultimate solution to the problem of school integration rested in altered housing patterns. This emphasis was clearly evident in a letter to a field representative of the Atlanta Community Relations Commission:

I appreciate your views, but disagree with them. Mandatory busing out of neighborhoods against the wishes of both parents & children is not the best solution to our school problems. I favor busing at public expense for children who desire to attend other schools if it will increase integration. . . . Other emphases than busing should be pursued. As you know, for instance, we are now trying to enforce our new state open housing legislation. There are many facets of the problem. . . .[29]

Regarding the issue of affirmative action, Carter strongly endorsed the principle of equity in minority hiring and greatly increased black employment at all levels of state government during his gubernatorial term. But he disliked quotas or any other regulations that would restrict the potential employment pool. The public interest, he argued, could only be served by hiring the best people available, and he believed that if strictly applied this policy would eventually result in minorities getting their fair share of jobs. In a long letter to the leadership of the Southern Christian Leadership Conference, the Governor clearly and frankly stated his position on the issue:

It is important to me, as it is to you, to see that Georgia makes use of the best talent and ability available to fill positions of employment in State government. More importantly, it is my duty to the taxpayers to see that those who handle the State's business are chosen for ability without regard to sex, race, or political considerations. . . .

I must tell you that I cannot agree to appoint only Blacks, or women, or any other type of person to policy making boards. This would be inconsistent with my duty to seek and appoint the best qualified people to positions of authority in State government. I also strongly believe that the adoption of such a policy by any Governor would work against the long-term best interests of Black citizens. I do give you my commitment that the representation of Blacks on major policy making boards and in top administrative positions will continue to increase during the remaining two years of my administration, at an equal or even accelerated rate.[30]

Interest groups lobbying for reforms beneficial to all of society won Carter's admiration and support, and whenever possible, he sought to utilize their influence. Pressure groups that pursued their own selfish interests without regard to the potential consequences for the public interest became, for Carter, an insidious threat to fair and just government and, indeed, the democratic process itself. Carter's disdainful view of special interest lobbying developed during the four years he sat in the Georgia Senate and hardened during his governorship. While assuming that most special interest representatives spoke for basically honest and good people, he believed they had a very narrow view of society and would never support any policy that conflicted with their own group interest.

The lobbyists who fill the halls of Congress, state capitols, county courthouses, and city halls often represent well-meaning and admirable groups. They are employees of school teachers, lawyers, doctors, labor union members, bankers, and businessmen. What is often forgotten, however, is that lobbyists seldom represent the average citizen, and often express the most selfish aspect of the character of their clients.

Physicians are compassionate and dedicated in alleviating the afflictions of their patients. School teachers serve their students in a self-sacrificial way, and lawyers are genuinely interested in the welfare of their clients. Our businessmen and bankers want to do a good job in serving their customers. But the lobbyists of the medical associations do not even profess to represent the best interests of medical patients; they represent what is best for medical doctors. The lobbyists who represent teachers work for what is best for their own employers. They would not try to cut teachers' salaries or retirement benefits in order to finance a new kindergarten program. Chambers of Commerce hire representatives to lobby for their business members, and not for the customers of the businesses.

It is hard to imagine lobbyists seeking lower interest payments and less abusive collection procedures if they work for bankers or small-loan organizations.

There is nothing illegal or immoral about all of this. But it must be recognized for what it is.[31]

A perception of the continuous economic struggle between the rich and the poor, or, more generally, between the haves and have-nots conditioned Carter's attitude toward the unfortunate effects of special interest involvement in government decision making. Because of their superior organization and political acuity, established economic interests consistently prevailed over the disadvantaged who exercised far less political power than their numbers warranted. Government, of necessity, had to intervene on the side of the weak and the voiceless; this was the "sad duty" of politics.

Clearly, Carter's sense of class conflict derived from Christian ethics rather than Marxist theory. Here again, Reinhold Niebuhr spoke eloquently to Carter's concept of human realism and social justice. Like so many others, Carter found wisdom and understanding in Niebuhr's observation that "Man's capacity for justice makes democracy possible; man's inclination to injustice makes democracy necessary." Special interest lobbyists manifested that "inclination to injustice" that had to be checked. "Love and kindness," he believed, "meant a great deal in one-to-one relationships but not in dealing with structures and corporate groups."[32]

Carter's attitude toward special interest influence often merged with the antiestablishment rhetoric he employed in his political campaigns. Carter tended to project his opponents as little more than leaders of private interest coalitions whose independence in office would be compromised by preelection commitments.[33] Certainly, Carter also sought and, in some instances, gained support from special interest groups, but these partnerships tended to be alliances of convenience that became increasingly tenuous after the election as each party attempted to use the other for its own ends.

Carter's antiestablishment rhetoric reflected a populist-progressive strain in his political personality more evident on the campaign trail than in office. Such rhetoric should not be too easily dismissed as the hyperbolic utterances of an ambitious political candidate. Carter believed a profound change had taken place in American society during the 1960s, that people were demanding and obtaining a greater influence in public policy making. The successful politicians in the future, he believed, would be those who recognized this and voluntarily adapted to it.[34] Moreover, Carter assumed that people could play a constructive role in government and, through the Goals for Georgia program, instituted a limited form of participatory democracy as a vehicle to facilitate citizen participation in the determination of public policy. Before citizens could rationally participate in the decision-making process, however, the veil of secrecy had to be removed from the governing process; this he sought to accomplish, in part at least, through the enactment of a state sunshine law.[35]

Politicians, the Governor concluded, needed to do less talking and more listening. Shortly after assuming office, Carter initiated a "taking the government to the people" program through which he symbolically moved the state capital to one of the smaller cities of south Georgia for a day. This, the Governor assumed, would give him a better understanding of the concerns of the people in the area and would permit them to discuss their problems directly with him.[36] While the program obviously was in part a public relations gimmick, at a time when so much cynicism about government existed, Carter believed government officials needed to make a special effort to convince the public that they understood and cared about the problems and concerns of average citizens. This same attitude appeared in a letter to Gerald Rafshoon concerning an anticipated gubernatorial tour of Georgia in 1973: "I see the program as a governor moving through the state visiting and listening to the people—asking questions and learning the good and bad opinions."[37]

A better reflection of Carter's sincerity in soliciting public views is illustrated by the attention paid to correspondence flowing into his office. Responses to citizen inquiries or suggestions were unusually substantive, and a surprising percentage of the letters eventually crossed his desk. In answering letters objecting to a particular policy or procedure, Carter, often in a handwritten note, endeavored to explain his position and convert the correspondent to his point of view. In responding to a critic who objected to the appointment of a woman to the state bench, for example, he urged tolerance. "I have confidence that she will do a good job," he wrote. "I hope that you will give Mrs. Robinson a chance to prove her ability."[38] On those occasions in which the critic appeared irreconcilable, Carter's characteristic advice was "if you're registered, vote against us."[39]

As the foregoing suggests, Carter had an acute awareness of the

significance of political imagery. In a note thanking an acquaint-
ance for a bust of John F. Kennedy, the Governor noted that
"Kennedy still occupies a position representing youth, idealism,
vigor, etc.—which he may or may not actually deserve. Politically, of course, the image is the reality."[40] Image-making is at best
a cynical process often used as much to deceive as to inform. Aware
of this possibility, Carter appears consciously to have sought to
project an image grounded in his own political character and social
commitments. In developing Carter's political image, Gerald Rafshoon did not attempt to sell a manufactured product but rather
a highly simplified version of the real product.

Even though simplified, the "real product" remained unconven-
tional and difficult to comprehend. Carter's campaign tactics served
only to further the confusion. He ran for state office three times.
In each campaign he adopted a different posture. When seeking a
seat in the state legislature in 1962, he ran as a good government,
anti-machine progressive. He ran as a moderate liberal in his first
gubernatorial campaign, and four years later he appealed to the
conservative vote. Although appearing hypocritical in adopting
these tactics, Carter simply emphasized those elements in his political character attractive to the voters neglected or ignored by
other candidates. While probably not consciously seeking to
deceive, Carter's appeal misled many voters who then became
disillusioned with his performance in office. Thus, Carter's opportunism often had a pernicious effect on the effort to educate
the public on the issues, a function Carter believed essential to
good political leadership.

To summarize, Carter's political character and social commitments grew from a basically conservative mentality, a pragmatic
temperament, a liberal faith in man's ability to control his own
destiny, and the flexibility and opportunism of a practical politician. Clinton Rossiter suggested that no visible line separates liberals from conservatives, "but somewhere between them stands a
man who is at once the most liberal of conservatives and most
conservative of liberals."[41] Unfortunately, Rossiter never had an
opportunity to observe Governor Jimmy Carter; he would have
been intrigued, for Carter was both and he was neither. Indeed,
in some important respects, he was not even a politician. If, as
Harold Lasswell has suggested, politics is the art of determining

who gets what, when, and how, Carter ignored most of the rules of the game.[42] He rejected the notion that a political leader should be merely a broker or umpire among contending interest groups making demands on the government; or that an invisible political hand functioned in such a way that as individual interest groups struggled to satisfy their particular demands it somehow redounded to the advantage of society as a whole. The common good, in Carter's judgment, represented the overriding interest, and it seldom profited from efforts to satisfy the desires of special interests. Before endorsing the particular demands of a special interest, he had to be convinced that the satisfaction of those demands served the public interest. Such organizations as Common Cause, the Georgia Conservancy, and Georgia affiliates of the National Organization of Women and the League of Women Voters convinced him, and he became an enthusiastic advocate of most of their causes. Other more self-interested groups did not, and they found in the Governor a formidable nemesis.

The public interest was predominate in the reform program Carter unveiled as Governor of Georgia. Conservation, welfare reform, the promotion of education, judicial reform, consumer protection, an overhaul of tax policy, budget reform, and above all an efficient, fiscally responsible government headed his list of reform priorities. Although in many ways a fiscal conservative, he did not slash government spending but rather sought to give the citizenry a better return on their tax dollar. Generally unimpressed with the typical liberal's faith in solving problems through increased spending, he nevertheless did not hesitate to spend when new expenditures clearly promoted the general welfare. It was not so much government spending but responsible management that concerned him.

Assuming state government in Georgia had been badly mismanaged in recent years, he sought to initiate a great variety of management reforms to correct the situation. Of all the reform proposals advanced, he considered reorganization one of the most crucial. Consequently, reorganization provides a useful case study of the practical consequences of Carter's philosophy of government, the manner in which he attempted to mobilize public support behind his programs, and his style of legislative leadership.

PART I

Goobers and Axe Handles: Jimmy Carter, Lester Maddox, and the Reorganization of State Government

Reorganization is as important to the future of Georgia's state government as education is to the future of our young people.

Governor Jimmy Carter

When I put my pennies into a peanut machine I don't expect to get bubble gum, and neither do the people.

Lieutenant Governor Lester Maddox

We have met the enemy face to face, and it are we.

Senate Majority Leader Al Holloway

chapter 1

HOUSE BILL No. 1:
THE BEGINNINGS OF THE
CARTER-MADDOX FEUD

Executive reorganization of state government became a major issue in the 1970 gubernatorial campaign. Surprisingly, it was not Jimmy Carter but Hal Suit, the Republican gubernatorial nominee, who made reorganization an issue in the November general election. Addressing delegates attending the annual convention of the Georgia Press Association meeting at Jekyll Island on June 27, 1970, Suit discussed the need for a general overhaul of the state government bureaucracy. Thereafter, the Republican gubernatorial candidate increasingly emphasized reorganization. Meanwhile, Carter, who had espoused it in his 1966 campaign, said little about reorganization during the Democratic primaries and exhibited little enthusiasm for the reform during the general election contest. Clearly, reorganization was Suit's issue, and the Democratic nominee had no desire to publicize it.[1] Given the election results, Suit's arguments concerning the necessity of government reorganization apparently failed to convince many voters, but it obviously impressed his opponent. A few days after the election, Carter began talking about the need for reorganization and, within a few weeks, it led his list of legislative priorities.[2]

Few observers of Georgia state government questioned the desirability of organizational reform. The executive branch had last been reorganized in 1931 when Governor Richard B. Russell reduced the number of state agencies from 107 to 18. Since that time a maze of commissions, boards, bureaus, and departments had been established, confusing areas of responsibility and disrupting lines of authority. Several governors prior to Carter had recognized the need for reorganization, but none had been willing to make either the necessary commitment of time or the expenditure of political capital required to effect a major reform of the state government bureaucracy.[3]

Because most state agencies existed by legislative statute, any reorganization plan required authorization from the General Assembly. Circumstances prevailing prior to or created during the gubernatorial campaign, however, severely restricted the new Governor's chances of securing a workable authorization bill.

One of the major obstacles to Carter's proposed reorganization effort resulted from the growth of factional divisions in the General Assembly, particularly the Senate, during the preceding four years. Previous to the Maddox administration, the state legislature had largely rubber stamped gubernatorial proposals, but during Maddox's term it had developed an unprecedented degree of independence and autonomy from gubernatorial leadership. In the process, personal factionalism grew to the extent that it took delicate negotiations between various power brokers to get major legislation through the General Assembly.[4]

The 1970 gubernatorial campaign contributed to the hardening of factional alliances. The bitter Democratic primary race between Carter and former Governor Carl Sanders divided state Democratic leaders into hostile factions. Sanders had many friends in the legislature, including his 1970 campaign manager and law partner, Eugene Holley. Chairman of the powerful Senate Banking and Finance Committee, Holley had developed an effective working alliance with Lester Maddox during the latter's governorship. The Sanders' loyalists who rallied around Holley had little inclination to permit their erstwhile antagonist, Jimmy Carter, to cover himself with glory during his gubernatorial term.

Carter offended another powerful Senate leader, Hugh Gillis, by attacking his father, State Highway Director Jim Gillis, during the campaign. Eventually Carter forced Gillis' resignation from the State Highway Department. Gillis had been associated with the department for over a quarter-century. One of the major patronage dispensers in state government, he ran the State Highway Department with an iron hand. For all intents and purposes, a road or highway could not be built, repaved, abandoned, or expanded without his approval. By 1970 charges of political intrigue, abuse of power, and corruption surrounded the administration of the State Highway Department, and Gillis became an issue in the gubernatorial campaign. Both Carter and his Republican opponent vowed to depose the highway director. While Gillis had made numerous enemies during his long tenure, he also had made many friends, some of whom sat in the General Assembly where his son Hugh, president pro tem of the Senate, marshalled their opposition to the new Governor.[5]

Others in the state legislature and in state government had their own reasons for opposing the new administration. Friends of Herman Talmadge feared a successful governorship would place Carter in a good position to challenge the state's junior United States senator. Moreover, a number of the individual power brokers in the legislature recognized that to some extent their power depended upon gubernatorial weakness.

The most visible and publicized legislative obstacle confronting Carter, however, was the new lieutenant governor, Lester Maddox, who by virtue of his office presided over the Senate and exercised considerable influence and power. Maddox quickly ingratiated himself with the various factions hostile to the new Governor. One of the few political candidates in 1970 to speak out in defense of Jim Gillis, he later strongly supported Hugh Gillis who successfully withstood a challenge to his Senate leadership post.[6] Moreover, a few weeks after the election, Maddox hired the Sanders-Holley law firm to represent him in certain "business and nonpolitical" matters.[7] The lieutenant governor also found common cause with other Carter antagonists and within a few months of the election had become the most visible leader of an anti-administration coalition which crystalized in the General Assembly during the 1971 legislative session.

The relationship between Lester Maddox and Jimmy Carter extended to the 1966 gubernatorial race during which Carter had narrowly missed overtaking Maddox for a position in the Democratic primary election runoff. Shortly thereafter, Maddox informed the press of his intention to appoint the Plains senator chairman of the State Education Committee. Before the November elections, Carter reciprocated, publicly announcing his support of all Democratic nominees including Maddox.[8] It was a difficult decision. The endorsement of a militant segregationist clearly violated the principles of a man whose liberalism on the race issue had incurred the wrath of his south Georgia neighbors.[9] Two major considerations influenced Carter's decision. First, he did not take the obligations of party loyalty lightly, especially since he had sworn to support all party nominees. Second, he distrusted and intensely disliked the Republican nominee, Howard "Bo" Callaway. The south Georgia senator undoubtedly assumed that while an embarrassment, Maddox was relatively harmless, but Callaway represented a more dangerous and less governable force in state politics.[10]

personality profile:
LESTER GARFIELD MADDOX

The son of a steelworker, Lester Maddox was born in Atlanta, Georgia, on September 30, 1915. An indifferent student, his formal education ended before he completed the eleventh grade. He worked for several years as a laborer and supervisor in several steel mills before opening a small restaurant. He eventually opened the Pickrick restaurant ("pick" means "to select" and "rick" means "to pile up;" thus, "You PICK it out . . . we'll RICK it up") near the Georgia Tech campus. He built the restaurant into a business grossing in excess of $1 million a year. During the early 1950s he began publishing a popular series of weekly advertisements in Atlanta newspapers under the heading, "Pickrick Says." After the 1954 Supreme Court desegregation decision, the column became increasingly political in content. He twice ran unsuccessfully for mayor of Atlanta and once for lieutenant governor of Georgia. Meanwhile, he steadfastly refused to serve blacks in his Pickrick restaurant, often using axe handles to drive away nonviolent civil rights activists attempting to integrate his business. Maddox closed the restaurant in 1964 rather than *accept integration. He parlayed his subsequent notoriety into the successful political career that previously had eluded him. In 1966 he ran second to former governor Ellis Arnall in the Democratic gubernatorial primary, edging out Jimmy Carter for a spot in the runoff election. He defeated Arnall in the second primary and faced Howard "Bo" Callaway, the Republican nominee, in the general election. Although winning a plurality of votes, Callaway failed to secure a majority, and the election was thrown into the Democratically controlled General Assembly which selected Maddox. Under state law, he was unable to run for relection in 1970 and therefore entered the race for lieutenant governor and easily won election.*[11]

Despite the controversial circumstances of his election in the Georgia General Assembly, Maddox had proven a popular governor. His surprisingly large margin of victory over a respected incumbent and two other candidates in the 1970 Democratic primary election for lieutenant governor greatly increased his clout in state politics. (Maddox won a majority of votes in the primary, thus avoiding a runoff.) Moreover, under Senate rules, the lieutenant governor not only presided over the Senate but also referred bills to appropriate committees and appointed the members of standing and ad hoc Senate committees. Lester Maddox obviously was a force to be reckoned with in state politics.

Anticipating that Carl Sanders, his more liberally identified opponent in the 1970 Democratic gubernatorial primary, would capture much of the urban vote, Carter assumed that his political fortunes rested with many of the same voters attracted to Maddox. Consequently, during the campaign, Carter tried whenever possible to identify with the governor, even to the extent of implying, much to Maddox's chagrin, that they were running as a team. Carter also stated, repeatedly, that if elected he could and would work closely with Maddox during his gubernatorial term.[12]

Shortly after winning the Democratic gubernatorial nomination, Carter and Maddox exchanged mutual pledges of support. At a press conference in September, the Democratic nominee announced that he had met with Maddox and they had discussed several legislative proposals including solutions to pollution problems, aid to cities, and support for education. Carter said he intended to work with the lieutenant governor in developing his legislative program. A few days later Maddox pledged his "total support" and praised the Democratic nominee for "running a Maddox-like campaign." Carter told the outgoing governor he planned to "continue a number of Maddox innovations, including 'Little People's Day'."[13]

Although it may have been good electoral politics for Carter to identify closely with Maddox during the 1970 campaign, it gave Maddox a sense of leverage over the gubernatorial nominee that complicated relations between the two men. During the campaign, the press noted a number of occasions during which Maddox appeared to be baiting Carter, contradicting him, and, at times, making him appear foolish.[14] Castigating the press for trying to drive a wedge between them, both men denied differences, but real problems existed and increased as the campaign progressed. At a meeting of the State Democratic Convention shortly after the primary runoff election, Maddox seemed bent on picking a fight with the party's gubernatorial nominee. He warned Carter not to get involved in the affairs of the General Assembly, particularly the Senate over which he would preside. "The people stated," he said,

that they will not accept encroachment of the executive branch of state government over the legislative branch. The people voted for an independent legislature, and they want to keep it that way. They want it kept free from disruptive pressures from the state's chief executives. . . . They don't want a chief executive to interfere with the internal affairs and operations of the legislature.[15]

Maddox added that he would be watching the new governor to see that he kept his campaign promises. "When I put my pennies into a peanut machine," he declared, "I don't expect to get bubble gum, and neither do the people."[16] While the outgoing governor's comments came during an exchange of congratulations, they were direct and challenging; the message was clear and unmistakable.

A few days later Carter felt compelled to issue a "blanket denial" of a rift between himself and Maddox. He said there had never been a "cross word or misunderstanding" between them and that any indication of a division "was a creation of Atlanta newspapers."[17] Despite Carter's denials, relations between the two deteriorated. Shortly after the first primary, Maddox had attempted to solicit a pledge from Carter and Sanders that they would not interfere in any way with the functions of the General Assembly. Sanders agreed, but Carter refused, informing Maddox that he wanted some voice in naming Senate committee chairmen.[18] Persistent rumors that Carter supporters in the Senate planned to offer a candidate for president pro tem of the Senate had inspired Maddox's outburst at the State Democratic Convention.

Conflict between the two strong-willed political leaders was inevitable. Although both were deeply religious and had a populist-conservative political philosophy, their religious convictions, conservative principles, and populist ideals differed significantly. Maddox's race-conscious religious fundalmentalism, his anti-intellectual, reactionary political ideology, and his demagoguery in the southern populist tradition offended Carter.

Other equally important differences divided them. An activist reformer with an extensive legislative program, Carter's agenda carried with it the implication that much was wrong with state government and an implicit criticism of the incumbent administration. Proud of his accomplishments in office, Maddox bristled at the suggestion that the state government needed overhauling.[19] Moreover, whether consciously or unconsciously, Maddox, like most persons in his situation, undoubtedly resented the man who took over his office.

Maddox might be leaving the governor's office, but he actively sought to retain as much power and influence as possible. In explaining his decision to run for lieutenant governor in 1970, Maddox reasoned

As lieutenant governor I would have an official position from which to help keep alive the work of the previous four years, a forum from which I could be heard and from which I could exert a positive influence on the direction of state government.[20]

Obviously, Maddox intended to have a major voice in government policy during the four years of the new administration, and this ultimately would put him on a collision course with Jimmy Carter.

Finally, Carter and Maddox had vastly different conceptions of the role of executive leadership. As an activist, Carter accepted literally the definition of leadership. Maddox, just as literally, espoused the constitutional division of power. He argued that any executive interference in legislative affairs, such as seeking to influence the selection of party leaders or committee chairmen, would result in a "virtual dictatorship with the executive branch controlling the legislature."[21] While simplistic to the point of naiveté, there is no reason to doubt the sincerity of Maddox's convictions. "I had respect for the function of the legislature," he wrote in his autobiography,

During my administration that body had achieved the greatest degree of independence in recent Georgia history. I worked for this independence. My refusal to resort to strong-arm tactics, threats, rewards, dealings in smoke-filled rooms, and other time-tested methods of subverting the constitutionally intended powers and functions of the legislature was misinterpreted by my critics as an indication of weakness on my part. Nothing could have been further from the truth.[22]

Bill Shipp, a political columnist for the *Atlanta Constitution*, agreed that legislative independence had grown significantly during Maddox's term but suggested a different reason. "Carter's predecessor," the reporter argued, "was so busy saving the world from Godless communism that the state levers at the governor's disposal were allowed to rust." They would have to be re-oiled, Shipp concluded, if Carter hoped to get any of his programs through the General Assembly.[23]

Carter's first effort to oil those squeaky levers of gubernatorial power proved disastrous. A few days after the November general election, the Senate Democratic Caucus convened to select party leaders for the upcoming General Assembly session. On the eve of the caucus meeting, Governor-elect Carter endorsed Senator Robert Smalley for the post of president pro tem, hoping to unseat the incumbent, Hugh Gillis. Because of his attacks on State Highway Director Jim Gillis during the primary and general election campaigns, Carter assumed he would get little cooperation from Hugh Gillis and wanted to replace him in the Senate leadership hierarchy with a more personally congenial senator. Moreover, both Gillises had campaigned for Carl Sanders in the Democratic gubernatorial primary.[24]

The following day the caucus met and voted 27 to 17 against the Carter-backed candidate. With the support of Lester Maddox, Hugh Gillis easily retained his leadership position.[25] Carter's prestige had suffered a devastating blow even before he took the oath of office. Meanwhile, an incensed Maddox denounced Carter for intervening in internal Senate affairs. Alarmed, Carter met with Maddox and was surprised by the intensity of the outgoing governor's anger. "He's really mad," a chastized Carter informed supporters after the meeting.[26]

A few days later, Carter again met with Maddox in an attempt to "calm troubled waters." After the meeting Carter reported to newsmen it had been a cordial discussion. Both he and Maddox, Carter said, regretted their differences in the president pro tem fight and had reassured each other it would not happen again.[27] Given the circumstances, however, little if any chance of a permanent reconciliation existed. Maddox considered the General Assembly, especially the Senate, his personal bailiwick, and he would brook no gubernatorial interference in it. Meanwhile, Carter had an extensive legislative agenda that had to be taken up by the General Assembly. To get any substantial part of that package through the state legislature would require active gubernatorial leadership.

Even before the convening of the General Assembly in January, Maddox again attacked the Governor and once more the two met in an attempt to resolve their differences. They provided vastly different accounts of their discussion. Carter described it as a cordial meeting in which they talked about their differences. He noted they had discussed the lieutenant governor's apparent opposition to all of his (Carter's) legislative proposals on economy, efficiency, tax revision and constitutional changes. Carter reported:

I told him I would like to have his support, but if he couldn't support my legislation, then I would have to do the best I could to get my bills passed, because I was pledged to the people to do so. He said that was all I could do and we parted with a handshake.[28]

According to the Maddox version of the meeting, after chatting amicably for a few minutes, he assured Carter he would support him in every possible way "to keep Georgia moving forward." Thanking him, the Governor noted he needed all the support he could get. "But I didn't call you in here to find out where and how you're going to support me," Carter coldly remarked. "I called you here to tell you that if you ever oppose me on *any* issue I'll meet you head on and fight you with all the resources under my command and authority." Taken aback, Maddox declared no one had ever spoken to him like that before. "Governor Carter, you shock me!" Maddox said. "I don't want to fight you; in fact, I sincerely hope we can avoid that. If it comes down to a fight, then you'll have to initiate it. But I can assure you that if you do, I'll be compelled to fight back!"[29]

Although the two versions of the meeting corresponded in some respects, each man accused the other of initiating the hostilities. The weight of evidence supports the Carter version. The Governor, who could be blunt on occasion, was usually more circumspect in such matters and less inclined to exaggerate. Moreover, in the earlier differences between them, Maddox clearly had been the aggressor; Carter had initiated the efforts to reconcile their differences. Throughout his career in public service, Maddox tended to overreact, dramatizing and exaggerating such incidents. Indeed, he apparently related different versions of his meeting with Carter to different people.[30]

By August the lieutenant governor charged Carter with "trying to destroy Lester Maddox" and create a dictatorship, and by autumn he wished the Governor would stop 'riding my back and trying to cut my throat."[31] In a letter to the Governor released earlier to the press, the lieutenant governor said he had attempted to cooperate with Carter despite his "open and sometimes undercover attempts to ridicule and discredit me."[32]

Although obviously displeased by Maddox's continual opposition, Carter usually refrained from responding in kind to these emotional attacks. While noting Maddox's opposition, Carter, in his correspondence, rarely displayed anger or personal animosity. His note to Billy Dilworth typified Carter's demeanor. In a column in the *Athens Banner-Herald*, Dilworth discussed the harmful effects of the Carter-Maddox feud in the General Assembly. The Governor told the reporter that his "point was well taken" and said he had had a series of private talks with Maddox, and while they had not resolved all their differences, some progress had been made. "With a mutual friend like you," Carter declared, "it is certain that neither of us is all bad."[33] Carter also managed to retain a sense of humor about his adversary. When asked during the 1971 General Assembly session whether he was trying to ignore Maddox, Carter responded, "It's impossible to ignore the lieutenant governor even if I wanted to."[34] And when Maddox's press secretary, Jack Thomas, resigned to join the army, Carter could not resist penciling the young man a tongue-in-cheek note. Because of his habit of extemporizing, Maddox delivered few of the speeches Thomas wrote for him. "It was with profound regret that I learned your decision to join the Army," Carter wrote:

Of course, your experience in scattershot verbal warfare should serve you well and provide a shield of armor against mealymouthed whimperings of mere mortal bureaucrats.

Your reputation as the author of the South's best unread speeches should follow you throughout your career. Here's hoping the Army will find more use for your material than did your previous employer.[35]

A few weeks after his Democratic Caucus defeat, the Governor-elect largely recovered his earlier losses by announcing he would use the Democratic leadership in both houses of the General Assembly to handle administration measures. Traditionally, Georgia governors had appointed administrative floor leaders separate from the regular party leadership elected by party caucuses; and, indeed, Carter earlier had announced his intention of appointing his cousin, Senator Hugh Carter, as his Senate floor leader. After the caucus defeat, however, Carter decided to work with the established leadership. It was a masterful stroke that brought into his camp two of the most influential and effective lawmakers in the Georgia General Assembly, Senate Majority Leader Al Holloway and Speaker of the House George L. Smith.[36]

Carter's decision to use these two influential state legislators to manage his proposals in the General Assembly stunned his legislative antagonists, who immediately began groping for some means of counteracting his strategy. A few days after the General Assembly convened, members of the Senate Democratic Caucus met to discuss Holloway's dual role. Under a new rule proposed by Lieutenant Governor Maddox and President Pro Tem Hugh Gillis, Holloway would have to gain the approval of seven of the ten members of the Senate Policy Committee before introducing an administration measure. Both Holloway and Carter objected to the restrictive nature of this requirement. After a hurried conference between Carter and Senate leaders, they reached a compromise under which Holloway would refrain from sponsoring administration measures if seven members of the policy committee objected.[37]

personality profile:
ALBERT WESTON HOLLOWAY

Born in York County, Virginia, on November 4, 1918, Albert Weston Holloway was educated in Virginia schools, including two years at the College of William and Mary. Shortly before World War II, he became an insurance adjuster and moved to Georgia. After the United States entered the war, he enlisted in the United States Army, received a lieutenant's commission, and began pilot training. The recipient of several decorations for valorous service, including the Air Medal and Distinguished Flying Cross with oak leaf clusters, he eventually rose to the rank of captain and served as lead and command pilot of several operational missions in the European theater, including the massive Berlin air raid on Christmas Day, 1944. Following the war, the insurance adjusting company for which he worked promoted him to the position of district manager with offices in Albany, Georgia. There he met and in 1950 married Ethel Hilsman Edmondson. Asked to assist in the operation of his wife's family business after the death of her father in 1953, Holloway soon rose to the position of president and general manager of the firm, a large wholesale plumbing and heating company. After serving one term in the Georgia House of Representatives, 1957-58, he ran successfully in 1962 for the state Senate from the twelfth senatorial district and joined a freshman Senate class that included Jimmy Carter from the neighboring fourteenth district. Described half-jokingly by his friend, George Busbee, as "the meanest man alive," Holloway soon earned the reputation of being a volatile, combative, and, at times, recalcitrant legislator whom other senators nevertheless grew to like and respect.[38]

Carter's strategy paid almost immediate dividends as both Holloway and Smith announced their enthusiastic support of the proposed government reorganization effort. Under the firm guidance of the Speaker, the House Democratic Policy Committee agreed in late December to introduce and support an authorization bill that would give the Governor authority to reorganize state government. Before winning the endorsement of the powerful House leadership panel, Carter agreed to a stipulation proposed by the Speaker that would give the General Assembly a veto of specific reorganization proposals before they went into effect. Under the original bill Carter would have had broad discretionary authority to transfer functions from one department to another before seeking the approval of the legislature.[39]

The authorization bill agreed to by Carter and the House Policy Committee, House Bill No. 1 (HB 1), gave the Governor authority to propose the transfer of functions among state agencies, abolish agencies and departments not constitutionally mandated, consolidate functions, delegate authority of non-elected department heads, and establish new departments or agencies. The reorganization plan was to be submitted to the General Assembly at the beginning of the regular 1972 session; legislators then would have ten days to veto provisions of the plan they found unacceptable. Provisions of the plan not vetoed during this time would automatically become law.

To many observers, HB 1 appeared weak and emasculated.

Carter critic Reg Murphy, editor of the *Atlanta Constitution*, exhibiting an uncanny ability to underestimate his nemesis, concluded after Carter's agreement with Speaker Smith and the House Policy Committee, "There is no need for alarm about Governor-elect Jimmy Carter's proposal to reorganize the state government. The legislature already has scuttled it."[40] To some extent Senate Majority Leader Holloway agreed. "It's the most harmless piece of legislation you ever saw," he said. "I don't see how anybody could disagree with it."[41]

Nevertheless, it did not take Lieutenant Governor Maddox long to do just that. He argued that the ten-day veto period should be extended to forty-five days and that the plan should not be implemented before July 1972 when the 1973 fiscal budget went into effect.[42] Several state officials, led by Labor Commissioner Sam Caldwell, also expressed opposition. Sounding an argument that would be monotonously repeated during the following months, Caldwell endorsed the principle of reorganization but opposed HB 1. Expressing a previously unenunciated concern about the integrity of the legislature, Caldwell challenged the constitutionality of the authorization act. The legislature, he said, should affirmatively approve any reorganization of government instead of having an automatic law that would require a legislative veto to stop.[43]

As the opposition to HB 1 grew, Carter scheduled a meeting with elected state officials, Speaker Smith, and Lieutenant Governor Maddox to discuss their differences. During the meeting, Carter agreed to give constitutional officers a veto over any proposed statutory changes in their departments and to provide legislators with a copy of the proposed reorganization plan at least fifteen days before the 1972 session of the General Assembly convened. He also extended the veto period from ten to fifteen days.[44] These concessions failed to pacify reorganization critics, who, adopting the legal argument first advanced by Caldwell, vowed to continue their opposition to the bill in the Senate. Conversely, Speaker Smith confidently expected his chamber to approve the bill.

Although Carter did not refer explicitly to reorganization during his twelve-minute inaugural address, he emphasized it at his first press conference and again during his "State of the State" address delivered to a joint session of the House and Senate. Repeating his prior statements that executive reorganization would be the first priority of his administration, he noted that in the forty years since the state government had been reorganized, the number of state agencies had grown from 18 to approximately 300 departments, boards, bureaus, commissions, councils, and authorities. Indeed, he told the lawmakers, "Every time I open a closet door in my office, I fear that a new state agency will fall out!"[45]

A few days after the General Assembly convened, the House leadership called up HB 1 for debate. After disposing of six weakening amendments by a voice vote, the House adopted two clarifying amendments before approving the authorization bill by a 163 to 8 vote. Despite its easy victory in the House, the administration still faced difficulties in the Senate where presiding officer Lester Maddox and much of the leadership raised numerous objections to the bill.

Upon receipt of HB 1 from the House, Maddox referred it to the Economy, Reorganization and Efficiency in Government Committee (EREG) of which he was a voting member. Perhaps the most powerful committee in the Georgia General Assembly and certainly the most controversial, the EREG was the only committee to be created by legislative statute. Organized during Carl

personality profile:_____
GEORGE LEON SMITH II
_____

Born in Stillmore, Georgia, on November 27, 1917, George Smith received his elementary and secondary schooling in Emanuel County and later attended the University of Georgia. After passing the state bar examination, he practiced law in Swainsboro where he served as solicitor of the city court, 1937-41. In 1941 he became city attorney, a position he held for the remainder of his life. First elected in 1945 to the Georgia House of Representatives from Emanuel County, he eventually rose to the office of Speaker of the House during the governorship of Ernest Vandiver, 1959-63. At the time, however, the Speaker served at the pleasure of the governor. Consequently, with the inauguration of Carl Sanders in 1963, Smith reluctantly vacated the office. The deadlocked gubernatorial election of 1966, however, gave Smith an opportunity to assert a measure of legislative independence that the General Assembly never again relinquished. Elected Speaker of the House by his colleagues in 1967, he soon gained recognition as one of the state's most powerful and effective political leaders. A master of parliamentary procedure, he ran the House with a firm hand but still managed to maintain warm, cordial relationships with most of his fellow legislators, friendships that not only added to his popularity but contributed significantly to his power.[46]

Sanders' administration to seek out "all reasonable and practical economies" and make "analytical and penetrating studies" of state government, the committee had subpoena powers and the authority to hire and set the compensation of its staff.[47] Maddox loaded the committee with reorganization opponents, including the committee chairman, Stanley Smith, who earlier had declared that the House-passed bill amounted to an abdication of legislative responsibility and a violation of constitutional principles.[48] Meanwhile, Governor Carter resolutely opposed major changes in the bill passed by the House, especially a Smith-Maddox proposal to substitute affirmative legislative approval for the legislative veto provision. At a Chamber of Commerce "Eggs and Issues" breakfast, Carter, urging businessmen actively to support his reorganization effort, argued that he could not submit 200 or 300 separate reorganization proposals to the legislature. In such a situation, he reasoned, "unbearable pressures by special interest lobbyists would be placed on the legislators."[49]

To slow the Governor's momentum on the bill, EREG Chairman Smith scheduled a hearing on the constitutionality of HB 1 during a two-week legislative recess for budget hearings. Carter used this time to meet individually with senators seeking their support. Bill Shipp, a reporter with good sources in the legislature and the administration, noted that Carter had "made a number of senators see the light by threatening to cancel pet projects, by calling some of their key constituents back home, and, on occasion, by simply berating them in front of friends."[50]

On January 26, Carter officially signed his first measure into law as Georgia's Governor. With Maddox at his side, he affixed his signature to House Bill 2, a tax reform measure, and then turning to the lieutenant governor, quipped, "I hope very shortly I'll be signing House Bill 1." With similar equanimity, Maddox smiled and replied, "I know you do, Governor." A few days later Carter again met with Maddox but again failed to convince him of the wisdom of HB 1.[51]

By repeatedly identifying reorganization as his major legislative objective in the 1971 General Assembly session and by making unqualified predictions that he "would get it," Carter precipitated an early test of his gubernatorial strength. Capitol observers speculated about his willingness to gamble so much on a "legislative dice roll."[52] Indeed, the stakes were high, and the Governor knew it. *The Atlanta Constitution* announced in bold headlines that Carter and Maddox had put the political heavyweight championship of Georgia on the line, and the Senate vote on the government reorganization bill would determine the victor.[53] A loss at this point could have been disastrous to the Governor. Confronted by a resurgent legislature whose independence had grown enormously during the four-year term of his predecessor, Carter needed to reassert the governor's traditional role as legislative leader if he hoped to win approval of any substantial part of his extensive reform program.

Carter acted wisely in accepting an early confrontation with the lieutenant governor. Even before his inauguration, it had become obvious to Carter that Maddox automatically would oppose any substantive measure he put forth. Carter would probably never be in a stronger position for such a struggle than during the early "honeymoon" period of his administration. HB 1 would determine whether Carter or Maddox would exercise the greatest degree of authority during the next four years. As is true of most legislative chambers, some members of the Georgia General Assembly would gravitate naturally toward power. The votes of these uncommitted legislators would be vital to Carter as he unveiled his legislative agenda. Moreover, the vote on HB 1 would come before Carter had to begin making those hard political decisions that would inevitably offend various lawmakers.[54]

One such decision became necessary during the reorganization struggle. Shortly after the General Assembly convened, Richard B. Russell, Georgia's respected senior United States senator, died, and Carter had to appoint someone to fill his unexpired term. Whomever the Governor selected, the choice undoubtedly would offend the numerous state politicos who aspired to the Senate seat; and when Carter announced the appointment of David Gambrell, this was the case. Gambrell, who had served as treasurer in Carter's gubernatorial campaign and later as chairman of the Democratic State Committee, was a young, ambitious politician who, as an incumbent a year later, would be a formidable candidate for election to a full Senate term. Carter antagonist Sam Caldwell immediately announced his candidacy for the Senate seat, and many political observers speculated that Lester Maddox would also enter the fray.

Meanwhile, in an unusual Sunday evening press conference on the eve of the reconvening of the legislature after its two-week recess, Maddox demonstrated that the real issue before the Senate was not HB 1 but a test of strength between himself and the Governor. Reading from a sixteen-page handwritten statement, Maddox charged that Carter had entered into a secret deal with key legislators to get his reorganization bill passed. Carter, Maddox claimed, had agreed to support a sizeable increase in the salaries of state officials and legislators. The participants in the conspiracy were:

cowardly and conniving politicians . . . special interests and the "in" crowd . . . persons who engender fear and cowardice and lust for power who conceived the plot in defeat and nurtured it in iniquity, in raw and rotten collusion . . . they would set up a dictatorship, a monarchy . . . they would sell their souls for a mess of porridge.[55]

Clearly the lieutenant governor had overstepped himself and seriously compromised his chances of defeating the bill his antagonist had designated his "No. 1 Legislative Priority." In his eagerness to condemn and discredit the new Governor, Maddox made the mistake of including influential House and Senate leaders in his bill of indictment. Capitol reporters concluded that Maddox's extravagant and excessive language had caused at least three senators, who previously had announced their intention of voting against HB 1 to change their minds and now support the Governor. Maddox's statements also annoyed several uncommitted senators whose support he needed. His aides previously had believed that they had enough votes to substantially alter the authorization bill, but the lieutenant governor's ill-timed, ill-tempered press conference shattered their careful, low key lobbying among state senators.[56]

As the Senate reassembled, few neutral observers were willing to hazard a guess regarding the outcome of the vote on HB 1. One veteran observer remarked. "There are eight senators who are uncommitted, and eight others who have lied to both sides."[57] Administration supporters assumed that the lieutenant governor would have his way in the EREG Committee but also assumed that the committee's recommendations could be overridden on the floor of the Senate.

And so it was. On February 8 the EREG Committee met and by a 7 to 2 vote rejected HB 1. The committee then adopted a substitute for the Carter proposal that required the General Assembly to take affirmative action on any reorganization proposal.[58] The Senate Policy Committee met a few days later and worked out a compromise under which the legislative veto would be restored but which would permit either house to withdraw from the Carter package "controversial" sections for an affirmative vote. Confident of victory, Carter rejected this "eleventh hour compromise" and vowed a fight on the floor of the Senate for the bill as passed by the House.[59]

Listening with his aides to the Senate debates on an extension loudspeaker connected to the Senate chamber, the Carter grin grew as the lawmakers rejected hostile amendments by ever growing margins. The EREG substitute providing affirmative legislative action on reorganization proposals lost by a vote of 30 to 26. The only significant change in HB 1 resulted from a compromise previously agreed to by Carter that would allow the General Assembly to take up the reorganization proposal item-by-item rather than as a whole package. On the final vote, HB 1 passed the Senate by a resounding 53 to 3 vote.[60]

During the Senate debate, reorganization critics made the constitutionality of HB 1 the major issue. The Governor's critics repeatedly argued that the legislature could and should reorganize state government through affirmative legislative action. "We have only one issue," shouted reorganization critic Bobby Rowan, "whether or not we are abdicating our responsibility."[61] Noting that for forty years the legislature had failed to use its power to reorganize, Senate Majority Leader Al Holloway, paraphrasing the cartoon character Pogo, declared: "We have met the enemy face to face, and it are we."[62] The Carter floor leader argued that reorganization would only be accomplished through gubernatorial initiative. He claimed that the legislature could not or would not reorganize state government on its own.[63]

Carter's Senate victory was widely heralded as a devastating defeat for the lieutenant governor. "MADDOX NOW IS OFFICIALLY NO. 2," headlined the *Atlanta Constitution*.[64] Magnanimous in victory, Carter extended the olive branch to Maddox only to have it harshly rejected. Characterizing the vote as "a loss for the people," Maddox vowed to spend the next four years traveling the state seeking the repeal of the reorganization bill. "I'm trying to prevent any dictatorship from moving in on our government," he declared.[65]

Because of the minor amendments it adopted, the Senate returned HB 1 to the House where once again efforts to substantially alter it failed.[66] Surrounded by key lawmakers from both chambers who had helped push the bill through the General Assembly, Carter signed HB 1 on February 15, 1971, declaring, "I know of no more significant measure that has been passed by the General Assembly in the past ten to fifteen years."[67]

The victory had not come easily, and the Governor had staked much on the outcome. Carter personally spent forty hours lobbying state senators and their constituents to gain support for the reorganization bill. Still, he was disappointed. He had expected more support on key amendments in the Senate. Carter carefully had underlined on a Senate voting list, the names of four senators

who he said had lied to him concerning support of the reorganization bill.[68]

The knowledge that the authorization bill was only the first of
many hurdles also muted the celebration in the Governor's office.
The reorganization plan still had to be written and then approved
by the same lawmakers who had found HB 1 so divisive and controversial; and the sides were divided too evenly to predict a
winner.

chapter 2

THE REORGANIZATION AND MAN-
AGEMENT IMPROVEMENT STUDY

Passage of HB 1 represented only the first step in the year-long effort to reorganize the state government of Georgia. Before any changes could be implemented, an extensive study of the existing governmental structure would have to be made, recommendations for change developed and reviewed, draft legislation prepared, and most importantly, the approval of state constitutional officers and state legislators secured. To meet the Governor's timetable, the reorganization study had to be completed by early fall and the draft legislation prepared by December 1, well before the General Assembly convened January 10, 1972.[1]

personality profile:
TOM M. LINDER, JR.

Born in Atlanta, Georgia, on August 12, 1937, Tom Linder was reared in Hawkinsville, Georgia. The Linder family had been influential in south Georgia politics for some time. His grandfather, Tom Mercer Linder, had served for many years as state Commissioner of Agriculture before making an unsuccessful race for governor in 1954.

Linder, who had attended the public schools of Hawkinsville, enrolled at the University of Georgia, where he graduated with a BA in history and political science. Meanwhile he served six years in the United States Marine Corps Active Reserve. He later attended Cumberland School of Law, Samford University, earning the JD degree in 1965. Shortly after graduating, he became an industrial representative for the Georgia Department of Industry and Trade. In that capacity he worked with many Georgia communities on local development plans and traveled throughout the country talking with industries about moving to Georgia. In 1969 he was named executive director of the Middle Georgia Area Planning Commission and served in that position until named state planning and community affairs officer by Jimmy Carter in 1971.

Linder immediately created a stir in his new position by establishing a strict dress code and requiring his departmental employees to do such routine maintenance as mopping floors and washing walls. The controversy, however, quickly died down, and the Governor retained confidence in his young state planning officer. After the General Assembly passed HB 1, Carter named Linder project director of the Reorganization and Management Improvement Study.²

The Governor's staff began developing operating procedures and an organizational structure even before the General Assembly adjourned in March. The Governor asked his youthful director of the Bureau of State Planning and Community Affairs, Tom M. Linder, Jr., to head the reorganization project. Under Linder's direction, the reform effort, formally titled the "Reorganization and Management Improvement Study," assumed a pyramidic organizational structure. He divided state government services into seven functional areas: education, human resources, natural resources, transportation, protection of persons and property, economic development, and general governmental activities. One or more study teams were then organized in each of these areas to review existing policies and procedures and to make recommendations for reform. The study teams reported to one of four group leaders, who, in turn, forwarded recommendations or suggestions to Assistant Project Director William H. Roper, a representative of the Management Review Section of the State Budget Bureau, or Project Director Linder. Roper and Linder forwarded all recommendations for change to Governor Carter who chaired the executive committee of the Reorganization and Management Improvement Study. Besides Carter and Linder, the executive committee consisted of Clifford Clarke, president of the Georgia Business and Industry Association; two state legislators, Lamar Plunkett, chairman of the Senate Appropriations Committee, and House Majority Leader George Busbee; and two state officers, State Auditor Ernest Davis and Budget Director Battle Hall.

Theoretically, the executive committee supervised the work of the various study teams, provided them with information, made suggestions regarding procedures, assisted in the recruitment of business volunteers, and reviewed recommendations channeled from the study teams. In reality, the executive committee played a much more important role in generating support for reorganization than it did in formulating the final plan. Clearly, Roper, Linder, and especially Governor Carter served as the ultimate arbiters of the recommendations emanating from the reorganization study teams.

House Bill No. 1 outlined the objectives of reorganization. Through structural reform and improved management practices, state legislators charged the administration with developing a reorganization plan that would

1. improve services rendered to the citizens of the state
2. promote economy in the operations of state government
3. improve efficiency in the management of state government
4. promote the orderly growth of the state and its government
5. avoid duplication of effort by agencies of state government[3]

Prior to undertaking the reorganization study, the Governor's office contacted other states whose governments had been recently reorganized and dispatched a small delegation to meet with Wisconsin state officials to discuss their experiences with reorganization.[4] As a result of this preliminary study, the administration determined that one of three groups usually conducted reorganization studies: professional management consultants, state employees, or business executives. Each group brought certain advantages and disadvantages to the reform effort. Management consultants and business executives provided great expertise in identifying potential economies in government operations and in the techniques of efficient management, but they lacked first-hand knowledge of government and would not be available when the inevitable problems arose during implementation. Conversely, state employees had an intimate knowledge of government and would still be around for the implementation of changes, but potential conflicts of interest qualified their objectivity. In an effort to resolve these difficulties, Carter and Linder decided to utilize all three groups.[5]

After a careful evaluation of several candidates, the administration selected Arthur Anderson and Company as the management consultant firm to assist in the reorganization study. Six firms had submitted bids. Linder and his staff systematically evaluated each on a 100-point system according to several established criteria: individual in charge (20 points); full-time on-site personnel (15); experience with statewide reorganization and other governmental studies (15); Atlanta staff size, capabilities and reputation in the state (20); research capabilities and availability of specialists (15); cost (10); participation in Georgia civic activities, conformity with approach explained to consultants, and willingness to make price concessions (5). Scoring high in all categories, Arthur Anderson and Company had a cumulative rating of 97. It had a large Atlanta office with 300 employees, good research capabilities, numerous Georgia clients, a good reputation throughout the state, and close contacts with major corporations in the Atlanta area, an important consideration in the recruitment of business volunteers for the reorganization study. George Kaiser, the designated leader of the management consultant team, had formerly served as secretary of administration for the state of Wisconsin and had participated in government reorganization projects in Wisconsin, Florida, Nebraska, and Colorado. Similar cost estimates from all but one of the competing firms removed price as a major consideration in the selection of a consultant firm, but the active involvement of its personnel in a variety of civic activities weighed in favor of Arthur Anderson.[6] In selecting a consulting firm, the administration manifested a keen sensitivity to the projected ability of each firm to make a favorable impression on state government officials and members of the General Assembly. The appraisal of one proposed head consultant, for example, noted that while the individual had extensive experience and excellent credentials, "his British accent and polished manner might make it difficult for him to deal with the General Assembly."[7] The Anderson firm's only liability was the presence of a company employee on the Governor's staff which, it was feared, might lead to charges of bias and favoritism in the selection of a consulting firm.[8]

Project Director Tom Linder then wrote to all the major business firms located in the Atlanta area asking them to contribute personnel to reorganization study teams for periods ranging from two to six months. He received an overwhelmingly favorable response. Among the major corporations contacted, only the Cox Broadcasting Corporation, which owned the two major newspapers in Atlanta and the National Broadcasting Company's radio and television affiliates in the area, refused to contribute. Forty-eight businesses contributed a total of sixty-five people to the effort. There is no evidence that anyone in the administration, including the Governor, questioned the propriety of relying on business volunteers, many of whom did business with state government and might have had potential conflicts of interest. Only organized labor seriously questioned the wisdom of employing business volunteers so extensively.[9] In a letter to James O. Moore, president of the Georgia state AFL-CIO, Carter, surprised by labor's criticism, explained that the reorganization project relied on management personnel "because they had expertise in such things as accounting and data processing. . . ." Nevertheless, the Governor moved quickly to involve organized labor in the reform effort.[10]

Before looking for volunteers from government agencies and departments, Carter described to state officials the type of employees he wanted. They should be aggressive with inquisitive tendencies, he said, "perhaps someone in line for promotion."[11] Ultimately, eighteen government agencies and departments diverted personnel to the project. The University System of Georgia contributed the most. Nine faculty members and administrators from the Georgia Institute of Technology, Georgia State University, and the University of Georgia participated full-time in the study, and several other University System employees contributed on a part-time basis. In an effort to acquaint Linder with the great variety of expertise available on the state's college and university campuses, Carter arranged an informal dinner at the governor's mansion where Linder met and talked with the presidents of the various colleges in the University System.[12]

A total of 117 people worked full-time on the Reorganization and Management Improvement Study, including 48 state employees, 65 volunteers from business and labor, and 4 representatives from Arthur Anderson and Company. According to the aggregate statistics the administration employed in publicizing the reorganization study, the business volunteers brought four centuries of experience to the project and state employees another three centuries of experience, most of it at government management levels. These participants devoted thirty-four man-years to the reorganization study.[13] Despite the heavy expenditure of time and resources, theoretically the study cost the state little. The Reorganization and Management Improvement Study operated on a $205,000 budget. Nearly half that sum came from a federal Department of Housing and Urban Development grant and much of the remainder from the Governor's emergency fund (see Table 1). Meanwhile, the reorganization staff computed the value of those thirty-four man-years of primarily volunteer labor at well over $500,000.[14]

Although it appeared a very good bargain for state government, the accounting procedures used on the reorganization study resembled a budgetary flimflam. The forty-eight state employees volunteered by government agencies were diverted from their regular duties and responsibilities. If their services had been charged to the reorganization budget at pro rata figures, the costs of the reorganization study would have risen considerably. The actual costs of the business volunteers is more difficult to assess. Few businesses invest money in purely altruistic causes. To the extent that businesses viewed their contribution as an investment in good public relations, it was relatively harmless; however, some business leaders no doubt assumed they had acquired a promissory note from the administration that could be used at a later date. On a less tangible level, participating companies acquired valuable

Table 1. *Reorganization and Management Improvement Program Expenditure Projection December 31, 1971*

	ACTUAL EXPENDI- TURES MARCH 1 THROUGH DECEMBER 31	PRO- JECTED TOTAL EXPENDI- TURES	UNEX- PENDED BAL- ANCE
Consultant Fees	$116,975	$125,000	$ 8,025
Travel of Project Team Members	9,188	14,000	4,812
Office Supplies and Postage	12,175	10,200	(1,975)
Printing	17,842	12,000	(5,842)
Equipment Rental and Repairs	3,039	1,500	(1,539)
HUD Inspection Fee	483	1,000	517
Telephone Expense	2,016	2,000	(16)
Film Production	5,013	5,000	(13)
Public Awareness Consultant	11,575	15,000	3,425
	$178,306	185,700	7,394
Add: Contingency		19,300	19,300
Total Projected Cost		$205,000	$26,694

PROPOSED SOURCE OF FUNDS

HUD Grant	$100,000
Donations for Public Awareness Program	5,000
Governor's Emergency Fund	100,000
Total	$205,0000

SOURCE: State of Georgia, "Reorganization and Management Improvement Study."

NOTE: Governor's Emergency Fund:
   $65,000 has been received from the Governor's Emergency Fund leaving a balance of $35,000 to be drawn

   Public Awareness:
   Further efforts are being made to obtain donations for paying the fees of the Public Awareness consultant. Mr. Al Bows is heading up this effort. As of December 31, 1971, $4,975 has been received.

new contacts in state government and probably received a more sympathetic hearing when conducting business with the state. To be sure, the administration recognized the existence of potential conflicts of interest. Thus, Linder took care to avoid having any state employee, regardless of his qualifications, involved in the study of his own department or, in the case of business volunteers, having any participant involved in the study of a department that regulated or did business with his firm.

From the initial review to the final implementation of recommended changes, the Reorganization and Management Improvement Study consisted of nine distinct phases.

Phase I—Project Administration and Planning

This initial phase included all preliminary planning, scheduling, personnel recruitment, and task assignments. It also provided a mechanism for continuous monitoring to insure that scheduled target dates for various projects were met. (See Figure 1.)

Phase II—Preliminary Review

Aimed at inventorying all functions of state government, this step encompassed the first substantive study activity. Each state agency conducted a self-study of its activities and procedures, completed a detailed questionnaire, and prepared a report of its findings and conclusions. Relevant study team members then conducted follow-up interviews with agency personnel before preparing a preliminary review summary. These surveys provided the means of assigning priorities and identifying areas in which detailed studies seemed appropriate.

Phase III—Public Awareness Program

(The public relations and information functions conducted under this heading are described in detail in Part II.)

Phase IV—Detailed Study

Based on the preliminary review of state government functions, assigned priorities, and the identified areas of reform, pertinent study teams conducted detailed studies of existing functions. Each study team then prepared a memorandum on its findings and recommendations. In making their proposals, the study teams considered not only the preliminary review but also the findings and conclusions of all previous reports, the reorganization reports of other states, relevant research reports, and pertinent General Assembly committee reports from the previous five years.

Each study team prepared a comprehensive work program that included a timetable identifying starting and completion dates as well as initiation dates for particular work steps, man-hour requirements, and personnel assignments.

Roper and Linder reviewed the study team recommendations' memoranda before forwarding them to Governor Carter for his study. A meeting between the Governor, project managers, and study team members followed. At this meeting they developed final recommendations and forwarded them to the executive committee for its review.

Phase V—Development of Reorganization Plan

The development of the reorganization plan occurred simultaneously with the detailed studies conducted by the various reorganization study teams. The final reorganization plan represented the cumulative product of the reviewed recommendations memoranda.

Phase VI—Report Preparation

The ultimate product of Phases II, IV, and V was a 219-page report published under the title "Reorganization and Management Improvement Study." The first section of the report, entitled "Proposed Departments," detailed anticipated structural changes, and the second section, "Special Studies," covered functional and procedural matters.

Phase VII—Draft Legislation

Under the direction of James T. McIntyre, Jr., the director of the Office of Planning and Budget and chief legal counsel for the reorganization study, a team of lawyers primarily from state agencies converted the recommendations into legislative bill form for introduction in the General Assembly. McIntyre's team wrote the fifty-seven page bill in such a way that each proposed change fell into a separate subsection. This permitted constitutional officers and state legislators to veto specific changes without abolishing the entire section in which it appeared.

Phase VIII—Constitutional Officer Review

After the final reorganization report, constitutional officers reviewed proposed changes in their departments and either accepted or rejected the inclusion of the recommendations in the reorganization plan submitted to the General Assembly. Many of the changes objected to by the constitutional officers were later introduced in the state legislature as separate legislation.

Phase IX—Implementation Follow-Up

Having secured approval from the General Assembly, the administration closely monitored the implementation of changes by state agencies to assure the successful completion of reforms and the realization of anticipated savings. Each state agency received an implementation notebook to use in preparing detailed plans for putting proposed reforms into effect. After approval by the Governor, these plans provided the basis for preparing monthly reports on the progress achieved in instituting the new procedures.[15]

From the beginning, structural reform, which included reducing the large number of state agencies, received the highest priority in the reorganization effort. Governor Carter justified this emphasis on three grounds:

First, government should be responsive and close to the people. It should be as easy as possible for a citizen to deal with. By combining several agencies which provide similar or closely related service, we eliminate the need for the citizen to deal with a large number of agencies in order to obtain services.

Second, present agencies overlap and duplicate each other in the services they provide and the equipment, personnel skills, and offices required to deliver these services. If we eliminate this overlap and duplication by combining agencies, we can expect the same services to be performed at a lower cost or, if we choose, we can provide increased services for the present cost.

Third, there are presently 300 agencies in the Executive Branch of State Government. It is very difficult, if not impossible, for the Governor or members of the General Assembly to deal effectively with this number of agencies. Reducing the number of agencies will alleviate this problem and thereby provide the opportunity for improved management of state Government.[16]

While most reorganization study teams concentrated on structural reform, several special management improvement studies that transcended functional divisions were conducted. These special teams studied cash receipts and cash management, electronic data

Figure 1. Reorganization and Management Improvement Study Project Schedule

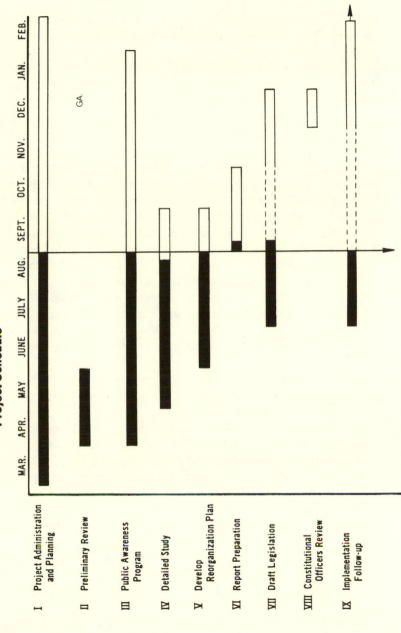

SOURCE: Carter Gubernatorial Papers, Record Group 1, Subgroup 15, Series 65.

processing, printing and publication, purchasing, and records management. The recommendations of the special study teams later proved to be among the most controversial and politically volatile of the entire reorganization project.

Governor Carter played an active role throughout the reorganization effort. He initially allocated 200 hours of his time to the reorganization effort and ultimately devoted many more hours to the Public Awareness Program. By his own estimate, the Governor devoted nearly one-quarter of his time to the reform.[17] He personally screened all recommendations put forth by the study teams and met at least three times with each group. During these meetings, which sometimes lasted three to four hours, he asked questions, made suggestions, and impressed study team members with his general knowledge of good management procedures, his quick grasp of administration details, and his commitment to organizational reform.[18] Repeatedly, he urged the study teams to make their recommendations on the basis of merit and without regard to political expediency or potential cost savings. "I have no intention of making a recommendation simply for political expediency, nor to avoid confrontation," he declared. "I don't intend to back down at all on what I consider to be the best plan for Georgia."[19]

At times, study team recommendations conflicted with the Governor's desires on particular issues. While sometimes overruling the study teams, usually the Governor accepted their contrary recommendations, albeit at times reluctantly. Carter, for example, wanted to remove civil defense from the state Department of Defense, but the reorganization study team objected and Carter ultimately agreed. He also proposed that mental health be separated from the state health department but again accepted a contrary recommendation from the study team in the area.[20] In areas in which he had greater knowledge and experience, such as education, he was less likely to accommodate suggestions contrary to his own inclinations. Overall, participants in the reform effort gave the Governor high marks for the quality of his contributions to the reorganization plan and for his willingness to abide by and support their recommendations.[21]

By September 1971, the various reorganization study teams had produced 2,500 pages of recommendations representing over 300 substantive proposals for governmental reform. Three different review groups studied each recommendation "to insure thoroughness, objectivity, and application of sound business principles."[22] For purposes of analysis, the recommended changes can be classified under the two broad categories identified in the "Reorganization and Management Improvement Study": (1) structural agency reform; and (2) management improvement reform related to common services which crossed departmental lines.

STRUCTURAL REFORM

As a result of the reorganization study, the existing sixty-five budgeted agencies were consolidated into twenty agencies (Figures 2 and 3). In addition, the functions of over 200 unbudgeted agencies were transferred to one or more of the twenty line departments. The functions of five departments remained relatively unchanged—the Office of Attorney General, Department of Defense, Department of Veterans Service, Department of Revenue, and the University System. Several existing departments either gained new responsibilities or lost jurisdiction over functions previously administered.

The Department of Education lost vocational rehabilitation to the new Department of Human Resources. In an effort to remove education from politics and permit the school superintendent to devote himself to the task of directing the public school system without the distracting and time-consuming problem of reelection, the administration recommended a constitutional amendment that would allow the selection of the state school superintendent to be made by the State Board of Education. The proposal, one of the more controversial features of the reorganization plan, would have greatly strengthened the governor's control over education, since he appointed members of the State Board of Education.[23]

While losing some functions, the Comptroller General assumed important new responsibilities. In an effort to consolidate all functions related to insurance, the Board of Workmen's Compensation, previously a separate agency, and the industrial safety activities previously supervised by the Department of Labor were transferred

Figure 2.   *Georgia State Government—Executive Branch Before Reorganization*

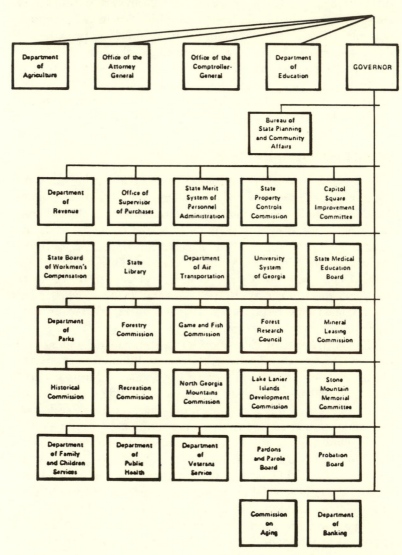

SOURCE: Copied from State of Georgia,

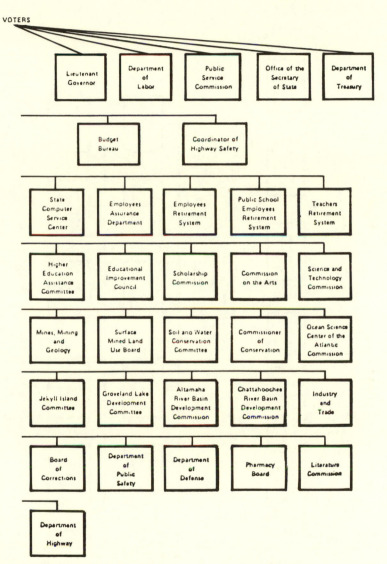

VOTERS

| Lieutenant Governor | Department of Labor | Public Service Commission | Office of the Secretary of State | Department of Treasury |

| Budget Bureau | Coordinator of Highway Safety |

| State Computer Service Center | Employees Assurance Department | Employees Retirement System | Public School Employees Retirement System | Teachers Retirement System |

| Higher Education Assistance Committee | Educational Improvement Council | Scholarship Commission | Commission on the Arts | Science and Technology Commission |

| Mines, Mining and Geology | Surface Mined Land Use Board | Soil and Water Conservation Committee | Commissioner of Conservation | Ocean Science Center of the Atlantic Commission |

| Jekyll Island Committee | Groveland Lake Development Committee | Altamaha River Basin Development Commission | Chattahoochee River Basin Development Commission | Industry and Trade |

| Board of Corrections | Department of Public Safety | Department of Defense | Pharmacy Board | Literature Commission |

| Department of Highway |

"Reorganization and Management Improvement Study."

Figure 3. Georgia State Government—Executive Branch After Reorganization

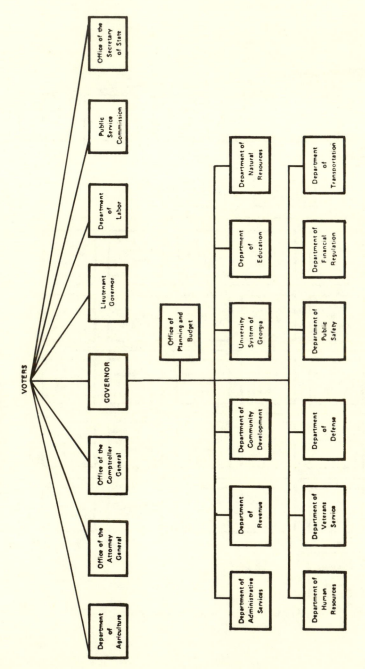

SOURCE: Copied from State of Georgia, "Reorganization and Management Improvement Study."

to the Office of the Comptroller General. This constituted the only significant change in the existing functions of the Department of Labor.

In addition to its regular constitutional responsibilities, under the reorganization plan, the Office of the Secretary of State acquired jurisdiction over the state library and if the necessary constitutional amendment passed, authority over business incorporation procedures. In addition, the secretary of state assumed responsibilities for the licensing of professionals and tradesmen. Meanwhile, the maintenance of real property records was transferred to the Office of the Attorney General and securities regulation to the Department of Financial Regulation.

In addition to its existing regulatory powers over transportation and utility companies, the Public Service Commission had its responsibilities expanded "to include certificate and regulatory powers, including financing, rates schedule, safety, etc., for water and sewerage, all communications, transportation, and energy resource use industries."[24] As a result of reorganization the five-member board would serve the dual function of a policy-making and appeal-hearing body with examiners assigned to handle complaints and conduct certificate hearings.

The Department of Agriculture retained all its previous functions except the inspection of eggs in eating establishments and nursing homes (reassigned to the Department of Human Resources). To eliminate duplication of effort, to save money, and to strengthen consumer protection activities, the department's existing consumer functions were expanded to include inspection of milk, shellfish canneries, and fuel oil, as well as cigarette, beer, and wine licensing.

Similarly, the jurisdiction and responsibilities of the Department of Public Safety grew significantly. All major state activities in the areas of public safety, criminal investigation, and law enforcement were transferred to this department as well as other functions relating to highway safety, drug abuse, arson investigation, and vehicle safety inspection, which had been scattered throughout state agencies.

The functions of several existing budgeted agencies were combined into four new departments. The Department of Financial Regulation assumed regulatory jurisdiction over securities sales and all state-chartered financial institutions including banks, credit unions, industrial loan companies, and savings and loan companies, all previously exercised by the Department of Banking, the comtroller general, and the secretary of state. It also assumed responsibility for enforcing the Georgia securities law pertaining to the registering of securities for sale and the licensing of broker-dealers and salesmen. The Department of Transportation retained all the functions previously administered by the State Highway Department as well as those of the Aviation Division and the Metropolitan Atlanta Rapid Transit Authority funding program that previously had been supervised by the Department of Industry and Trade. The budgetary and state planning functions exercised by the Budget Bureau and the Bureau of Planning and Community Affairs were combined in the new Office of Planning and Budget, which also assumed the advisory functions of the Science and Technology Commission and the Georgia Commission on the Arts. The Department of Community Development combined the local and regional planning and development assistance activities previously exercised by the Bureau of Planning and Community Affairs with the functions of the Department of Industry and Trade.

Much of the controversy inspired by the reorganization plan swirled around the creation of three umbrella departments, or super-agencies as they came to be called, the Departments of Administrative Services, Natural Resources, and Human Resources. The functions and responsibilities of sixty-two existing state agencies were incorporated into the activities of these three departments.

The Department of Administrative Services was designed to deliver a wide variety of support services to other state agencies in the areas of purchasing, personnel administration, printing, data processing, payroll, communications, property management, and motor pool operations. The department assumed responsibility for the functions previously performed by the following seventeen state agencies:

Advisory Council on Georgia Government Documents
Capitol Square Improvement Committee
Department of Air Transportation
Employees Retirement System
Federal Surplus Property Unit (from the Department of Education)
Georgia Building Authority

Georgia Education Authority
Mineral Leasing Commission
Real Property Inventory Unit (from the Secretary of State)
State Communications Committee
State Computer Service Center
State Merit System of Personnel Administration
State Properties Acquisition Commission
State Properties Control Commission
Supervisor of Purchases
Teachers Retirement System of Georgia
Treasury Department

Divided into six functional divisions, the Department of Administrative Services was headed by a commissioner appointed by the governor with the consent of the Senate. The report also proposed the development of guidelines and procedures related to the disposal of state-owned surplus real and personal property, the Social Security Trust Fund, cleaning and maintenance of capitol office space, and working hours of state personnel.

The Department of Natural Resources incorporated the natural resource use and protection activities previously exercised by thirty-six separate state agencies:

Game and Fish Commission
State Parks Department
State Forestry Commission
Department of Mines, Mining and Geology
Department of Public Health (air, water, solid waste disposal)
Commissioner of Conservation
Georgia Recreation Commission
Groveland Lake Development Authority
Stone Mountain Memorial Authority
Jekyll Island State Parks Authority
North Georgia Mountains Authority
Lake Lanier Islands Development Authority
Soil and Water Conservation Committee
Forest Research Council
Mineral Leasing Commission

Figure 4. *Department of Administrative Services*

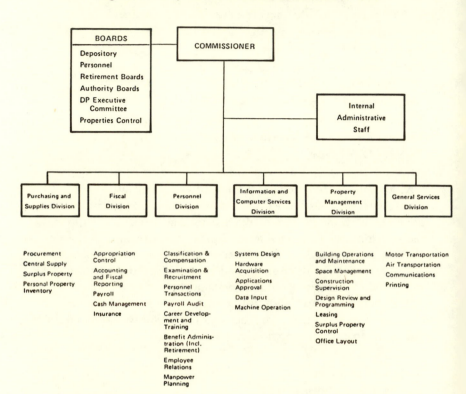

SOURCE: Copied from State of Georgia, "Reorganization and Management Improvement Study."

Surface Mined Land Use Board
Georgia Natural Areas Council
Altamaha River Basin Development Commission
Chattahoochee River Basin Development Commission
Ocean Science Center of the Atlantic
Resources Advisory Board, South East River Basins
Governor's Citizens Advisory Council on Environmental Affairs
Southern Regional Environmental Conservation Council
Franklin Delano Roosevelt Warm Springs Memorial Commission
Interagency Council on Outdoor Recreation
Herty Foundation
Southeastern Interstate Forest Fire Protection Advisory Committee
Coastal Marshlands Protection Agency
Atlantic State Marine Fisheries Committee
Governor's Commission on Coastal Zone Management
Georgia Waterways Commission
Pesticide Review Board
Rivers and Harbors Development Commission
Citizens Environmental Council
Interstate Environment Compact
Ty Cobb Memorial Committee

The department, separated into seven divisions, was headed by a commissioner appointed by a reconstituted Game and Fish Commission with the governor's advice and consent.

None of the new departments evoked as much controversy as the proposed Department of Human Resources. In an effort to consolidate state social services, the new department assumed responsibility for administering programs in such areas as physical and mental health, welfare, probation and parole, drug treatment, and housing. The functions of eight separate state agencies and the activities encompassed in over fifty different programs were transferred to the Department of Human Resources. The consolidated agencies included

Department of Public Health
Department of Family and Children Services
Office of Rehabilitation Services (from the Department of Education)

Figure 5. *Department of Natural Resources*

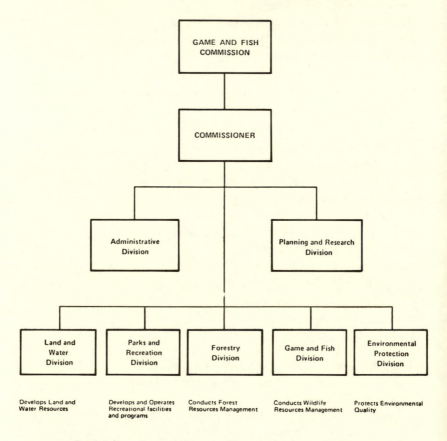

SOURCE: Copied from State of Georgia, "Reorganization and Management Improvement Study."

Board of Corrections
Board of Pardons and Paroles
Board of Probation
Commission on Aging
Cooperative Area Manpower Planning Systems (includes Youth Opportunity Council from the Office of the Governor)

The abolition of the Board of Health, whose members were nominated by the Georgia Medical Association and appointed by the governor, and its replacement by a Board of Human Resources on which licensed physicians would constitute a minority aroused great concern, especially among the state's doctors. The proposal to combine criminal justice activities and public health and welfare functions also aroused considerable controversy.

MANAGEMENT IMPROVEMENT REFORM

In addition to the proposals for structural reform, reorganization study teams conducted sixteen different special inquiries in an effort to improve management efficiency and reduce the costs of services common to all agencies of state government. The special studies included

Air Transportation
Capital Construction and Financing
Cash Management
Cash Receipts
Communications
Data Processing
Insurance
Laboratories
Motor Vehicles
Payroll
Personal Property Management
Personnel
Printing and Publications

Figure 6.   *Department of Human Resources*

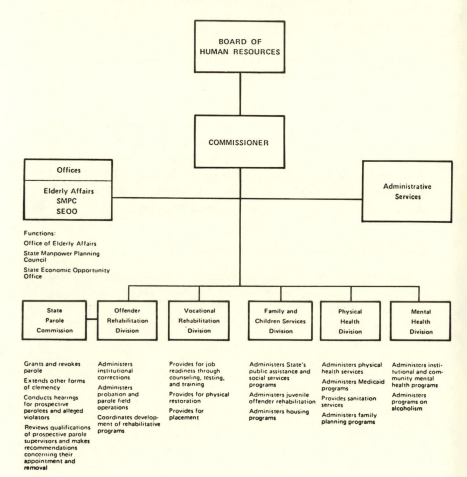

SOURCE: Copied from State of Georgia, "Reorganization and Management Improvement Study."

Purchasing
Record Management
Space Management

The special studies resulted in several far-reaching proposals for change that aroused considerable opposition, especially from the state's constitutional officers. One of the more controversial involved the consolidation of computing and data processing services in the Department of Administrative Services. Prior to reorganization, the state operated 14 administrative data processing centers and 3 instructional and research centers utilizing a total of 135 computers. Linder found that some of these computers were used at less than 10 percent of their capabilities.[25] Consolidation in a single agency, the administration argued, would provide great savings.

The reorganization plan also included a proposal to consolidate the state's 42 printing units and approximately 100 photocopy machines into 8 printing units and 8 rapid copy centers. Adoption of this recommendation, according to the special study team that investigated the matter, would not only produce substantial cost savings but would also permit the disposal of old and obsolete machinery and the upgrading of equipment and techniques.[26]

Other significant proposals produced by the special management improvement study teams included the creation of a central motor vehicle pool, centralized purchasing, reform in revenue collection procedures and cash management, and an overhaul of the state's insurance programs.

The reorganization team estimated that the adoption of structural and management improvement reforms would not only greatly improve the delivery of state services but also would produce a one-time financial windfall of $20 million and an annual cost savings of $60 million. The windfall would come from requiring semi-monthly rather than monthly deposit of sales tax receipts and from requiring payment of insurance premium taxes monthly rather than annually. Meanwhile, the cost reduction, cost avoidance, and revenue increases would derive from the adoption of the various proposals for structural and management improvement reform (Table 2).

Table 2. *Reorganization and Management Improvement Study*
ESTIMATED FINANCIAL BENEFITS TO THE STATE

Proposed Departments	COST REDUCTIONS*		ANNUAL COST AVOIDANCE	REVENUE INCREASES	
	ONE-TIME	ANNUAL		ONE-TIME	ANNUAL
Governor's Office					
Dept. of Agriculture					
Attorney General					$ 69,000
Comptroller General		$ 348,000			
Dept. of Labor					
Public Service Commission					
Secretary of State	$ 260,000	73,000			
Planning and Budget					
Dept. of Admin. Services		20,000			300,000
Dept. of Revenue				$ 2,000,000	
Dept. of Community Development					
University System of Georgia		563,000			6,972,000
Dept. of Education					
Dept. of Natural Resources		1,884,000			
Dept. of Human Resources	(60,000)	852,700	$ 280,000		1,370,000
Dept. of Veterans Service					
Dept. of Defense					
Dept. of Public Safety			470,000		
Dept. of Financial Regulations		43,000			
Dept. of Transportation		9,394,800	4,900,000		760,000

70

Table 2. Reorganization and Management Improvement Study (continued)

	(A)	(B)	(C)	(D)	(E)
Special Studies					
Air Transportation					
Capital Construction		600,000			
Cash Management					2,000,000
Cash Receipts		147,000		30,500,000	10,799,000
Communications		800,000			
Data Processing		570,000	2,670,000		
Insurance	(4,000,000)	(1,746,000)			
Laboratories	(3,000,000)	2,485,950			
Motor Vehicles	(2,000,000)	1,500,000			317,500
Payroll		132,000			
Personal Property Management					
Personnel		65,000			
Printing and Publications		605,000	12,000		
Purchasing		9,600,000			
Records Management	746,000	176,000	274,000		
Space Management			830,000		726,750
Special Implementation Cost	(4,000,000)				
Total	($12,054,000)**	$28,113,450	$9,436,000	$32,500,000	$23,314,250

SOURCE: State of Georgia, "Reorganization and Management Improvement Study."

Note: Net Annual Financial Benefit $60,863,700 (B + C + E)
Net one-time Financial Benefit $20,446,000 (A + D)

*These figures are net of costs to implement.
**Brackets indicate net costs to the State.

71

Most of those involved in the reorganization study expressed satisfaction with the final plan the Governor forwarded to the state's constitutional officers and the General Assembly. George Kaiser, the Arthur Anderson consultant who had participated in numerous such studies, told Tom Linder it was one of the most well-conceived and comprehensive plans he had seen.[27] Participants in the study realized that problems would arise with the implementation of proposed changes, but they believed the plan was fundamentally sound and would accomplish the objectives set forth in HB 1.

Before any of the changes recommended in the Reorganization and Management Improvement Study could go into effect, however, they had to survive the review of constitutional officers and the Georgia General Assembly. Opposition to the reorganization plan began to grow well before the publication of the final recommendations. But opposition had been anticipated, and the administration launched an elaborate public relations campaign simultaneously with the reorganization study. The character, methods employed, and effectiveness of that effort are considered in Part II.

PART II

The Selling of Government Reorganization: The Public Awareness Program

Interest and strong grass roots support for reorganization by Georgians will be vital in the deliberations of the General Assembly in assuring successful passage.

Tom Linder, Project Director

After discussing the subject matter with Mr. Tom Linder and being given information by others involved in selling reorganization, I have concluded that I must refuse the request to be used as part of what I believe to be an attempted snow-job of the people and their elected representatives in the Georgia General Assembly.

Lester Maddox, Lieutenant Governor

chapter 3

SELLING REORGANIZATION
TO THE PEOPLE

In principle, everyone favors a reform that promises to promote economy and greater efficiency in government as well as better delivery of state services. But, reorganization is a complex, somewhat abstract reform that usually fails to generate great public enthusiasm. Thus, it is an issue that is often debated and resolved by political activists.

The abolition of some agencies and the consolidation of others, as well as a general reshuffling of administrative duties and responsibilities, inevitably causes the disruption of prevailing divisions of authority. It is at this point that the principle of reorganization succumbs to the fact of reorganization. The major resistance comes from the losers in the general redistribution of administrative power and authority. It also comes from those legislators who have established cordial working relationships with the heads of existing executive departments and agencies and do not want those arrangements disrupted. Moreover, there appears to be a prevailing assumption that reorganization will inevitably result in a redistribution of power favoring the governor at the expense of the legislature.

Thus, reorganization has no natural constituency, but any governmental reorganization plan will encounter several natural points of resistance. Well aware of this, the Carter forces realized they would have to create a constituency for reorganization if they hoped to put their plan into effect. Consequently, the administration launched an elaborate Public Awareness Program shortly after the end of the General Assembly session. Through the campaign, the administration sought to inform the public of the progress being made in developing the reorganization plan, to encourage citizen interest and participation through questions and suggestions, and, most importantly, to generate public awareness and support.[1]

The Public Awareness Advisory Committee provided professional advice and direction for the public relations effort. Bert Hatch, president of the Georgia Association of Broadcasters, and Glenn McCollough, an official in the Georgia Press Association, represented the media on the committee. Rod O'Connor, a professor of industrial management at the Georgia Institute of Technology, and Earl Leonard of the Coca Cola Bottling Company represented the academic and business communities respectively. Gerald Rafshoon of Rafshoon Advertising, Inc. supervised the public relations campaign, and Carter's press secretary, Jody Powell, provided the necessary liaison between the committee and the Governor's office.

Organizers of the awareness program sought to sell the reorganization plan to three important constituencies: Georgia citizens, state government officials and employees, and members of the General Assembly. Cloyd Hall, special assistant to the Governor, assumed responsibility for coordinating the Public Awareness Program and for maintaining close contact with department heads and members of the General Assembly.

Soon after the creation of the Public Awareness Program, Hall met with each member of the advisory committee seeking guidance on the nature and scope of the public relations effort. Committee members generally agreed on the need to launch the program immediately and to maintain an extremely active campaign throughout the period reorganization was being studied and the plan developed. They also agreed that the opposition to reorganization should be discredited by associating it with special interest pressures. This would put the antagonists on the defensive and place their objections in an unfavorable light.[2]

Hall divided the program into two chronological periods. The need for reorganization would be stressed during Phase I; and, after release of the plan, Phase II would be initiated with an emphasis on explaining and justifying the proposal. He then developed an elaborate "Work Plan," listing individual assignments and establishing initiation and completion dates for assigned responsibilities.[3]

However, planning is important but execution is crucial. A good plan poorly executed seldom results in victory; thus it was with the Public Awareness Program. It was highly organized and well-planned, but success depended upon execution.

The administration attached great importance to generating public enthusiasm for the reorganization program. Success in the public relations effort, Carter staffers agreed, would greatly facilitate the lobbying activities among government officials and members of the General Assembly. Gerald Rafshoon masterminded the reorganization public relations campaign. In a memorandum to the Public Awareness Advisory Committee, he outlined the public relations effort that would be needed to accomplish the objectives of the Public Awareness Program.[4]

The campaign Rafshoon recommended included both a direct and indirect appeal to public opinion. The media, including radio, television, and newspapers, provided an invaluable means of direct communication. Films, brochures, newsletters, and people-to-people contacts similar to those employed during election campaigns constituted another medium. The indirect means of generating awareness and building support included favorable coverage and editorial support from the press and broadcast media and endorsements from individuals, associations, and civic clubs. All of this, Rafshoon concluded, would help build the necessary "bandwagon" psychology needed to overcome the resistance to change.[5]

Rafshoon reserved the "star role" in the Public Awareness Program for Governor Carter. By virtue of his office, the Governor had the ability to attract great publicity to the reorganization effort, and Rafshoon desired to exploit that influence to the fullest. He recommended a "roadshow" for the Governor during which he would sell reorganization to the people of Georgia in the same way that he had sold his gubernatorial candidacy a few months earlier.[6] Besides taking up the campaign trail, the Governor, through news conferences, film clips, and speeches to state-wide organizations, civic clubs, and professional associations, would create a public awareness of the positive aspects of reorganization. Private meetings at the governor's mansion were also to be utilized extensively. Carter could use these occasions to brief and solicit support from media executives, community leaders, department heads, and key legislators.[7]

Despite elaborate planning, the Public Awareness Program had fallen far behind schedule by early summer. Recognizing the need for a larger staff commitment, Tom Linder increased the assigned personnel from three to nine, including Peter Banks, a registered lobbyist for Atlanta Gas Light Company, and Bill Wells, a special assistant in the Governor's office. Rafshoon also agreed to devote more of his time to the effort, especially in providing professional guidance, and Linder committed half his time to the Public Awareness campaign. These changes had the desired effect. By midsummer the Public Awareness Program was on schedule, and the results were beginning to be felt in the three targeted areas: the general public, state departments and agencies, and members of the Georgia General Assembly.[8]

personality profile:_____
GERALD RAFSHOON
_____

The son of a career Air Force officer, Gerald Rafshoon was born in Brooklyn, New York, in 1934. He attended a series of schools connected with the various Air Force bases to which his father was assigned before enrolling at the University of Texas, where he earned a degree in journalism in 1955. Thereafter, he wrote advertising copy for Lyndon Johnson's Austin radio station, and, among other things, served a four-year term in the United States Navy. By 1963, he had joined Twentieth Century-Fox as its national advertising manager. Three years later, he resigned his position at the movie studio to found Gerald Rafshoon Advertising, Inc., in Atlanta. Impressed by the poor quality of Carter's political advertising during the 1966 gubernatorial campaign, he called Hal Gulliver, who was covering Carter for the Atlanta Constitution, *to tell him, "Your friend Carter needs help."*

Gulliver arranged a meeting, and Rafshoon quickly convinced the gubernatorial aspirant he needed an entirely new approach to political advertising. The two men liked each other immediately. Rafshoon, who would later describe himself as Carter's "media masturbator," managed Carter's media campaign during the successful 1970 gubernatorial contest. He then served as an unofficial media and public relations advisor during Carter's governorship.[9]

Earlier, Rafshoon had agreed to produce an eight-minute film which, in a "low key manner," would depict the need for and the advantages of reorganization. Because the administration contemplated using television extensively in its public relations campaign, it considered the documentary film an especially important means of direct communication. Along with the executive committee of the Reorganization and Management Improvement Study and the advisory committee of the Public Awareness Program, the Governor previewed a film used in Montana to promote government reorganization. Rafshoon then read a script he had written based on his reaction to the Montana film. Noting that a recent poll of Georgians indicated that 85 percent of them felt government generally neglected the concerns of the average person, Rafshoon concluded that "responsive" should be the key word of the public awareness campaign. "If we are *responsive* to the public in what we do," he said, "the public will be *responsive* to the program." While he recognized the importance of reaching legislators, constitutional officers, and department heads, the advertising executive concluded that if the public is responsive to reorganization, the politicians and bureaucrats will be too . . . they follow, they don't lead."[10]

Rafshoon sought to involve Georgia citizens as much as possible in the film. Factory workers, farmers, small businessmen, teachers, and welfare mothers would all be given an opportunity to have their say. This approach, Rafshoon argued, was not just a gimmick but a way of actually involving average citizens in the reorganization effort. He felt the film should not be hard-sell but should leave the viewer with a warm, favorable feeling toward the reorganization concept. "Let him see this and then the next time he sees his legislator, he'll voluntarily say, 'Man, I really like Carter's plan to save money, give more services, etc'."[11]

The executive committee analyzed Rafshoon's script in much the same manner it earlier had studied the Montana film. The Governor felt his role in reorganization should be deemphasized and that of legislators and state department heads stressed. Committee members, especially the legislators, also considered Rafshoon's approach too soft-sell. Senator Lamar Plunkett and House Majority Leader George Busbee agreed the film should include a message urging viewers to contact the senators and representatives in their districts. Busbee said the approach should be to "support your legislator in his brave effort to carry reorganization through."[12] He noted that lawmakers would come under intense pressures from certain quarters and would need this type of moral support.

Revised along the lines suggested and expanded to eleven minutes, Rafshoon completed the film in August and ordered twenty-five copies for use on public and commercial television, at county fairs, civic club meetings, and a variety of other public functions. It was shown extensively throughout the state during the summer and fall months and proved an effective and popular public relations gambit.[13]

The Public Awareness staff utilized broadcast and television media in a variety of other ways. Every radio station in the state received, and most aired, a fifteen-minute interview with the Governor conducted by Bert Hatch, president of the Georgia Broadcasters Association. "Spot" and "fact" tapes made by reorganization personnel, sympathetic department heads, favorable legislators and prominent individuals regularly appeared in the mail of radio stations. Before the reorganization fight ended, every radio and television interview and talk show had been exploited at least once —some several times. Finally, during the last two months of the year, the Public Awareness staff distributed to both public and commercial television stations a series of educational programs promoting reorganization.[14]

Throughout the campaign, Tom Linder remained a veritable whirlwind of activity. He made three or more speeches a week to civic clubs and statewide organizations and associations, eagerly submitted to radio and television interviews, and participated on numerous talk shows. He virtually accepted all invitations to speak, and when he found it necessary, actively solicited them. The overwhelmingly positive response to his efforts established Linder as one of the most effective spokesmen for the reorganization cause.[15]

Meanwhile, Rafshoon Advertising produced and distributed 145,000 brochures to explain reorganization to the average voter. In these handbills, which bore the slogan, "Economize, Revitalize, Reorganize State Government," the Public Awareness staff employed a question and answer format to correct prevailing misconceptions and to answer reorganization critics. In discussing this promotion, Carter again wanted his role minimized and that of the General Assembly emphasized.[16] In an effort to show unity of purpose and to dramatize the important role of the legislature, Rafshoon wanted to adorn the cover of the brochure with a picture of the Governor flanked by George L. Smith and Lester Maddox, presiding officers of the Georgia House and Senate. In a long, acrimonious memorandum to Cloyd Hall, Maddox said he wanted no part of it. He reiterated his constitutional objections to HB 1 and refused to have anything to do with an attempted "snow-job of the people and their elected representatives in the Georgia General Assembly."[17] The distribution of a second twenty-page brochure summarizing proposed changes in the executive branch accompanied the release of the reorganization plan. Over 200,000 copies of this pamphlet went out to interested citizens throughout the state. The administration also had 2,500 copies of the complete 219-page report printed and sent to state legislators, department heads, daily newspaper editors, selected radio and television news directors, members of state boards, and reorganization project personnel.[18]

Near the end of the year, the Carter campaign organization created during the 1970 gubernatorial campaign was revived as the Citizens' Committee for Reorganization. Headed by Robert Lipshutz, an Atlanta attorney and advisor to the Governor, a twenty-three member steering committee coordinated the organization's activities throughout the state. The committee's membership came primarily from the state's more populous areas and included a Democratic national committeeman, some of the Governor's largest campaign contributors, and several of his county campaign chairmen. Members of the Citizens' Committee for Reorganization devoted their time and money to building grass-roots support for the reorganization program. They wrote letters and telephoned friends and acquaintances arguing the merits of reorganization and urging them to contact their senators and representatives in behalf of the program.[19]

The committee also mailed out thousands of copies of a newsletter bearing the banner: "JIMMY CARTER NEEDS YOUR HELP." The cover consisted of a cartoon in which the Governor appeared as a sword-swinging St. George slaying "a multi-headed dragon named Waste, Inefficiency, Special Interests and Petty Politics."[20] The Public Awareness staff mailed 50,000 copies of these handbills in late December and two weeks later distributed a second newsletter. The question and answer format again was employed in these pamphlets to explain the reorganization plan and to respond to the charges made against it by highly vocal critics. The Citizens' Committee for Reorganization remained active throughout the period during which the General Assembly debated reorganization.[21]

The administration utilized every conceivable means of publicizing reorganization. The Sumter County Grand Jury endorsed state government reorganization and formally urged that it be approved by the General Assembly.[22] The Governor's Plains home was located in Sumter County. Tom Linder also sought to have reorganization promotionals inserted in the football programs of state universities and colleges, but the chancellor of the University System vetoed that scheme.[23] Finally, as the date for the convening of the General Assembly approached, officials of the Public Awareness Program hired Bell and Stanton, an Atlanta-based public relations firm, in a further effort to mobilize support behind the reorganization proposal. Bell and Stanton officials agreed to a 50 percent reduction in their normal fee, and the firm's $15,000 bill was paid primarily from private donations, the largest a check for $5,000 from Delta Airlines.[24]

Efforts to secure support from the numerous statewide organizations and associations that were influential throughout the state accompanied direct appeals to public opinion. The administration especially wanted the endorsement of two influential public lobbying groups: Common Cause and the League of Women Voters. Leah and Sidney Q. Janus, a politically active Atlanta couple, held the key to support from these organizations. Leah was president of the League of Women Voters, and Sidney headed Common Cause. Fortunately for the reorganization program, they both early expressed their support for the reform effort.[25]

JoAnn Hawkins, a member of the Public Awareness team, served as the principal contact with Common Cause. In a long memorandum to Tom Linder, she described the early development of Common Cause, including the role played in it by such Georgians as Julian Bond, Andrew Young, and Vivian Henderson. She went on to explain the way in which Common Cause operated:

> The usual procedure, once a mutual agreement is reached, is that the Washington office of Common Cause writes its members in the state (1,500 in Georgia) and asks them to write their legislators supporting the idea. The members also ask five of their friends to write their legislators, and rarely do they identify themselves as members of Common Cause. In most cases, all the legislator is aware of is that he is getting lots of mail from concerned citizens, which is, in truth, exactly what the members of Common Cause are.[26]

Shortly after endorsing the reorganization program, Common Cause established a campaign committee of six members to coordinate the organization's efforts on behalf of reorganization. Sidney Janus reported that his group had a special interest in the new Department of Human Resources, since it best exemplified the Common Cause theme of "nearer my government to me." Support in this area was especially welcome as the projected Human Resources Department was the most controversial feature of the reorganization plan and would be difficult to get through the General Assembly.[27]

The active support of the influential League of Women Voters was also an important coup for the administration. Leah Janus enthusiastically endorsed the principle of reorganization shortly after Carter proposed it, but with the formation of the study teams, a problem arose. Commenting on a reorganization article in the Sunday magazine supplement in the *Atlanta Journal and Constitution*, Ms. Janus remarked that reorganization had "everything, *almost*: vision, careful planning, youth, brain power, manpower, but no womanpower!" "Centuries of experience," she added facetiously, "have given women expertise in housecleaning."[28] In responding, Hamilton Jordan pleaded guilty. He explained that the Governor had recruited business volunteers for the reorganization study teams, and, unfortunately, the various companies contributing personnel had all selected men. He emphasized, however, the important contributions that women like herself could make to the reorganization effort.[29]

Governor Carter also maintained a close, personal contact with Ms. Janus. He invited her to meetings at the governor's mansion, and the two carried on an active correspondence. At one point the Governor declared: "I want and need your personal help and the active support of the League of Women Voters. I have asked Hamilton Jordan to contact you and work closely with you in educating and involving the League in the Reorganization effort."[30]

Although it would be difficult, if not impossible, to assess the significance of the League's endorsement, many state legislators respected the manner in which the women's organization diligently researched and carefully evaluated legislation before placing its stamp of approval on it. If nothing else, the League's support gave reorganization an added measure of respectability.

The Public Awareness staff sought support from other women's organizations and gained endorsements from such varied groups as the National Council of Jewish Women of Georgia, the Atlanta Women's Chamber of Commerce, the Chi Omega Alumnae Association of Atlanta, the Northside [Atlanta] Women's Club, and the American Association of University Women. Local branches of AAUW, under the direction of the Legislative Program Committee of the Georgia division, were especially important to the reorganization campaign.[31]

Endorsements of reorganization and promises of active support flowed in from a large number of other statewide associations.

The state Chamber of Commerce threw its support behind the reform effort and volunteered two men to travel the state calling on local chapters, the news media, and business leaders. Such other diverse organizations as the Georgia Association of Private Employment Agencies, the Georgia Motor Trucking Association, Georgia LP-Gas Association, and the Georgia Association of Realtors all expressed their support of reorganization.[32]

The Georgia Jaycees' active support of reorganization, however, proved to be the administration's most significant endorsement. Shortly after putting together the reorganization study teams, Tom Linder solicited the support of Larry Colet, the newly elected president of the Georgia Jaycees, Sam Roberts, a Georgia member of the National Jaycee Board of Directors, and Robert A. Rushton, chairman of the Georgia Jaycees Governmental Affairs Program. All three responded favorably, and after visiting the state Jaycee convention, Hall and Linder returned with an endorsement of reorganization and promises of an active Jaycee campaign to publicize the reform.[33]

Through the summer of 1971 endorsements flowed in from local Jaycee organizations throughout the state. The response of Talbert C. Bryant, Jr., president of the Atlanta Jaycees, was typical. After a luncheon meeting with Tom Linder, Bryant wrote: "On behalf of our entire Executive Committee, I would like to thank you for being with us for lunch yesterday. We enjoyed your comments and look forward to working with you to participate in and sell the Governor's Reorganization Program. We will be in touch with you within the next two weeks concerning our plans and sincerely hope that we might be of service to you and Governor Carter."[34]

The staff of the Public Awareness team prepared a series of radio spot messages for use by local Jaycee organizations. A typical message read:

Hello, this is _____ of the _____ Jaycees. Government reorganization is something we've long been interested in. Not too many folks like State Government the way it is. The reorganization plan offers us change and improvement. It also shows us how to get $60 million in yearly financial benefits. It's the answer to our complaints about big, uncaring government. Write your legislator and let him know you care. Ask him to vote for reorganization. Tell him to vote for economy and efficiency.[35]

Local radio stations throughout the state used these messages extensively, and if the stations refused to carry them as public service messages, the Jaycees sponsored them.

The Jaycees' first statewide effort on behalf of reorganization came in September when the Jaycees, cooperating with Peggy Rainwater of the Governor's staff, established reorganization exhibits at the numerous county fairs held in Georgia during the autumn months. The Jaycees built and manned the exhibits, while Ms. Rainwater made the arrangements with county fair managers, supplied the materials, and organized seminars for those Jaycees who would be working at the displays. Between September 3 and November 6, the Jaycees established exhibits at fifty-nine county fairs.[36]

As the campaign for reorganization heated up near the end of the year, the Jaycees' increased their efforts. By November, twenty teams of Jaycees were actively promoting reorganization through slide presentations, speeches, and showings of Rafshoon's film. During a ten-day period in November, Jaycee teams conducted nearly fifty presentations. Meanwhile, local Jaycee organizations sponsored a series of radio programs and newspaper articles explaining and endorsing reorganization.[37] The November issue of the Jaycee *Rambler*, a magazine distributed to the 9,000 Georgia Jaycees, also featured reorganization. The organization printed an additional 8,000 copies of the issue and circulated them among all public officials in Georgia and to others expressing an interest in reorganization.[38] Tom Linder later attributed much of the success of the public relations effort to the Jaycees' extraordinary campaign.[39]

The importance of these organizational activities in building support for reorganization and influencing legislators is difficult to measure. There can be little doubt, however, that the active support of these organizations did build public awareness. It, as well as other aspects of the Public Awareness Program, had the effect of putting those opposing reorganization on the defensive.

Opponents found themselves having to make a strong case against reorganization to justify their opposition.

Newspaper and media endorsements for the reorganization effort was another indirect means of building public awareness and support. Newspapers could be especially valuable in winning the favor of community leaders and developing a bandwagon psychology state legislators would find hard to resist. Although it failed to gain the endorsement of a few of the state's largest newspapers as well as several smaller, local papers, the administration did secure a remarkable degree of editorial support for the reorganization plan.

A dinner party at the governor's mansion on July 8, 1971, for 199 Georgia broadcasters and their wives marked the first step in the drive to gain the active support of the news media. Following the dinner, Governor Carter informally briefed his guests on the progress of the reorganization program, and Tom Linder presented a program using slides and other visual materials to illustrate the advantages of reorganization. The Georgia Association of Broadcasters' endorsement of reorganization at its statewide convention a few days earlier made the occasion even more pleasurable for the Governor and his staff.[40]

A week later, on July 15, Carter treated 170 members of the Georgia press and their wives to a similar dinner at the governor's mansion. Thereafter, through the summer and fall of the year, the Governor and members of the reorganization staff held periodic background sessions, often at the governor's mansion, for editors, publishers, reporters, and radio and television personnel. Based on the response of those attending these functions and the enthusiasm with which the news media supported the reorganization effort, these meetings were a stunning success.[41]

Many of the state's smaller newspapers printed editorials prepared by the Public Awareness team. Other editors wrote their own columns praising the reorganization effort. Elimination of bureaucratic confusion and overlapping responsibilities, increased efficiency, and better delivery of government services received favorable mention in these editorials, but the editors placed their greatest emphasis on the prospective cost savings to be derived from reorganization.[42]

The reorganization staff also prepared editorials and articles for publication in the periodicals and newsletters issued by statewide organizations and associations, from the *Georgia Poultry News* to the *Christian Index*, a publication of the Georgia Baptist Convention with a circulation in excess of 130,000. Tom Linder actively assisted Don Wilson of the *Savannah Morning News* and Selby McCash of the *Macon Telegraph and News* in the preparation of a series of articles explaining the reorganization program and justifying the need for change. Meanwhile, numerous radio and television stations throughout the state promoted the reorganization drive. Radio broadcasters carried reorganization promotionals, often as public service messages, and made their facilities available to project personnel, who explained and defended the program.[43]

Although less successful in manipulating the Atlanta news media than that in other towns and cities, the Public Awareness staff secured important endorsements as well as favorable publicity in the capital. Jack Spalding, editor of the *Atlanta Journal*, added his prestigious voice to those advocating the Governor's reorganization plan; moreover, with the assistance of Tom Linder, *Journal* reporters developed a thirteen-part series on reorganization largely reflecting the administration's position.[44] The *Atlanta Constitution* remained editorially cool toward the reform effort, however. Dating back to the early 1960s when Carter had sat in the Georgia Senate and Reg Murphy covered the General Assembly, the *Constitution*'s editor had developed a passionate dislike for the Governor. In a column containing a cynical analysis of Carter's motives in urging government reform, Murphy left little doubt concerning his hostility to the Governor's program.[45] Nevertheless, Hal Gulliver, managing editor of the *Constitution*, and Bill Shipp, the paper's political reporter, remained professional and objective in their coverage of the reorganization effort. Indeed, Shipp's often critical columns contained the most factually accurate and insightful analyses to appear in the press during the long campaign for executive reorganization.[46]

The administration also gained important Atlanta radio and television endorsements. Ray Moore, the respected news director of WAGA-TV, delivered several editorials supporting the reorganization proposal.[47] Similarly, Elmo Ellis, general manager of WSB radio, the oldest and most powerful radio station in Georgia, gave the reform his endorsement.[48]

The administration considered news media support of the reorganization campaign vital to the success of the public awareness effort. The media contributed significantly to the administration's objective of educating the Georgia people concerning the need for reorganization and in mobilizing public opinion behind the program. The Public Awareness staff especially welcomed the strong editorial support from newspapers in the rural areas of the state. Many legislators in those areas exhibited little enthusiasm for reorganization, but home-town newspaper support could force them to consider the proposal more carefully.

As had been anticipated by the planners of the Public Awareness Program, Jimmy Carter assumed a leading role in selling government reorganization to the people of Georgia. During the months of study and debate concerning reorganization, the Governor capitalized on every opportunity to promote the program. No matter what the occasion, official or informal, he usually managed to plug reorganization. After a storm ravaged Savannah Beach, for example, Carter toured the area and discussed with the press difficulties limiting the state's ability to respond quickly and effectively in such emergencies. He said that any one of thirty-five agencies could be involved in any effort to initiate a beach anti-erosion project. He described the problems local officials had in determining the appropriate agency to turn to and the likelihood of being shuffled from one agency to another. With the present organization of state government, the Governor told Savannah Beach officials, he could make no promises as to when aid would be forthcoming.[49]

Like Tom Linder, Carter maintained a heavy calendar of speaking engagements throughout the state. He participated in numerous radio and television talk shows and interview programs and used his weekly radio broadcast and twice-monthly educational television program to explain and defend reorganization. He also used a weekly news column, distributed through the Press Ready News Service, to promote governmental reform.[50]

As the campaign for reorganization continued through the year,

Carter increasingly emphasized the projected $60.8 million in savings that would result from reorganization. In the early stages of the reform effort, the Governor had placed little emphasis on cost reduction. He told the various reorganization study teams that savings should not be a consideration in determining their proposals. Cost benefits, he concluded, would accrue naturally from the effort to organize government more efficiently.[51] Carter, instead, stressed better delivery of state services. It soon became evident, however, that the projected savings attracted more favorable public comment than any other feature of the reorganization plan. Although, from time to time, Carter reiterated his earlier theme that reorganization would be well worthwhile even if no savings resulted, he could not resist placing greater emphasis on the savings figure which attracted so much favorable publicity.

Carter accelerated his public awareness efforts after the printing of the final draft of the reorganization plan. For several years the Georgia Chamber of Commerce had sponsored a pre-legislative forum which traveled to several of the state's larger cities where the participants discussed the issues to be considered in the upcoming General Assembly session. Although no previous governor had participated in the forum, Carter decided to use it to reveal the proposed changes in state government. The Chamber of Commerce had scheduled meetings in fifteen cities during November, and the Governor planned to release to the public one phase of the plan at each stop. By the end of the tour the entire plan would be made public. This was to be the "Governor's Roadshow" that Gerald Rafshoon had urged Carter to undertake to sell reorganization. Accompanied by Bert Lance, the Governor made his first appearance in Toccoa on November 10, where he discussed the proposed Department of Transportation. Then he discussed taxation (Gainesville), public safety (Valdosta), natural resources (Savannah), and human resources (Thomasville), until the tour concluded in Columbus where Carter released the entire plan and discussed the advantages that would result from its adoption. It was a publicity bonanza. The press followed the Governor from city to city reporting on his activities, assessing local reaction (usually favorable), and speculating about future revelations.[52]

With each stop, however, the chorus of opposition emanating

from the capitol grew, reaching a crescendo with the release of the human resources proposal in Thomasville. At each stop the Governor patiently explained how the plan had been developed and advantages that would accrue from its implementation. He noted that some of the state's most successful and influential business and professional people had participated in the effort at almost no state expense. Appealing to existing innate anti-intellectual and youth prejudices, he repeatedly noted, "We had very few professors and young people working on this. We are afraid the professors and young people might come up with a lot of theorized ideas. We wanted practical ideas."[53]

In defending the proposal, he denounced those who resisted change. What the people who oppose change fail to realize, he said, "is that change is occurring anyway, it is the change of deterioration."[54] He repeatedly attacked opponents of reorganization as spokesmen for special interest groups who obviously feared a reduction in their power and influence if state government became more efficient and responsive. "It would be easy to compromise," he said, "but I'd rather not do it. It may be another forty years before we have another chance to reorganize."[55]

Carter also used regional press conferences held in the state's larger cities to explain and defend executive reorganization. In a series of these meetings with the press in late August and early September, he explained the way in which the Reorganization and Management Improvement Study had been conducted and how the final plan would be written. Following the official release of the proposal in early December, the Governor scheduled another series of press conferences. During these sessions he blasted representatives of special interest groups for their obstructionism. In Macon, home of the chairman of the State Board of Health, Dr. Beverly Forester, he leveled a withering attack on those opposing changes in state health and welfare services and the abolition of the Board of Health.[56] Carter also used his "taking the government to the people" program to advertise the merits of government reorganization. On December 30, 1971, for example, Carter moved the state capital to Moultrie, where he spent much of his time lobbying for reorganization.[57]

George Kaiser, the Arthur Anderson and Company consultant

who had participated in numerous state government reorganization projects, considered the Georgia public relations program the most comprehensive and successful such effort he had seen.[58] There can be little doubt that sponsors of the Public Awareness Program did make the general public more aware of reorganization and the arguments for reform. Available evidence, moreover, suggests that a substantial majority of Georgians approved the proposal. Perhaps Senator Stanley Smith, one of the most persistent critics of the reorganization plan, provided the best evidence of the success of the program. Smith told other antagonistic senators they could not simply kill the administration's bill but had to come up with their own plan. As Smith's statement indicates, the Public Awareness Program placed the opponents of reform on the defensive and created a positive momentum in favor of reorganization that state legislators would have to consider as they debated the merits of the proposal and cast their votes in the General Assembly.[59]

chapter 4

SELLING REORGANIZATION TO THE BUREAUCRACY

Members of the Carter administration had few illusions about elected state officials passively accepting a fundamental reorganization of the executive branch of state government. Several state government departments existed by constitutional provision with popularly elected department heads. This, along with the veto provision given such constitutional officers in the authorization act (HB 1), insulated them from gubernatorial pressures. Department heads could be expected to oppose any change that reassigned their duties and responsibilities; moreover, such reassignment of functions carried with it the implication that the administrator had failed to fulfill his duties.

Through the efforts of the Public Awareness Program among state department and agency heads, the administration hoped to eliminate as much of this anticipated opposition as possible. Realizing that reorganization would affect the employees as well as the administrators of existing state agencies and departments, the Public Awareness staff made a special effort to keep these people fully informed at every stage of the reorganization study. The situation bred an atmosphere conducive to the rampant spread of demoralizing rumors that could generate unnecessary resistance and seriously damage the reform effort. Administrative spokesmen wanted state employees to feel that reorganization was to be done with them and for them, not to them. They encouraged agency personnel to ask questions, make proposals, and generally contribute to the reform effort. Project Director Tom Linder agreed to meet with department heads at least once a month to brief them on the status of the study, and Governor Carter vowed to make himself available whenever these officials desired a meeting. Both men urged state officials to seek out and implement changes in the organization and administration of their departments and promised to give these efforts as much favorable publicity as possible.[1]

Shortly after the General Assembly adjourned in the early spring of 1971, Carter met with elected and appointed state department heads to assure them that their employees had no reason to fear "widespread firings or discharges." The Governor told members of the group their ideas and suggestions would be given careful consideration, and when disagreements arose, they would have ample opportunity to explain them to him personally. Carter reminded his guests, however, that while he would be reluctant to contravene their wishes, he had the responsibility to make the final decisions subject, of course, to the approval of the General Assembly or, as the case might be, the general electorate.[2]

Through the summer and early autumn months, Carter held a series of meetings at the governor's mansion that brought together relevant reorganization study teams and officials of individual departments and agencies to discuss the study teams' findings and recommendations. Meanwhile, study team group leaders met with each affected department or agency head at least weekly to inform them of the status of the project and solicit their suggestions and comments.[3]

Most appointed officials and several elected officers initially had voiced support of reorganization, but as the plan began to crystallize, the early enthusiasm of many of these officials waned, especially among elected department heads. Carter anticipated considerable resistance from Secretary of State Ben Fortson and State School Superintendent Jack Nix because of the major changes suggested for their departments.[4] They did not disappoint him. Both men publicly denounced the plan several months before the release of the final draft.

By its very nature, reorganization was destined to incur the wrath of some state officials, but breakdowns in the execution of the Public Awareness Program created unnecessary problems— problems that might have been mitigated had state officials been fully informed of the progress of the study and more actively consulted in their areas of concern.

The administration's handling of the influential Ben Fortson illustrates the problem. Fortson was something of an institution in Georgia politics. A colorful speaker with a magnetic personality, he was simply "Mr. Ben" to thousands of Georgians. Fortson's influence in political circles throughout the state, especially among members of the General Assembly, made him a dangerous potential adversary. Neither the Governor nor his reorganization staff could afford to antagonize him. Moreover, Fortson warned Carter about contemplated changes in his office even before the reorganization study had begun. "I'm not going to lie still like a catfish and be gutted," he said. "I'm going to wiggle."[5]

Nevertheless, at a July press conference Carter released to the media his plans for removing all licensing and regulatory functions from the office of the Secretary of State.[6] Fortson exploded. He told the press he had never been informed of or consulted about such changes. When questioned about Fortson's charges, Tom Linder conceded, "We never got together with Mr. Ben." Carter concurred. "No one," he said, "had discussed the proposal with Mr. Fortson."[7] The Governor immediately scheduled an appointment with the secretary to discuss their differences. During the meeting, Fortson put on one of his classic performances. Gesturing wildly and stomping the footrail of his wheelchair for emphasis, he used his most colorful rhetoric to denounce the proposed changes. "I've got on an old suit," Fortson told the Governor, "but it's going to take some stripping to strip me."[8] The proposed

personality profile: _____

BENJAMIN WYNN FORTSON, JR.

Born in Tignall, Georgia, on December 19, 1904, Ben Fortson was reared in Arlington, Georgia, where he received a public school education. He later matriculated at Emory University's Oxford branch, Starkes University in Montgomery,

Alabama, the Georgia Institute of Technology, and the John Marshall Law School.

At the age of nineteen, he took a job at the Citizen's National Bank in Washington, Georgia, and thus launched a banking career that absorbed him for the next several years. After he was seriously injured in an automobile accident in 1929, he was confined to a wheelchair and continued to pursue a banking career. He became increasingly interested and involved in politics. He served two terms in the state Senate. When the Senate districts were reorganized following the 1940 census, he ran for the state House of Representatives from Wilkes county. He served in the House until February 25, 1946, when he was appointed secretary of state to fill the unexpired term of John B. Wilson who had died in office. Thereafter, Fortson was returned to office by increasingly comfortable margins. His obvious love for his native state and his devotion to its history and traditions made Fortson one of the most popular and revered figures in state government. It also made him one of the most powerful.[9]

---

removal of securities regulation from his office especially upset the secretary. Fortson, while admitting that little had been done to curb shady securities salesmen in Georgia, declared that the major problem was an inadequate and unenforceable law and not lax enforcement. "I'm registering some stock now that I wouldn't put up on my wall out in the outhouse," he conceded, but said there was little he could do about it.[10] Fortson, moreover, had been informed shortly before his meeting with the Governor that he had been elected president of the National Association of Commissioners of Securities. He told the Governor he cherished the honor and removed his shoe and rubbed his foot on the Governor's carpet. "I am on hallowed ground. . . . I come in supplication," he said.[11] Observers unfamiliar with the secretary's antics were alternately amazed and bemused. The Governor was distraught. The reorganization study team ultimately reversed itself on the licensing issue but still failed to pacify the incorrigible secretary of state.[12]

Fortson then took to the stump denouncing reorganization in

terms soon to be adopted by other administration critics. The proposed changes in executive departments and agencies, he charged, would place excessive power in the governor's office and endanger the checks and balances system of state government. Hurt by Carter's failure to consult with him and embarrassed by the implicit criticism of his administration, Fortson lashed out at the Governor.[13]

Several weeks too late, gubernatorial assistant Richard Harden, who served as an administration troubleshooter, held a series of meetings with the secretary and reported that Fortson had expressed a willingness to compromise in several areas and in others had sound, reasonable arguments for opposing the changes. Clearly differences between the secretary and the Governor had been exaggerated. Regarding the transfer of securities regulation to the office of the Comptroller General, Fortson told Harden he had no great objection to the transfer but had been greatly embarrassed by the Governor's charges of lax enforcement of the regulations governing the sale of securities. After reiterating his earlier observation about the inadequacies in the existing securities law, he offered to cooperate with the Governor in drafting stronger legislation that could be effectively enforced.[14]

Similar breakdowns in communications alienated other previously friendly state officials. Carter stunned Comptroller General Johnnie Caldwell with highly publicized charges that 30 percent of the state's hotels and motels operated without fire and health permits.[15] Caldwell had opposed the transfer of these functions to a proposed new law enforcement agency. Admitting the validity of the Governor's charges, Caldwell, nevertheless denounced criticism of his office as both unjustified and unfair. The comptroller general reported that he had lobbied for increased appropriations to hire additional inspectors, but, for economy reasons, the Governor had cut the appropriation. The problem, in Caldwell's estimation, lay in the Governor's office, not in the comptroller general's department.[16]

In a scenario becoming increasingly familiar, the announcement that the agricultural laboratory would be taken from the Department of Agriculture also surprised Agriculture Commissioner Tommy Irvin. Irvin, one of the administration's most consistent supporters among elected state officials, had not only actively co-operated with the reorganization study team in his area but also voluntarily had instituted many of its recommendations. He thought he had a firm commitment from the Governor that an in-depth study would be made before the announcement of any decision regarding the laboratory. The special study team that recommended the removal, he noted, "spent less time in the laboratory of the Department of Agriculture than do the school children who are conducted on guided tours of the Agriculture building."[17]

State School Superintendent Jack Nix claimed to have been victimized by a similar breach of faith. In a letter to Carter concerning changes in the State Department of Education, Nix charged that it

was a clear violation of your August commitment to me in which you agreed to discuss with me personally any proposal affecting this department prior to adopting it as your final recommendation to the General Assembly. It was my understanding that no public release of reorganization information would be made until I had an opportunity to review and react to your proposals.[18]

personality profile:_____
S. SAM CALDWELL

Born January 22, 1929, in East Point, Georgia, and reared in one of the city's more economically depressed sections, Sam Caldwell became a high school dropout at the age of sixteen. Thereafter, he worked at odd jobs including driving a taxicab, selling encyclopedias, and for eighteen months working as a merchant seaman. After he was stranded in California by a maritime strike following World War II, he enlisted in the United States Marine Corps and served twenty-two months before securing an early discharge to enroll in North Georgia College. He later transferred to the University of Georgia and in 1952, earned a BA in journalism. Before he could launch his anticipated career in journalism, however, he was drafted into the United States Army during the Korean War, eventually rising to the rank of first lieutenant. Following his discharge in 1954, he worked as a public information writer for several state government agencies before becoming a speech writer for Governor Marvin Griffin. In 1962 he accepted a position as personnel director in the State Highway Department and soon became a protege of Jim Gillis, the influential director of that department. Meanwhile, Caldwell developed close ties with United States Senator Herman Talmadge and his Georgia supporters. In 1966 Caldwell ran successfully for the office of labor commissioner and soon became a major power in state politics. He parlayed the Department of Labor's thirty-four field offices into an efficient network of capable political operatives. An efficient and able administrator, he inspired an unusual degree of loyalty among departmental employees while at the same time developing strong ties to the black community and to organized labor.[19]

It was the volatile state labor commissioner, Sam Caldwell, however, who most eagerly aligned himself with the legislative opponents of reorganization and became the Governor's most vitriolic antagonist. Caldwell had originally opposed House Bill No. 1 but later wrote Carter pledging his support and cooperation in the reorganization effort.[20] The labor commissioner's allegiance proved short-lived. Although the reorganization plan involved relatively few changes in the Labor Department, Caldwell once again became the administration's most searing critic. Echoing Fortson's earlier charges, Caldwell declared that executive reorganization represented little more than a "power grab" by a governor bent on establishing a dictatorship in Georgia. Caldwell, who announced his intention of vetoing all provisions of the reorganization plan affecting the Labor Department, took his campaign against the proposal to the public, utilizing letter to the editor columns, radio interviews, and press conferences to attack the plan. "The way the Governor's been acting," Caldwell commented, "it appears he might eliminate Santa Claus before Christmas."[21] Caldwell's motives in so virulently attacking Carter are unclear, but, like several other state political leaders, the labor commissioner coveted the United States Senate seat of the late Richard Russell. Carter's appointment of David Gambrell to the vacancy and the Governor's obvious desire to see his appointee elected to a full term undoubtedly offended Caldwell. Furthermore, Caldwell obviously had allied himself with the supporters of Senator Herman Talmadge who feared that Carter might attempt to unseat the state's senior senator.[22] Sabotaging the reorganization plan would dull whatever luster Carter might acquire during his governorship.[23]

Even before the official release of the reorganization plan, Carter and Caldwell were totally estranged. The Governor asked all state department heads to distribute a statement to their employees outlining the way in which reorganization would affect personnel practices and fringe benefits. Caldwell refused. "We do not use our equipment to reproduce political propaganda." Caldwell wrote the Governor. "Neither are we in favor of misinforming our employees with false statements such as the ones contained in almost every paragraph of your news release."[24] When asked at a press conference to comment on Caldwell's charges, Carter responded acidly, "I don't have any comment on that and probably never will have any comment on any statements by the Commissioner of Labor."[25] The two men remained bitter antagonists throughout Carter's gubernatorial term.

Opposition arose from other quarters as well. State Treasurer Bill Burson initially had supported reorganization enthusiastically even though the plan included a recommendation that his office be abolished by constitutional amendment. Burson changed his mind, however, after entering the race for the Democratic nomination to fill the same United States Senate seat to which Caldwell aspired. By the end of the year, he characterized reorganization "as nothing more than a calculated effort in the guise of a noble purpose to gain control of state government in Georgia for the next 50 years or longer."[26] Veterans' organizations, especially the American Legion, opposed the elimination of the Department of Veterans Service as an independent agency and its incorporation into the Department of Human Resources.[27] The Board of Regents of the University System opposed the centralizing and budgetary aspects of the reorganization proposal as it affected them. Numerous agency and department heads grieved over the centralization of printing, purchasing, and computer services in the new Department of Administrative Services.[28] The most sustained and highly publicized opposition, however, resulted from the administration's decision to abolish the State Board of Health.

Carter defended the fundamental reorganization of the state's activities in this field citing as the reason "widely-recognized deficiencies" in the delivery of health services. He especially criticized inadequacies in dental care and the board's "abysmal performance in establishing a drug abuse treatment program." The Governor, who wanted to decentralize services through the establishment of thirty-three community health centers around the state, considered the Department of Human Resources the most important proposal in the reorganization plan.[29]

Under the Department of Human Resources, a new nine-member governing body composed of laymen and professionals representing various divisions in public health and welfare fields would replace the physician-dominated Board of Health. The Medical Association of Georgia (MAG), which had controlled nominations to the Board of Health, immediately registered its disapproval. The specter of laymen supervising professionals horrified the leaders of the association. Using all the considerable resources at their command, doctors waged their own public awareness campaign in hopes of saving the State Board of Health. MAG officials implied that members of the Carter administration had conspired with Secretary Elliott Richardson of the United States Department of Health, Education and Welfare to institute a form of socialized medicine in Georgia. They charged, moreover, that Carter intended to appoint chiropractors and podiatrists to the governing board of the Department of Human Resources.[30] (He appointed neither but did appoint his mother.) The Governor made concessions and offered compromises to the board and the MAG, but they repeatedly rebuffed his overtures. The doctors, who were convinced they could win in the General Assembly, gambled that they could save the existing board without making any concessions.[31]

Although most of the state's doctors supported the MAG campaign, they underestimated the latent hostility that existed among professionals in other health fields. Support for the administration poured in from pharmacists, dentists, nursing home operators, psychiatrists, nurses, and other health-related professionals who felt they had been treated too cavalierly by the MAG and the State Board of Health. To this support, the administration added the endorsement of several influential physicians despite the adamant hostility of the medical association. Dr. John H. Venable, director of the Georgia Department of Public Health, approved the changes after members of the State Board of Health demanded his resignation, blaming him for deficiencies in the delivery of health services. Venable refused to resign, and Carter supported him, arguing the problem was not with the director but rather with the chaotic, irrational organization of state services in the area.[32] Dean Arthur P. Richardson of the School of Medicine, Woodruff Medical Center of Emory University, added his prestigious endorsement of the Department of Human Resources, and several other practicing and teaching physicians followed his example.[33]

Although the Department of Human Resources remained the most controversial proposal in the reorganization plan and seemed likely to encounter the strongest opposition in the General Assembly, the administration, unlike its handling of changes in numerous other state departments, executed its campaign for the Department of Human Resources in a nearly flawless manner. It cleverly exploited the board's effort to make Dr. Venable a scapegoat, the MAG's isolation from other professionals in the health field, and its unyielding and dogmatic refusal to compromise. Meanwhile, the administration counterattacked in the MAG's own constituency, working hard to convince doctors that the proposed changes did not threaten their interests. The Governor contributed with an effective "Dear Bud" letter to his family physician explaining and justifying the need for change. The Public Awareness staff mailed copies of the letter to other physicians throughout the state.[34]

The opposition encountered from some department heads and constitutional officers was ameliorated by the support the administration received from numerous other state officials. State Highway Director Bert Lance, Welfare Director Jim Parham, director of the Department of Game and Fish Joe D. Tanner, Budget Officer Battle Hall, Auditor Ernest Davis, and Corrections Director Ellis MacDougall endorsed the proposal and actively participated in the Public Awareness Program.[35]

In other cases, the Governor managed to convert potential adversaries into advocates by making them offers they could not refuse. One such case involved George Beattie, executive director of the Georgia Commission on the Arts. When the director protested the abolition of the Arts Commission, Carter promptly replied that he wanted to enhance the state's commitment to the arts, not diminish it. Moving this function directly into the governor's office, he hoped, would have such an effect. He told Beattie he "would like to help personally to

a) expand your pilot Projects throughout the state as rapidly as possible;

b) let you, as the full-time spokesman, work with me and the Chancellor and Jack Nix within our top level coordinating committee;

c) with you, appoint several small advisory committees on different forms of the arts to develop a comprehensive statewide program;

d) investigate the advisibility of a school for the performing arts;

e) add the influence and stature of the governor's office to this effort;

f) eliminate the present isolation of the commission."

If after a year it appears as though we have made a mistake, the Governor declared, I will be "glad to make a suitable change more in consonance with your inclinations."[36]

After making last minute concessions to the comptroller general and the Health Board, Carter officially released the reorganization plan to constitutional officers on December 10. According to the provisions of the authorization act, the officers had ten days to veto provisions of the plan that affected their constitutional duties. The reorganization plan met a fusillade of vetoes which, if allowed to stand, would have left the reorganization program in shambles. Labor Commissioner Sam Caldwell personally accounted for twenty-nine of the forty-five vetoes cast by constitutional officers. Agriculture Commissioner Tommy Irvin, Comptroller General Johnnie Caldwell, School Superintendent Jack Nix, Treasurer Bill Burson, and Secretary of State Ben Fortson cast the remaining vetoes.

Although inviting a court challenge, the Governor abruptly disallowed all but six of the vetoes. He accepted two of Johnnie Caldwell's vetoes and one each from Nix, Fortson, Burson, and Sam Caldwell. Clearly the labor commissioner had made a mockery of the veto provisions and compromised the best weapon constitutional officers had to resist change. "If we let the Commissioner of Labor veto the whole thing," Carter declared, "we wouldn't need a legislature would we?"[37] Taking advantage of Caldwell's excesses, the Governor charged that at best the rejected vetoes were illegal and, at worst, frivolous. Under the provisions of HB 1, constitutional officers could veto only those portions of the plan that affected functions assigned to them by constitution or law. Attorney General Arthur Bolton, supporting the Governor's position, refused to override Carter's actions.[38]

Carter once again reassured state employees that rumors of mass firings were false and "anyone who tells you that . . . is just trying to stir up unnecessary trouble."[39] After reiterating that employees affected by the reorganization would be reassigned to other state positions, the Governor discussed the advantages government workers would derive from organizational reform. State employees, he said, would have an opportunity to expand their knowledge and understanding of state government; and, consequently, they would be better able to utilize their skills and abilities for career advancement. He also described insurance, retirement, and other fringe benefits that would accompany government reform. Finally, he associated an increased wage scale for hard-pressed teachers and other government employees with the savings to be derived from reorganization.[40] A few weeks later, Carter held a meeting at the governor's mansion for 150 state officials. Casually dressed in a tan cardigan sweater, he spoke informally to the group about reorganization and the advantages it would bring in terms of the more efficient delivery of government services and cost savings.[41]

The large number of vetoes exercised by constitutional officers and the adamant hostility of numerous state officials demonstrated the failure of the Public Awareness Program to subdue the anticipated resistance from the state government bureaucracy. Although a reorganization plan satisfactory to everyone could not have been drafted, breakdowns in the implementation of the Public Awareness Program resulted in unnecessary antagonism and opposition.[42] Nevertheless, the major reorganization battles remained to be fought; this time in the General Assembly or perhaps in the state courts.

chapter 5

SELLING REORGANIZATION
TO THE LEGISLATURE

The close vote on House Bill No. 1 clearly and unmistakably illustrated the fragile nature of the support for reform in the General Assembly. The resistance to reorganization, moreover, would inevitably grow as details of the plan became known. The vote on HB 1 indicated the plan would encounter its greatest opposition in the upper chamber, where Senate leaders, including the presiding officer, Lieutenant Governor Maddox, had urged their colleagues to vote against the authorization bill. Conversely, Speaker of the House George L. Smith early announced his support of reorganization; thus, in the lower house, Carter needed only to strike an agreement with the influential Speaker to enhance his chances of success in that chamber. Clearly, the major battles over reorganization were destined to be fought in the Senate chamber.

In an effort to defuse the opposition and allay criticism, the administration wanted to involve legislators as much as possible in the reorganization program. House Majority Leader George Busbee and Lamar Plunkett, a respected veteran senator and Carter loyalist, agreed to serve on the six-member executive committee that initiated the preliminary study and supervised the drafting of the final reorganization plan. Soon after the study began, Carter briefed General Assembly members at the governor's mansion, explaining the objectives of the reform effort and describing the ways in which the plan would be developed.[1]

Carter coordinated his lobbying efforts among state legislators with those of the Public Awareness staff. Cloyd Hall, director of the Public Awareness Program, assumed personal responsibility for maintaining close contact with General Assembly members during the months the reorganization study was under way and the reform proposals were drafted. Hall's assigned responsibilities among state legislators included

Furnishing speech material for members of the Executive Committee, key staff members, department heads and key legislators

Maintaining a personal contact with General Assembly members by giving them individual or group briefings, and asking them for input in the study

Reviewing legislative committee reports and resolutions in order to identify legislators' specific areas of interest

Keeping key legislators informed of status of project on a continuing basis, and prepare a list of key legislators to be included in the program

Relaying to Governor and Executive Committee any problem areas that might be encountered with legislators

Maintaining personal contact with key department heads and obtaining their recommendations on overall project[2]

Through the Public Awareness campaign among General Assembly members, the administration hoped to avoid the impression that reorganization was being foisted upon them by the Governor and his staff. Hall endeavored to give the members a stake in reorganization by consulting with them in the reform effort. Ultimately, he hoped to convince them that reorganization was not a power play by the Governor that would undermine established legislative prerogatives. The lawmakers had to be convinced of the legitimate need for governmental reform.

In August, Hall prepared for the Public Awareness Advisory Committee a status report on the activities and achievements of the Public Awareness effort among the state legislators to that point. He noted that besides the contacts made by the Governor and Tom Linder, he personally had consulted with 152 legislators. Hall mailed monthly status reports to General Assembly members that kept them informed of the progress of the reorganization effort. Under Hall's direction, the reorganization staff reviewed and catalogued legislative committee reports covering the previous seven years. After soliciting the counsel and advice of the legislators who had been involved in the preparation of those reports,

Hall forwarded their suggestions to the pertinent reorganization study teams with the recommendation that they meet with the legislator and report the results of those discussions to Tom Linder. The Public Awareness staff then drafted press releases reflecting the particular lawmaker's role in the preparation of the original report and the manner in which the report had been utilized by the reorganization study teams. By late summer, 103 such news releases had been sent to the media in the pertinent legislator's district.[3]

These activities continued through the fall months and until the convening of the General Assembly in January. Meanwhile, as the study teams began formulating their recommendations and the date for the release of the plan approached, the Governor accelerated his lobbying activities among state legislators. On July 28 and 29 and again on August 10 and 11, Carter held a series of dinners at the governor's mansion for key legislators from both houses.[4] While endorsing such dinners, an influential Senate supporter told the Governor that he still needed to make a special effort to win the votes of a relatively small number of uncommitted senators who would determine the fate of reorganization. Acting on this advice, the Carters entertained several uncommitted legislators and their wives at small, informal dinners or evenings at the governor's mansion.[5] In a similar manner, legislators visiting Atlanta between legislative sessions often found themselves recipients of invitations to spend the night at the mansion.[6]

The administration also subscribed to a clipping service that monitored newspapers throughout the state. Whenever a legislator made a public statement on the reorganization effort, he was likely to receive one of the Governor's famous handwritten notes defending or explaining the point in question, or, if appropriate, thanking the legislator for his support. Similarly, the numerous private citizens who wrote to the Governor expressing their support of the reorganization effort often received a handwritten note as well as the inevitable suggestion that they communicate their support of the program to the General Assembly members in their district.[7]

The Governor's estrangement from several powerful Senate leaders, however, limited and qualified Hall's success in building legislative support for reorganization. Through the summer and fall of 1971, Carter sustained a series of defeats from these Senate antagonists that appeared to doom chances of gaining General Assembly approval of the reorganization plan.

Following the adjournment of the 1971 General Assembly session, Carter moved to strengthen his support among state legislators. Punctuated by the increasingly bitter war of words between Carter and Maddox, the adjourned General Assembly had been an acrimonious session during which the Governor's contacts with legislative leaders were often tense and at times hostile.

Carter's political style was one source of difficulty. Reluctant to wheel and deal in the traditional fashion, he had problems pacifying legislators and building coalitions of support for his programs. Carter's relationship with the powerful Speaker of the House, George L. Smith, was typical. "The Speaker is a horse trader. He wants to do something for you, if you want to do something for him," a Carter associate remarked. "Jimmy is not like that. He doesn't like to trade. He's stubborn. He and the Speaker will eventually have to reach some compromise if either is to continue to be effective."[8] Arguing that the problem lay with the Governor, himself, and not with his staff or Hamilton Jordan, Bill Shipp, *Atlanta Constitution* political columnist, suggested, "If Carter listens to his top advisors, the cliff hanging battles of the 1971 Senate will be a thing of the past next year."[9]

Although Carter practiced an unorthodox style of legislative leadership, even the wisdom of Solomon would not have assisted the Governor in dealing with a few powerful Senate leaders. Cooly rejecting the Governor's overtures, these politicos, for reasons of their own, simply declared war on the Governor. Undoubtedly, they sought to run the state from their Senate seats, which, to some extent, they had been able to do during Lester Maddox's governorship. Culver Kidd, one of Carter's most resourceful Senate foes, provided a dramatic illustration of this mentality. "If Carter were really serious about reorganization," Kidd informed the press, "he would permit the General Assembly to name such department heads as public safety commissioner, revenue commissioner, purchasing superintendent and director of the Department of Family and Children Services."[10]

Existing personal factionalism and political cleavages severely limited Carter's range of effective action. In dealing with these problems, the Governor had only two feasible courses of action: confrontation or compromise and conciliation. In his relations with the House of Representatives and Speaker Smith, he chose the latter, but his antagonists in the upper chamber left him little alternative than confrontation.

Compromise and conciliation worked well among House leaders. The Speaker's commitment to reorganization remained firm through the summer and fall months. As a member of the executive committee of the Reorganization and Management Improvement Study, Majority Leader George Busbee faithfully supported the endeavor. Meanwhile, the administration actively cultivated Majority Whip Tom Murphy, one of the least enthusiastic members of the House leadership, and frequently consulted such influential House members as Sam Nunn, Elliott Levitas and Al Burrus, all of whom were given large responsibilities in related areas.[11] As he had done in winning approval of HB 1 (the authorization for reorganization), the Governor realized that at some point he would have to sit down with the Speaker and deal with reference to the reorganization plan itself, but prospects for its approval in the lower house appeared excellent.

Senate opponents never gave Carter an opportunity to employ the same conciliatory tactics in their chamber. While House leaders had supported the authorization bill [HB 1] and generally had voiced support for the reorganization program, powerful Senate leaders, including presiding officer Lester Maddox, opposed HB 1 and seemed bent on sabotaging any reorganization plan proposed by the Governor. Without much substance, they reiterated the argument that reorganization could and should be carried out by the legislature.

The Governor's Senate antagonists initiated the hostilities during a July meeting of the Senate Democratic Caucus. Shortly after the meeting convened the Maddox forces proposed a new rule barring the majority leader from serving as the Governor's floor leader.[12] It was a thinly disguised effort to unseat Majority Leader Al Holloway who, prior to the 1971 General Assembly session, had broken precedent by agreeing to serve as Carter's Senate floor leader. In an effort to short circuit this ploy, Holloway, with the Governor's approval, submitted his resignation as floor leader, and Carter immediately announced he would appoint a new administration floor leader before the next General Assembly session.[13] The Governor's Senate foes, however, were not so easily frustrated. Eugene Holley, an Augusta senator closely allied with former governor Carl Sanders and Carter's Senate opponents, announced his candidacy for Holloway's leadership position.[14] Elections were to be held at an August 24 caucus meeting.

personality profile:_____
RUDOLPH EUGENE HOLLEY

Born on February 15, 1926, in Aiken, South Carolina, Eugene Holley was orphaned at age eight and raised by an aunt in nearby Augusta, Georgia. He graduated Phi Beta Kappa from the University of Georgia in 1949, where, in 1958, he also earned a LLB degree. Previously, he had enlisted in the United States Air Force during World War II and served as a flight engineer on a B-24 bomber. During the Korean War he served as a forward air controller and military advisor to a Korean infantry division. He later flew an all-weather F-86 jet fighter and won the Air Medal with cluster and the Distinguished Flying Cross.

In 1958 Holley joined an Augusta law firm and in 1967 entered into a law partnership with former Georgia Governor Carl Sanders. Elected to the Georgia Senate from the twenty-second senatorial district in 1964, he developed a close working relationship with then Governor Lester Maddox, an alliance that continued during Maddox's term as lieutenant governor and presiding officer of the Senate. Holley secured the coveted chairmanship of the powerful Senate Banking and Finance Committee in 1969 and from that position led a successful fight to secure the enactment of a Georgia bank holding company bill that permitted banks to expand beyond the county in which they were chartered. In the 1970 Democratic primary elections, Holley managed the cam-

paign of his law partner, Carl Sanders, in the latter's unsuccessful bid for the gubernatorial nomination.[15]

Controversy over the Senate Democratic Caucus was nothing new. Because only six Republicans held Senate seats, many questioned the rationale for the caucus's existence. Moreover, as it had functioned in the past, the caucus promoted more disharmony than party unity. Through the manipulation of factional divisions and at times by browbeating their colleagues, a few powerful Senate leaders had managed to exert considerable control over the caucus, using that power in their own interests, not that of the party. Nevertheless, there was never any likelihood that the caucus would be abolished. Those who controlled it had no desire to see its termination, while a larger number of state senators, recognizing that it served no useful purpose, supported it out of fear of retaliation by Senate leaders or from simple inertia. Reflecting a fairly common attitude, one senator reported that if forced to vote on it, "I'd vote to keep the Caucus, but I'd probably enter a ping pong tournament if the Senate voted to have one."[16] While seeking support from Democratic senators, Holley admitted that the caucus had not functioned effectively in the past but defended it and vowed to make it a more useful instrument in establishing party policy in the future.[17]

In an astonishing miscalculation of its own strength, the administration decided shortly before the August 24 meeting to put up its own slate of candidates for Senate leadership positions. In addition to supporting Holloway's campaign for reelection as majority leader, the Governor's cousin, Hugh Carter, announced his own candidacy for the position of majority whip, and another Carter ally, Sam Doss, announced for caucus secretary.[18]

The administration suffered a stinging defeat in the caucus elections. Holley defeated Holloway by a vote of 28 to 20, and other administration candidates lost by even larger margins. By injecting himself into a conflict he could not win, Carter not only suffered a needless humiliation but also compromised whatever chances Holloway had of retaining his leadership position. Hugh Carter termed it the Governor's worst defeat.[19] Senate Republican Minority Leader Oliver Bateman of Macon said Lester Maddox and his cohorts had put the "kiss of death" on Carter's reorganization plan. "I don't envision now that the governor will be able to salvage any victories out of the Senate," declared the disappointed Macon Republican who strongly supported the reorganization effort.[20] In reality, the caucus vote provided a poor reflection of the Governor's strength in the Senate, but he had committed a major blunder in permitting his antagonists to manipulate a test of strength on their terms and in their forum.

While denying that the caucus elections were a test vote on reorganization, the Governor recognized that he had problems. Agreeing with his cousin Hugh's conclusion that he needed to pay more attention to legislative affairs, Carter told newsmen he had concentrated on the reorganization study and the state's revenue crisis and simply did not have "enough time to work adequately with the legislature. But this is a deficiency I am trying to correct."[21] A few days after the caucus meeting, the Governor invited Eugene Holley to spend the night at the governor's mansion while visiting Atlanta. Carter told Holley he could be an extraordinarily effective Senate leader and promised to work closely with him. Carter then asked the new majority leader to convene a meeting of the Senate Democratic Policy Committee in an effort to promote a reconciliation between himself and the Senate leadership.[22] Before the meeting took place, however, the Governor suffered yet another defeat at the hands of his Senate antagonists.

House and Senate districts had to be redrawn after tabulation of the 1970 census. To accomplish this task, the Governor called a special session of the General Assembly in September. Under the effective leadership of Speaker George Smith, the House developed a satisfactory plan for redrawing its districts with relatively little controversy. As could be expected, the Governor found the Senate plan less satisfactory. Rejecting the proposals put forth by Carter allies in the Senate and ignoring threats of a gubernatorial veto, the upper chamber adopted a plan written by arch-Carter antagonists Stanley Smith and Culver Kidd. The Smith-Kidd plan, which passed by a vote of 36 to 19, made substantial changes in the districts of numerous Carter supporters in the Senate, especially in metropolitan Atlanta districts. Meanwhile, the Senate districts of most administration foes were either strengthened or left unchanged.[23]

The Governor carefully studied the plan, decided he could live with it, and signed the redistricting plan into law, perhaps, by this time, simply anxious to see the General Assembly adjourn and disappear. The press again heralded the special legislative session as a major defeat for the Governor, further compromising his chances of getting reorganization through the Senate. Columnist Bill Shipp reflected a sentiment held by many: "Unless he [Carter] pulls off a political miracle by January, his governmental reorganization will be doomed in the regular session of the General Assembly."[24]

In view of the pessimism projected in the state's newspapers and, indeed, by many Carter supporters in the legislature, the Governor's confident predictions that he would get his program through the General Assembly ("I'm going to get it because it is right") appeared unrealistic to the point of wishful thinking.[25] But Carter's optimism was not as contrived as it appeared. The Public Awareness Program, he believed, would place pressures on legislators not reflected either in the Democratic Caucus elections or in the special session. He also counted on his pre-legislative forum tour to build additional public support for his program. Moreover, as he figured it, the voting arithmetic, particularly in the Senate, was much more evenly balanced than most observers recognized. To be sure, a hard-core, anti-Carter bloc of twenty to twenty-five senators existed, but it would take twenty-nine votes to kill reorganization, and the Governor, by virtue of his office, had political leverage that was unavailable to his antagonists and that could be used to influence the small group of wavering senators who would decide the fate of reorganization. In this context the accelerated lobbying activities of State Highway Director Bert Lance became increasingly significant. By virtue of his control over highway construction projects and because of his influence in Georgia banking circles, Lance had the ability to exert considerable pressure on uncommitted legislators, and he effectively used that leverage.[26]

personality profile:_____
THOMAS BERTRAM LANCE

Born in Young Harris, Georgia, on June 3, 1931, Bert Lance acquired his early education in the public schools of Calhoun, Georgia. He then attended Emory University for two years and the University of Georgia for one year, dropping out of school shortly before his scheduled graduation. He later took graduate courses in banking at Louisiana State University and Rutgers University.

Lance launched his banking career in 1951 as a teller at the Calhoun First National Bank founded by his wife's grandfather. In 1958, with a group of business associates, he acquired a controlling interest in the bank and five years later became its president and chief executive officer. Under his direction, Calhoun First National Bank rapidly increased its assets. It also successfully stimulated the depressed local economy by attracting rug manufacturers to the area and upgrading the region's cattle industry.

Lance and Jimmy Carter met during a regional planning meeting in 1966 and struck up an immediate friendship. In a few weeks Lance began recruiting business support for Carter's unsuccessful gubernatorial candidacy. After supporting Carter's candidacy for the same office four years later, Lance was appointed director of the State Highway Department. An able and resourceful administrator, Lance transformed the reconstituted Department of Transportation into one of the most efficient departments of state government while at the same time he proved a potent lobbyist for the Governor's programs among state legislators.[27]

Carter also gained leverage by incorporating $55 million in reorganization savings and revenue generated by his reform proposals into his 1973 state budget. In an August column in the *Bainbridge Post-Searchlight*, former Governor Marvin Griffin speculated:

A Governor who goes to the General Assembly with a plan to reorganize state government and carries a companion appropriation bill along with him that is reduced by an amount of $50 million, will have little trouble getting it adopted.[28]

Carter wrote the former governor thanking him for the advice and indicating his intention of mirroring reorganization savings in the 1973 budget request.[29] The tactic created an uncomfortable dilemma for legislators. They either would have to approve the reorganization plan, devise a legislative cost-cutting program, or increase taxes to produce a balanced budget. For many wavering legislators, the first alternative undoubtedly seemed the easiest.[30]

Another key element in the Carter strategy involved winning the support of Republican legislators in both houses of the General Assembly. While small—twenty-six representatives and six senators—the support of the Republican contingent in a close vote could make the difference between winning and losing. Fortunately for the Governor, most Republican legislators were reform-mined, business progressives who found much to support in Carter's programs, particularly reorganization. Hal Suit, Carter's opponent in the 1970 gubernatorial race, publicly endorsed the program, as did House Minority Leader Mike Egan and Senate Minority Leader Oliver Bateman.[31] Most House Republicans and five of the six Republican senators followed their lead. Carter's occasional blasts at the Nixon administration and his criticism of Republican federal appointments in Georgia sometimes placed strains on his relationship with Republican legislators,[32] but until the adjournment of the 1972 General Assembly session, Carter avoided obvious displays of partisanship. Meanwhile, he sought the counsel of Republican legislative leaders and in small ways assisted them whenever possible.[33]

Upon receipt of the first draft of the reorganization plan, Carter invited fifty key House and Senate leaders to the mansion where after a two-hour presentation of the proposal, he answered questions and sought suggestions before the drafting of the final version of the plan. The legislators gave the draft mixed reviews. House Speaker George Smith liked the plan and announced his intention of supporting it with a few minor revisions. Lester Maddox, however, urged the General Assembly to veto the entire package.[34] Commenting on the lieutenant governor's opposition, Carter declared "that is his privilege. He tried to veto the whole thing last session and I've never had any substantial support from him."[35]

Although the Governor generally dominated the headlines from the adjournment of the September special session until the convening of the regular session in January, Carter's critics stole the spotlight during three days in December. Stanley Smith, chairman of the powerful Senate Economy, Reorganization and Efficiency in Government (EREG) Committee, provided the forum. Smith called a special session of the committee, to which Maddox would refer the reorganization plan, to hear testimony from state officers. The purpose of the session quickly became apparent. Maddox had stacked EREG with Carter antagonists, and they gave department heads critical of reorganization free rein to publicize their discontents. Meanwhile, those favoring reorganization were treated as hostile witnesses, and their testimony was constantly interrupted by a long series of unfriendly questions.[36]

Chairman Smith closely questioned Project Director Tom Linder about the projected $60.8 million in savings that would result from reorganization. Smith, trying to reduce the figure substantially, argued that new revenue collection procedures and indirect taxes unrelated to reorganization had been used to inflate the savings figure. Linder's breakdown of the figure failed to quiet his detractor. Even Carter's supporters admitted that many of the economies could be effected without reorganization and much of the projected savings figure represented temporary, one-year budget reductions that would not be realized in the subsequent years. According to Smith's arithmetic real savings amounted to less than $5 million.[38]

personality profile:_____
STANLEY EUGENE SMITH, JR.

Born in Liberty, Missouri, on September 7, 1919, Stanley Smith graduated from Fairport High School, Fairport, New York, in 1937. He attended William Jewell College, Wagner

College, Brooklyn Law School, and St. Lawrence University. His pursuit of a law degree ended when he enlisted in the United States Army, eventually rising to the rank of captain in the Signal Corps during World War II. Assigned to Georgia's Warner Robins Air Force Base in 1943, he was attracted to the area and, after the war, settled in nearby Perry, where he worked as an insurance and real estate broker. He later owned and operated the Travel Host Inn in Perry.

Actively involved in church and civic affairs, Smith turned to politics and in 1953 was elected mayor of Perry, a position he held until 1960. In 1962 he ran successfully for the Georgia Senate from the eighteenth senatorial district. During his first General Assembly session, the Perry businessman struck up a friendship with another freshman senator, Jimmy Carter, who agreed with his emphasis on promoting legislative independence from the executive branch of state government. Four years later, Carter ran unsuccessfully for the Democratic gubernatorial nomination, and Smith secured the chairmanship of the powerful Senate Economy, Reorganization and Efficiency in Government Committee from which he eventually led the opposition to his erstwhile friend's effort to reorganize state government in Georgia.[39]

Despite the hostile environment, administration supporters acquitted themselves well before Smith's committee. Administration spokesmen, who were generally better informed than their inquisitors in their areas of concern, occasionally put their interrogators on the defensive and exposed their ignorance about matters under discussion. Smith and his cohorts obviously preferred soliciting the testimony of administration critics. In the role of critic the flamboyant Secretary of State Ben Fortson put on a lively show but warned Senate critics not to underestimate their antagonist. "I've known Jimmy Carter all my life," Fortson told the committee,

Don't pay any attention to that smile. That don't mean a thing. That man is made of steel, determination and stubbornness. Carter reminds me of a South Georgia turtle. He doesn't go around a log. He just sticks his head in the middle and pushes and pushes until the log gives way.[40]

Near the end of the year, Carter invited all members of the General Assembly to an all-day session at the Georgia Center for Continuing Education on the University of Georgia campus, where he promised to review with the legislators all major changes proposed in the reorganization plan. Although less than 100 of the 251 lawmakers attended, the participants included a number of House and Senate members who were not yet committed on the reorganization issue.[41] Those in attendance witnessed one of Jimmy Carter's virtuoso performances. He exhibited an impressive command of virtually every detail in the long, fifty-seven page bill, answered questions put to him by the lawmakers in an informed, straightforward manner, and vigorously defended each section of the plan with thoughtful, well-developed arguments that critics found difficult to refute. As one reporter observed, the Governor had indeed done his homework well. Many legislators in attendance were equally impressed.[42] "I feel good about it," the Governor declared afterwards. "The only persistent questions that came up were related to the Board of Health."[43]

As senators and representatives from across the state converged on Atlanta for the 1972 session of the Georgia General Assembly, the lawmakers generally agreed on three points: 1) Jimmy Carter's government reorganization plan would be the dominant issue before the legislature; 2) it would be an unusually divisive session; and 3) the General Assembly would pass relatively little of the Governor's reorganization plan. Senator Maylon London predicted only "the caption of the bill and its effective date will be approved by the legislature." To be acceptable, he said, many sections of the plan would have to be taken out or rewritten, and the proposed departments of Human Resources and Natural Resources had to go.[44] Reflecting a similarly hostile sentiment, Ed Zipperer, a member of the Senate EREG Committee, declared: "This bill has got to be studied very carefully because we don't want to reorganize and . . . form a dictatorial type of government just because a dictatorship is the cheapest form of government."[45] The Governor and his staff found even more frustrating comments, such as those of Senator Joe Kennedy, who told the press, "personally, I don't see how you can be against it," but who then proceeded to attack the plan, concluding it would do more harm than good.[46]

Even Carter's friends in the legislature exhibited little optimism. Cy Chapman, one of the Governor's key Senate supporters, thought it would take a "minor miracle" on Carter's part to get the reorganization plan through the Senate. "We think we probably have about 25 votes on our side of the fence now," he said, "while the opposition has 31. This means we would need a switch of four votes to pass the major portion of the reorganization project."[47] Another pro-Carter senator expressing pessimism about getting any of the plan through the Senate noted, "The opposition is awfully agile, I'm afraid."[48] House Speaker George Smith, one of the few to express even limited optimism, predicted that "a great majority of it will pass in the House," but, he concluded, "I can't speak for the Senate."[49]

Only the Governor and his immediate staff maintained a posture of unqualified optimism. Carter remained confident and refused to concede anything unnecessarily. He adopted a resolute, uncompromising attitude, branding efforts to stop reorganization as "foolish" and "ridiculous."[50] The Governor charged that some of the legislators opposing reorganization were "simply mouthpieces for some special interest" and vowed "to meet them head on."[51] Indeed, Carter appeared quite willing, if necessary, to fight a war of legislative attrition. "I'm going to get it," he declared,

I'll be the governor for three more years and almost the complete reorganization plan will be in effect before I go out of office. If I don't get all I want this year, I'll introduce revisions next year and keep trying.[52]

Carter vowed to introduce as separate legislation all vetoed items and fight hard to gain their acceptance in the General Assembly. "I had to browbeat people and twist arms to get this bill through," he declared, "and I'll do the same thing this time to get the plan passed. I'll do everything legally permissible."[53]

The Governor also hinted, none too subtly, that he could retaliate against those opposing him. While disclaiming any intention of going into legislative districts to tell voters how to mark their ballots, he did feel lawmakers had an obligation to tell the voters precisely where they stood on reorganization. "As a statewide effort," Carter declared, "I think it would be a legitimate thing for me to do, to acquaint the people with the facts and to acquaint them with the voting record of those running for reelection."[54]

General objections to the reorganization plan were abstract and to some extent contrived. Legislative critics rarely discussed the specifics of the proposal but instead concentrated on related issues of questionable relevancy. Clearly Carter's antagonists preferred debating reorganization on a hypothetical or emotional plane to confronting the more complex and perhaps politically unprofitable task of analyzing the specifics of reorganization.

One of the objections, endlessly repeated, involved the "reverse veto" provision of HB 1. Under the provisions of the authorization act, the reorganization plan automatically became law unless vetoed by either house of the General Assembly within fifteen days of the convening of the session. Administration critics argued that this left too little time to study and analyze responsibly the far-ranging proposals to be placed before them. They placed greater emphasis, however, on the constitutionality of the procedure which reversed the traditional roles of the executive and legislative branches and gave the governor the power to initiate legislation while the General Assembly sat in judgment.[55] Actually, ample precedent in administration law existed for such a procedure, and it previously had been used in Georgia on a number of occasions with little controversy. Moreover, Georgia Attorney General Arthur Bolton wrote the bill after carefully reviewing pertinent constitutional provisions and related judicial decisions.[56]

While undoubtedly some reorganization critics had serious reservations about the legality of the procedure, most administration opponents worried more about the tactical advantage it gave the Governor than constitutional niceties. In what virtually everyone expected to be a close vote, especially in the Senate, the opposition to reform had to build majorities, not the administration.

Charges that the Carter plan would greatly increase the powers of the executive ranked next to the reverse veto argument in the litany of objections to reorganization. Lieutenant Governor Maddox, legislative critics, and at least three department heads used the term "dictatorship" to characterize the effect of the plan on state government.[57] Exaggerated to the point of absurdity, such charges, more than anything else, reflected the demagogic strain of Georgia politics. Other than making administrative agencies more responsible to the chief executive, which theoretically, they should have been, the most significant new power given to the governor in the reorganization plan was the power to appoint chairmen of government boards who previously had been elected by the full board and to determine whether the boards had a policy-making or administrative function.[58] In answering these charges, Carter repeatedly denied that reorganization was a power play. "I have enough power through appointments and my position as director of the budget," he declared.[59] In fact, during the development of the plan, Carter studiously had avoided proposals that significantly increased gubernatorial powers, realizing that opponents could use such proposals to discredit governmental reform.[60] The argument that Carter desired extraordinary power made little sense logically as he would be leaving office and would be barred by the state constitution from succeeding himself before the full implementation of reorganization. Furthermore, most political observers assumed Lieutenant Governor Maddox, one of those most fervent in making the dictatorship charge, would succeed Carter in the governor's mansion.

Although administration critics did have legitimate objections to specific proposals contained in the reorganization plan, they also realized that the more outrageous their charges, the bigger and bolder headlines they could attract. Thus in their own way Carter's foes manipulated the press and media as effectively as the administration by using outrageous charges rather than careful analyses of the complex issues.

PART III

Confronting the Legislature: The Fight for Reorganization

Let me point out to you that there is no division in purpose between me as Governor and you as legislators. Your people are my people. Governors do not pass laws—*you* have given me an overwhelming mandate in House Bill No. 1 to reform the executive branch of Government. For a year now I have been carrying out that mandate.

Governor Jimmy Carter,
State of the State Message, 1972

Rather than twisting arms, I held your hands. Thus I am more than grieved when, at this very moment, a brazen, unbelievable and illegal attempt is being made to set up a dictatorship in state government designed to wreck constitutional and representative government.

Lieutenant Governor Lester Maddox

chapter 6

THE FRUITS OF PLANNING: GEORGIA LEGISLATORS DEBATE REORGANIZATION

Reflecting on the events of the past year, Jimmy Carter celebrated New Year's Day 1972 knowing that within a few weeks the fate of his long struggle for reorganization would be determined. The success of his governorship and, most likely, any future political ambitions he might entertain rested upon the outcome of this campaign. Thus, he had little time for holiday celebration. Reorganization opponents were busily at work seeking to frustrate him. Hostile senators hoped to veto the entire plan developed through the Reorganization and Management Improvement Study, or failing that, to challenge the constitutionality of HB 1 in the courts. With similar motives, State Representative Lamar Northcutt announced his intention of introducing a resolution postponing action on the reorganization bill for another twelve months; during which time, the plan would be studied by a twenty-five member commission with instructions to report its recommendations to the 1973 session of the General Assembly.[1]

The Governor and his staff spent the week preceding the convening of the General Assembly session pressing legislators for commitments on "key elements" of the plan, which included new financial regulations, creation of the departments of Human Resources, Administrative Services, and Natural Resources, and the transfer of the state treasurer's duties to the new Administrative Services Department. Although he refused to speculate about the extent of his numerical support in either house, Carter found reports from sympathetic legislators encouraging and observed that two leading Senate reorganization critics apparently had decided against seeking a veto of the entire proposal. "I think these legislators are beginning to feel the pressure from back home where the people support reorganization," Carter concluded.[2]

Nevertheless, an *Atlanta Constitution* postcard poll of legislators on the eve of the General Assembly session evidenced only moderate enthusiasm for the reorganization plan. Of the thirty-six senators and ninety-one representatives responding to the poll, only eight senators and twenty-seven representatives found it a "good" plan. While fewer senators (four) and representatives (eleven) termed it a "bad" plan, the remainder gave it only a lukewarm "fair" rating. Thirty senators and seventy-two representatives said they would support efforts to veto significant parts of the bill; five representatives (but no senators) favored vetoing the entire plan. A mere five members in each chamber approved the plan in its entirety. The most frequent reservations expressed by those responding to the poll concerned a perceived increase in gubernatorial power, the proposal to have the state school superintendent appointed by the State Board of Education, and the abolition of the State Board of Health whose functions would be assumed by a nine-member policy board in the new Department of Human Resources. The most astonishing objections came from a suburban Atlanta senator who somehow found the reorganization proposal a sinister Marxist plot.[3]

As opening day of the 1972 General Assembly session approached, the Governor and his staff intensified their lobbying activities on Georgia's capitol hill. They also moved to bring in reinforcements from those businesses that had participated in the Reorganization and Management Improvement Study. Project Director Tom Linder contacted those corporations furnishing personnel to the reorganization study and asked company officials to use their legislative contacts to support reorganization. Almost all responded favorably, promising to work quietly behind the scenes and to commit either the individual who had participated in the study or their regular legislative lobbyist to the cause.[4] Seeking to allay criticism of his controversial plan to make the state school superintendent an appointive office, Carter promised legislation providing for the election of the State Board of Education, whose members previously had been appointed by the governor.[5]

A few days prior to the scheduled opening of the legislative session, twenty senators and several state officials held a closed-door strategy session in the Marriott Motor Hotel's Whitehall Salon. Stanley Smith, Culver Kidd, and Senate Majority Leader Eugene Holley, leaders of the anti-Carter bloc in the Senate, called the meeting. Other Carter foes, including Labor Commissioner Caldwell, Dr. Carl Pruett of the State Board of Health, State School Superintendent Nix, and Lieutenant Governor Maddox, also attended the meeting. Stanley Smith firmly rebuffed efforts by newsmen to cover the session. After first refusing to acknowledge the existence of a meeting, Smith later declared it was a private session. During the meeting, which was infiltrated by at least one Carter loyalist, anti-reorganization strategists discussed a contemplated suit challenging the constitutionality of HB 1, substitute legislation for Carter's reorganization bill, and the possibility of delaying any consideration of the Governor's proposed budget for fiscal 1973 until the resolution of the reorganization bill. After the meeting, newsmen found Senate Majority Leader Holley in the hotel parking lot, where, after persistent questioning, he revealed that affirmative legislation probably would be introduced on the first day of the session as a substitute for sections of Carter's plan on which "there is widespread disagreement."[6]

The following day Fulton County officials served Carter with three separate lawsuits challenging the constitutionality of HB 1. The suits, filed by Sam Caldwell, Carl Pruett, and Eldridge W. Perry, a member of the Georgia Development Authority, sought to enjoin the secretary of state from printing any portion of the reorganization bill in the state's lawbooks until the court ruled on the constiutionality of HB 1. As the litigants were confident that the reorganization plan would be greatly altered in the legislature, they requested that hearings on their petition be delayed until January 26, the day following the fifteen-day period legislators had to vote on the reorganization bill. Evidence of United States Senator Herman Talmadge's quiet, behind-the-scenes efforts to discredit the Governor surfaced once again. Lamar W. Sizemore, a long-time personal friend and political ally of the senator, headed the Atlanta law firm filing the lawsuits challenging reorganization.

Sizemore probably would not have involved himself in such an explosive political issue without first consulting with the state's senior senator.[7]

Meanwhile, beginning its hearings before the General Assembly convened, Senate Efficiency, Reorganization and Economy in Government Committee resumed hearings on the reorganization bill on January 5. The following day committee members voted 9 to 2 to veto the proposed departments of Administrative Services, Human Resources, and Natural Resources.[8]

While Senate critics plotted strategy in the Whitehall Salon, filed petitions in the state courts, and sought to decimate the bill in committee, Carter prepared for a critically important meeting with members of the powerful House Democratic Policy Committee. During the three-hour meeting, Carter explained the reorganization plan in detail and agreed to a revision of Section 105 of the bill concerning the creation of the Department of Administrative Services. Several legislators worried that under Section 105 smaller state agencies would lose their ability to function autonomously in personnel matters. The Governor agreed to a revision that would clarify the rights of smaller agencies integrated into larger departments to hire and fire their own personnel.[9] The compromise cleared the way for House leadership support of the reorganization bill.

Although government reorganization certainly would be the dominant issue during the General Assembly session, the Governor's legislative agenda included a number of other items certain to anger some lawmakers and consequently to complicate further efforts to gain approval of the reorganization plan. Carter's legislative package included environmental and consumer protection legislation, judicial reform measures to modernize the state's antiquated court system, property tax equalization, a state sunshine law, antiblockbusting legislation, no-fault insurance, a bill permitting fourteen-foot mobile home producers to use state highways, and a bill providing stricter controls over land developers.[10] The Governor also had to prepare a budget for fiscal 1973 for submission to the General Assembly. In this case, Carter developed two budgets, one reflecting $40 million in projected reorganization savings and another, somewhat lower, in which such savings were not included.[11] Clearly, the Governor used the two-budget tactic to increase pressures on legislators to approve the reorganization plan. The budgets illustrated the savings to be derived from reorganization and the resulting expanded services available to Georgia citizens without a general tax increase.

On the opening day of the General Assembly session, Carter predicted that "almost all' of his reorganization plan would survive the legislative review. Despite the "highly publicized opposition," he believed each proposal "perfectly capable of standing on its own merits." As legislators debated the bill, Carter reasoned, this would become increasingly obvious and support for the plan would grow. Opposition to reorganization, he concluded, consisted of the same group which had opposed reorganization "ever since it was first mentioned a year ago. They fought against House Bill One which directed me to reorganize state government, they fought all year the specific reorganization recommendations, they are still opposing reorganization."[12]

The Governor received a mixture of good and bad news just prior to the convening of the legislative session. Because of reservations about certain provisions of the reorganization bill, House Majority Leader George Busbee unexpectedly refused to manage the reorganization bill on the floor of the House. Carter then decided to use several sympathetic lawmakers to shepherd various sections of the proposal through the House.[13] The good news came shortly before the opening of the General Assembly session when Senate Majority Leader Eugene Holley convened a meeting of the policy committee of the Senate Democratic Caucus to report that Senate critics of the Carter proposal had been unable to draft an acceptable alternative. Instead, they would seek to amend the Governor's proposal on the floor of the Senate.[14]

Lieutenant Governor Maddox gaveled the 1972 Senate session to order at 10 A.M. on January 10, and a few hours later EREG Committee chairman Stanley Smith introduced three bills as substitutes for key provisions in the reorganization bill. The substitutes would have drastically altered and diminished the functions of the proposed departments of Human Resources, Natural Resources, and Administrative Services.[15]

At noon the following day Governor Carter strode briskly into the House chamber to deliver his "State of the State" address to a joint session of the legislature. Although he received the traditional standing ovation at the end of his speech, most observers agreed that the legislators' reception had been distinctly cool. Indeed, legislators did not once interrupt the Governor's address with applause. Deferring any mention of reorganization until the last portion of his address, Carter hit the subject hard. While speaking on the subject, his voice hardened and flashes of anger crossed his face as he defended the proposal and denounced those seeking to frustrate reform. Continuing a theme developed earlier in the Public Awareness campaign, Carter linked reorganization critics to special interest groups. "The choice we have," he told the lawmakers, "is to yield to the pressures of our good friends, special groups of interests and tell the people their rights shall be denied, or we can summon our courage and act for the people."[16] Reactions to the speech were predictable. The Governor's friends described it as "sincere," "moving," and "compassionate," while his foes were less charitable. House Speaker Pro Tem Tom Murphy, perhaps reflecting the opinions of many legislators, said, " I thought he made a beautiful speech. I just didn't happen to agree with much of it."[17] Less sanguine, Senate Majority Leader Holley, stung by Carter's caustic references to pressure group influence, declared: "I think reorganization and the methods of how you implement it should be a topic that honorable men can disagree on. I think I have the best interest of the people at heart, as do the group of senators I am working with to amend this bill. I have no selfish interests."[18] Although commending Carter for having the courage of his convictions, Maddox said the Governor "sounded embittered, hurt and angered. I didn't see him extending the carrot stick to anyone."[19] Later in the day, Maddox concluded the speech was decidedly "political" and demanded equal time from the state's radio and television stations which had carried the Governor's address.[20]

A flurry of activity enveloped legislators during the opening days of the legislative session. House Republicans caucused and voted unanimously to support the reorganization bill but reserved the right to oppose individual sections of the proposal.[21] Senate Democrats also were busy. A few hours after Carter's "State of the State" speech, some thirty senators met in a room at the Henry Grady Hotel to discuss the reorganization proposal. Afterwards, Lieutenant Governor Maddox, inadvertently testifying to the effectiveness of the Public Awareness Program, disclosed that those attending the meeting generally conceded that "the people" did not want an outright veto of the reorganization bill. It was also agreed, Maddox said, that it would be preferable for the Governor to come back with affirmative legislation when a section was vetoed rather than having someone else propose substitutes.[22]

Meanwhile, the Governor made plans for personal appearances in both houses of the legislature to explain and defend the reorganization bill and, surprising Senate critics, asked Holley to convene a special meeting of the Senate Democratic Policy Committee to see whether they could resolve their differences. "I need their help," Carter told the press. "I want to reestablish a working relationship with the Senators. I just want to open up. I want to know what their concerns are."[23] A conciliatory atmosphere prevailed during the meetings and a compromise was reached on the Governor's controversial plan to centralize printing and computer services in the proposed Department of Administrative Services.[24]

Compromise and conciliation continued the following day during a Carter appearance before the Senate to defend the reorganization plan. He indicated his willingness to compromise on several provisions but reaffirmed his determination to fight for the key elements of the proposal. The Governor's most significant concession involved a decision to allow policy-making boards to elect their own chairmen. Under the original proposal, the Governor would have appointed board chairmen.[25] Later the same day, Carter moved to the House where for nearly three hours he discussed the reorganization plan with members of the lower house.[26]

The Governor's conciliatory efforts, however, had little lasting effect. In testimony before the House, Maddox continued his yearlong harangue against the "reverse veto" method established in HB 1. While admitting that many of the Carter proposals had merit, the volatile lieutenant governor declared that, if implemented, the plan "would cost the taxpayers millions more, not less and help set up a dictatorship that was both sinister and insidious." Maddox was followed by eleven state constitutional officers, most of whom criticized various provisions of the reorganization bill with equal fervor.[27]

On the third day of the session, leaders in both chambers published the rules and procedures to be used in the consideration of the reorganization bill.

Senate:

1. Read the bill chapter by chapter. The chair will entertain a motion at the end of each chapter reading on whether to take up that chapter or any section of the chapter for vetoing.
2. When all the sections within a chapter have been disposed of by lack of veto motion, failure of a veto motion, or a final vote to veto a section, action on the chapter shall be considered complete. When a chapter has been completed, a motion to reconsider can be made but at no time thereafter.
3. When the action on all chapters has been completed and debate terminated, it will then be in order to vote on whether to veto the entire remaining plan.
4. After the final vote on the plan as described above, a motion to reconsider may be given. It will be in order for the Senate to take up the reconsideration question as first business the next day.

House:

1. Read the plan section by section. After each section is read, any member will be given the opportunity to say whether he wants a particular section to be considered for veto.
2. After all sections have been read, the House will take up for consideration and debate the sections which have been marked for consideration for veto.
3. After all sections have been acted upon, a motion to veto the entire plan will then be in order.
4. Once final action is taken on an individual section or on the entire plan, a motion for reconsideration will not be in order (as is provided for in the Senate).[28]

After a reading of the reorganization measure in the House on Thursday, January 13, lawmakers registered their objections to 108 of the bill's 243 sections. Carter supporters sponsored a number of these vetoes to fulfill earlier compromises or to clarify language and make necessary editorial changes. Other vetoes, however, if sustained, would have gutted the reorganization plan.[29]

The following day—a good one for the Governor—House members began voting on the proposed vetoes. By votes of 37 to 145 and 59 to 115, they refused to kill Carter's controversial plans to consolidate state printing plants and computer services. Moreover, Speaker Pro Tem Tom Murphy's proposed veto of the entire section creating the Department of Administrative Services received little support (32 to 145). Although encountering opposition from both Democratic and Republican House leaders, Murphy sought to introduce a substitute section eliminating the governor's right to fire appointed department heads.[30] While the "key elements" of the plan easily survived the first day's voting, House critics succeeded in vetoing several minor provisions, the most significant of which gave the director of the proposed Department of Administrative Services, a gubernatorial appointee, a voice in the selection of the state's personnel director. Civil servants as well as legislators worried that the proposal might politicize the state merit system. Although Carter disagreed, he neverthless announced that he would not seek to have the vetoed section restored. As with his earlier agreement with the House Policy Committee, the Governor again revealed a flexibility and willingness to compromise on lesser issues to further prospects of gaining larger objectives.[31]

The following week Carter's conciliatory skills became vitally important as the House debated the proposal to abolish the State Board of Health and create a new Department of Human Resources. The first day's balloting left the Human Resources Department in a shambles. In a series of irreconcilable votes, House members approved the section of the reorganization bill creating the department but vetoed the proposal to abolish the state health board. Along similar lines, they vetoed the establishment of a nine-member policy board for the new department but approved the section creating the office of commissioner with responsibility for carrying out policy board decisions.[32] Moreover, during the first day's voting, the representatives did not reach the controversial section merging offender rehabilitation with health and welfare services.[33] Obviously, the Governor had problems.

Hoping to save what he considered the most important innovation in his reorganization plan, the Governor moved to reconcile differences with House leaders. In a letter to Speaker Smith,
Carter reviewed his perception of the House's major objections
to the human resources proposal and then offered a compromise
he hoped would win approval in the lower chamber. The compromise consisted of three major changes in the original bill: 1) the
removal of the probation and parole supervision agencies from the
new Department of Human Resources; 2) the increase from nine
to fifteen in the membership of the policy board; and 3) the stipulation that at least three practicing physicians and two other representatives of the medical profession would serve on the board.[34]

Carter's timely compromise effectively undermined opposition
to reorganization in the House. After resolving the impasse over
human resources, the House voted down veto after veto and then
overwhelmingly (24 to 158) rejected a proposed veto of the entire
bill.[35] Ultimately, the lower house vetoed 34 of the 243 sections
of the bill. Most reflected compromises reached earlier between
the lawmakers and the Governor or were friendly vetoes to permit editorial changes. The House votes could only be viewed as
an overwhelming endorsement of the reorganization bill. Yet
the lower chamber still had to act on vital elements of the reorganization plan, especially the proposal to abolish the State Board of
Health and the various compromises agreed to by the Governor
and the lawmakers.[36]

While the House voted on the reorganization bill, Senate leaders
continued hearings on the measure, giving hostile state officials a
forum from which to rehash their already well-known objections
to the plan.[37] The motivation behind these stalling tactics quickly
became apparent as the Senate, facing the fifteen-day deadline,
finally began voting on attempted vetoes. Senate leaders simply
did not have the votes to make major changes in the reorganization
bill. Votes on key provisions of the plan were close, but in most
instances, the opposition could not muster the necessary twenty-
nine votes to effect a veto. The Senate added only eleven new
vetoes to the thirty-four voted earlier in the House; however, those
sustained in the upper chamber constituted the Governor's most
serious reorganization setbacks. Carter characterized the Senate

vote against including the Forestry Department in the new Department of Natural Resources as his worst defeat. The senators also rejected the proposal to house the Forest Research Council and the state's Soil and Water Conservation Agency in the Department of Natural Resources, the plan to consolidate the state's seventy-eight printing plants into eight units, and the effort to move the employee and teacher retirement systems into the proposed Administrative Services Department.[38]

Although Carter had suffered serious setbacks in the Senate, the reorganization bill survived the legislative review remarkably intact. One hundred and ninety-eight of the 243 sections of the bill were left entirely unchanged; moreover, Carter supporters initiated most of the forty-five vetoes with administration approval. Nevertheless, while both houses of the General Assembly had completed action on the bill in the prescribed fifteen days, much still needed to be done before the lawmakers completed work on state government reorganization. The various compromises would be introduced as regular legislation, and the Governor still contemplated reversing some of the vetoes of state constitutional officers through affirmative legislation. Realizing that he did not have the votes, Carter reluctantly abandoned hopes of merging the Forestry Department in the new Department of Natural Resources.[39]

To fill the voids the legislative vetoes had left in the reorganization plan, the administration staff began drawing up an omnibus bill for introduction in the House that included earlier compromises made with legislators during their deliberations on the bill.[40] Meanwhile, at a meeting with members of the Urban Caucus, Carter revealed he would move to have the approved sections of the reorganization bill reintroduced as affirmative legislation. This action, Carter reasoned, would eliminate legal challenges and permit immediate implementation of governmental changes.[41] At the same time, by promising not to implement any reorganization changes until after the adjournment of the General Assembly, the administration gained a postponement of the scheduled January 26 hearing on court challenges to the legality of HB 1.[42]

Taking advantage of the Governor's own apparent doubts concerning the constitutionality of HB 1, hostile legislators attached to an administration measure an amendment that would strip the

Governor of future authority to reorganize state government by means of the legislative veto. Unperturbed, Carter declared: "If we continue to make the kind of progress on reorganization that's evidently in prospect, I don't see any need for the reverse veto to be used again."[43]

Indeed, matters did seem to be going the Governor's way. A few days later the House voted 145 to 6 to reaffirm through traditional legislative procedures its earlier action on the reorganization bill. On the same day, the House Rules Committee voted 10 to 2 to send to the floor a bill transferring the functions of the State Board of Health to the Department of Human Resources. This action was facilitated by Carter's willingness to give licensed medical personnel seven of the fifteen seats on the departmental governing board. However, the House's failure to take final action on the human resources bill before a scheduled two-week recess for budget hearings disappointed the Governor and bred unfounded rumors that the proposal was in trouble.[44]

Despite the positive steps taken in the House, threatening clouds still drifted across the Governor's horizon, in the form of Stanley Smith's Senate EREG Committee which sent a bill to the floor postponing the transfer of the State Board of Health to the Human Resources Department for one year pending further study. The following day the Senate refused to adopt the Governor's proposal for the consolidation of the state's printing and computer operations. This action especially incensed Carter, because it violated the agreement reached with Senate leaders a week earlier. Meeting with the press following th Senate action, Carter contrasted the constructive role of the House, "which has acted responsibly on these matters" to the "irresponsible" role of the Senate which had "completely gutted that portion of the reorganization plan that would have saved the most money for the taxpayers of Georgia."[45] Carter's only hope for saving the proposal rested with House leaders in a Senate-House conference committee.

Aggrieved by the Senate leadership's breach of faith and frustrated by major setbacks at a time when the reorganization plan seemed on the verge of acceptance, the Governor took the offensive, bitterly attacking Senate leaders, particularly Maddox, Smith, and Holley, whom he accused of bottling up or drastically alter-

ing legislation in the EREG Committee through secret meetings and obstructionist parliamentary maneuvers. The Governor
charged there had been "an almost complete breakdown of the
legislative process in the Senate."[46] Until that time, the critically
important EREG Committee had held only two formal meetings
during the entire legislative session, yet Chairman Smith reported
numerous measures to the floor of the Senate without consulting
the full committee. Smith simply circulated bills and resolutions
among anti-administration senators and then reported them out
with committee recommendations. Carter's floor leader, the iras-
cible Al Holloway, who was barely able to contain his pent-up
fury, took to the well of the Senate to denounce Smith and his
cohorts in terms similar to those used earlier by the Governor.[47]

One of the more bizarre incidents in the entire reorganization
struggle occurred on the eve of the legislative recess. Culver Kidd,
one of Carter's most resourceful and intransigent Senate foes, suddenly announced his willingness to sponsor an amendment to the
human resources bill undercutting the EREG Committee substitute and assuring passage of the Carter proposal. Carter easily
could have lived with the relatively harmless amendment suggested
by Kidd. In explaining his sudden change of position, Kidd simply
told the press he planned to do a little negotiating with Carter on
new staff allotments for the Milledgeville mental health facility
in his district.[48] Despite a big splash in the newspapers at the time,
little more was heard of the proposal until the spring of 1978 when
Carter, now president of the United States, gave unusual video-
taped testimony against Kidd on federal charges of conspiring to
obstruct enforcement of state gambling laws. Carter testified that
during the debates on the human resources proposal, Senate Majority Leader Holley approached him with a proposal from Kidd.
Kidd offered to support Carter's reorganization proposal in exchange for advance notice of gambling raids by state agents in his
district. Ray Pope, then Georgia Public Safety commissioner,
supported the Carter account, but Holley's recollection of the
incident varied in significant details from Carter's, and Kidd won
acquittal.[49] Whatever the truth of the matter, Kidd ultimately
voted against the administration on every reorganization roll call,
the only senator to do so.

personality profile:_____

EDWARDS CULVER KIDD, JR.

Widely known as the "Silver Fox" of Georgia politics, Culver Kidd was born in Milledgeville, Georgia, on July 17, 1914. His father and grandfather had operated a small Milledgeville family drugstore where they concocted and sold a variety of home remedies including "Kidd's One-Minute Toothache Drops." Culver Kidd graduated from Georgia Military College in 1932 and four years later earned a BS degree at the Georgia Institute of Technology. An officer in the United States Army during World War II, he received the Purple Heart after being wounded at Okinawa and held the rank of major at the conclusion of the war.

Following the war, Kidd, like so many young veterans, entered politics and was elected to the Georgia House of Representatives. In 1962, after serving twelve terms in the House and making an unsuccessful bid for the Democratic nomination for lieutenant governor, he ran successfully for the Georgia Senate from the newly created twenty-fifth senatorial district. His capacity for hard work and his considerable political skills soon made him a major power broker in the General Assembly. A prolific bill writer, he introduced as many as 200 bills during a single legislative session and managed to successfully shepherd many of them through the General Assembly. His major legislative interests included the administration of the large Central Georgia Regional Hospital in his district and legislation of interest to small loan companies. Kidd served as president of Middle Georgia Management Services, Inc., a holding company for six small loan companies.[50]

During the legislative recess, Carter and his staff feverishly redrafted proposals, shored up support in both houses, and sought accommodations and compromises that might swing a critical vote in their direction. Given the close divisions in the Senate, a single vote could mean the difference between winning or losing. The Governor courted the support of such outspoken foes as Sam Caldwell, Lester Maddox, and officials of the Medical Association of Georgia (MAG). In an effort to pacify the latter, the Governor offered yet another compromise on the composition of the fifteen-member governing board of the Human Resources Department. He announced he would seek amendment of the reorganization bill to create a ten-member screening committee—five members appointed by the MAG and five by the governor—to recommend appointments of practicing physicians to the department governing board. He also agreed to increase the number of licensed physicians on the board from three to five.[51] The MAG, however, resolutely refused to compromise, thus setting the stage for a showdown with the Governor when the General Assembly reconvened on February 21.

Exhibiting the confidence that had characterized his public posture throughout the long reorganization struggle, Jimmy Carter flew to Washington to attend the winter meeting of the National Governors' Conference as the House opened debates on the proposal to abolish the State Board of Health. Most observers expected a close vote, and MAG lobbyists, who swarmed around the capitol, predicted victory. Surprisingly, the vote gave the Governor a lopsided 130 to 55 victory over the powerful medical association. The House immediately transmitted the bill to the Senate where Lieutenant Governor Maddox referred it to the EREG Committee. Although many House members believed the administration's victory had been facilitated by the obdurant, uncompromising stance adopted by the doctors, MAG officials, still hoping to get their way in the Senate, continued dogmatically to resist any change in the State Board of Health.[52]

The tactic anti-administration forces would use in the Senate quickly became apparent as Stanley Smith and his EREG Committee refused to take action on the reorganization bills. The committee met and considered minor bills but totally ignored the various reorganization measures. When Al Holloway asked the committee to take up the reorganization bills, Smith promptly adjourned the meeting. He also artfully dodged a Carter request to meet with the committee but later relented when Carter made a public issue of it at a press conference.[53] During the subsequent meeting, Smith promised to report out of committee a bill abolishing the State Board of Health, but he warned the Governor it would not be a bill to his liking.[54] A few days later Smith did report out a substitute for the House bill abolishing the State Health Board, and, as predicted, Carter found it unacceptable. Smith attached the substitute to a House bill that would create the Department of Offender Rehabilitation. In excruciatingly close votes, the Senate rejected the Smith substitute (28 to 27) and by a bare constitutional majority (29 to 26) approved the House bill abolishing the State Board of Health. It was a stunning victory for the Governor in which he not only gained Senate approval of the human resources proposal but also, when senators voted down the Smith substitute, secured the Department of Offender Rehabilitation. Two senators usually aligned with the opposition assured Carter's victory by voting for the House bill. This support became vitally important when two Republican senators who normally supported the administration defected to the opposition on the issue.[55]

Shortly after the human resources vote, Carter again publicly urged Smith to release the House omnibus bills that had been stalled in the EREG Committee since January 28.[56] With the forty-day constitutional limit for General Assembly sessions rapidly approaching, Smith obviously hoped to keep the remaining reorganization bills bottled up in committee during the remainder of the session. But the Carter forces had skillful parliamentary strategists of their own, particularly George Smith and Al Holloway. When responding to questions about the reorganization bills languishing in the Senate EREG Committee, Holloway revealed that House leaders had promised to hold a Senate bill in the House Rules Committee to be used, if necessary, as a vehicle for bringing the remaining reorganization bills directly to the floor of the Senate without passing through Smith's Committee.[57]

Confronted with this threat to bypass his committee, Smith caucused with other anti-administration senators to devise a counter strategy. The following day the EREG Committee reported an omnibus bill of its own to which Smith attached an amendment significantly changing the composition of the governing board of the Human Resources Department. When the issue reached the Senate floor, however, the Carter forces easily brushed aside this last-ditch effort to reopen the human resources issue and to scuttle reorganization.[58]

Only the Senate bill drastically altering the proposed consolidation of printing and computer services remained on the Senate Calendar. Through the adoption of several amendments, the House had revised the bill in a form similar to Carter's original proposal and returned it to the Senate. On the last day of the session, Holloway successfully moved that the Senate not concur in the House amendments, thus necessitating a House-Senate conference committee on the issue. Lieutenant Governor Maddox, however, delayed appointing Senate members to the conference committee. At 9:05 P.M., less than three hours before the scheduled adjournment of the session, Holloway finally gained the floor to introduce a motion instructing the "yet-to-be-named" Senate members of the conference committee. Holloway's motion passed, but Maddox continued to stall. Julian Webb, another Carter ally, then moved that the Senate instruct the "conference committee-to-be-named" to report to the Senate in one hour. After the Senate approved the motion, Webb sought to make the time limit more explicit. "That will be at 10:31 P.M.," he informed the lieutenant governor. "You sound like some of those people visiting my moonlighting operation," Maddox retorted.* "They seem to think I can't tell time."[59]

To save the proposed consolidation of printing and computer services in the conference committee, Carter reluctantly made his last reorganization compromise and agreed to exempt Labor Department computers. The concession to his archenemy, Sam Caldwell, pained the Governor. With the agreement in hand, the conference committee reported back to the Senate at 11:50 P.M., an hour and nineteen minutes late. The drama, however, still had not ended. Stanley Smith, one of the Senate conferees, mysteriously had disappeared. After the head of the House delegation, Majority Leader George Busbee, threatened to stand in the well of the Senate until the sergeant-at-arms found the errant senator, Smith finally appeared, signed the conference report, and informed

---

*Maddox operated a gift-souvenir shop in Underground Atlanta where one of the more popular items was a "Lester Maddox watch" that ran backwards.

the Senate that an agreement had been reached. This last item of business on reorganization had been concluded virtually at the stroke of midnight.[60]

Before the General Assembly session, few observers and prognosticators had given Carter much chance of getting any substantial part of the reorganization bill through the legislature, especially the Senate. Yet at the end of the session, the Governor could claim, without contradiction, that 90 to 95 percent of the plan had been approved by the General Assembly. Moreover, Carter had other significant successes during the session, including action on early childhood education, tax reform, environmental protection, a state sunshine bill, judicial reform, consumer protection, and a bill conferring full rights to eighteen year olds.[61] To be sure, the Governor did not get everything he wanted in all of these areas, but the legislative scorecard was impressive when considering the intransigent opposition of the Senate leadership to most of his legislative proposals.

chapter 7

HOW CARTER DID IT: AN ANALYSIS OF LEGISLATIVE VOTING BEHAVIOR IN THE GEORGIA SENATE

Seasoned capitol watchers, newspaper reporters, political activists, and legislators marveled at Jimmy Carter's success in pushing the reorganization bill through the state legislature. Few had given him much chance of success prior to the General Assembly session, and afterwards they speculated as to how Jimmy did it. In retrospect, Carter's success resulted from a complex, interrelated combination of circumstances that included the long Public Awareness campaign preceding the General Assembly session, the administration's effective management of the bill in the legislature, the cooperative attitude of House leaders, Carter's timely compromises and personal lobbying among legislators, Republican support of the measure, and the arrogant pettiness of the Senate opposition.

Tom Linder, Cloyd Hall, and the staff of the Public Awareness Program did their jobs thoroughly and professionally. Informed citizens could hardly have been unaware of the need for reorganization, the major changes proposed in the Reorganization and Management Improvement Study, or the administration's arguments in defense of those recommendations. The effectiveness of the Public Awareness effort clearly strengthened the position of administration supporters in both houses and undoubtedly caused many undecided or uncommitted legislators to favor parts of the Carter program. Even such staunch critics as Lester Maddox and Stanley Smith affirmed the effectiveness of the administration's

Public Awareness effort. Both men were forced to concede that public opinion in Georgia favored reorganization.

Along with the Public Awareness Program, the supportive attitude of George L. Smith, George Busbee, and most other House leaders proved of inestimable value in gaining legislative approval of the reorganization bill. Other than Carter, himself, perhaps no one contributed more significantly to the adoption of the reorganization plan than House Speaker Smith. In a letter to the Speaker following the adjournment of the General Assembly session, Carter acknowledged his debt to the veteran legislator not only in securing approval of the reorganization bill but in the passage of numerous other administration measures.[1] House Majority Leader Busbee similarly contributed to the Governor's success during the legislative session.

The House leadership's cooperative relationship with Carter and the effective, businesslike manner with which it managed the reorganization bill contrasted markedly with the Senate's handling of the measure. Naturally, Carter repeatedly compared the manner in which the two houses conducted their business, much to the detriment of the upper chamber.[2]

Moreover, the House leadership's prompt disposition of the various reorganization bills constantly compelled Senate leaders to act. Thus, public attention focused on the upper chamber, and the resulting exposure proved disastrous to that less-than-august body of the legislature. Indeed, the Senate's reputation sank to such low esteem that before the session ended the Senate leadership hired a public relations expert to improve its image. Shortly after the General Assembly convened, Culver Kidd recommended to the members of the Senate Democratic Policy Committee that they employ Joe W. Andrews to coordinate a public relations program for state senators. Andrews, a registered lobbyist for several Georgia business associations, had agreed to perform this service without charge.[3] As the Senate was confronting attacks from all quarters for its perceived close association with special interests, Kidd's suggestion was remarkably ill-timed, and the policy committee promptly rejected it. Six weeks later, however, Majority Leader Holley announced the Senate would in fact hire a public relations expert. Artfully justifying the proposed $20,000 expenditure of public funds, Holley explained:

The public relations program will really be for the benefit of the public. The idea is not to sell the Senate to the public, but to let the public see what the Senate is doing.[4]

That, however, was precisely the problem; the public already had seen too much of how the Senate conducted its business.

The Georgia Senate did not come to its unenviable reputation easily. Even before the General Assembly convened, a private study group, the Citizens' Conference on State Legislatures, had ranked the Georgia General Assembly forty-fifth among the fifty state legislatures in overall effectiveness. Although the study ranked a state's legislature as a whole, the Georgia Senate's poor performance certainly contributed to the entire legislature's poor rating. Five categories were used to evaluate state legislature assemblies: functional, accountable, informed, independent, and representative. The Georgia legislature received its highest ranking (thirty-third) in the "independent" category, and its lowest (forty-ninth) on "accountable."[5] The Senate's performance during the 1972 legislative session did little to challenge the reliability of that assessment.

The widely perceived relationship between legislators and lobbyists also did little to enhance the reputation of the General Assembly. On the eve of the legislative session, *Atlanta Constitution* editor Reg Murphy predicted:

Within two weeks one of the major lobbying groups will have a spectacular cocktail party for the legislators. The reason I can forecast that with no fear of contradiction is that there always is a spectacular cocktail party given by some lobbying groups early in the session.[6]

A vivid example of the Senate leadership's accommodating attitude toward special-interest lobbyists occurred during Senate debates on the controversial plan to abolish the State Board of Health. On the same day the Senate leadership scheduled a vote on the proposal, it chose as its honorary "Doctor of the Day," with full floor privileges, Dr. James Kaufmann, the chief lobbyist for the Medical Association of Georgia.[7] It was an enviable position for a lobbyist but a poor way to conduct the public's business. Such conduct reflected the Senate hierarchy's arrogance and indifference to accepted standards of proper legislative behavior.

Lester Maddox, the presiding officer of the Senate, created a carnival-like atmosphere that further contributed to the Senate's shoddy performance. To emphasize a reactionary philosophy that he confused with conservatism, he rode bicycles backwards around the capitol grounds and sold backward running watches at his Underground Atlanta souvenir shop, where he also peddled T-shirts with a Maddox caricature inscribed with his favorite epithet, "Phooey."[8] Maddox's antics provided an unfortunate reflection of the quality and style of the leadership he exercised in the Georgia Senate. In an editorial entitled, "Maddox's Senate," the editors of the *Atlanta Constitution* characterized the lieutenant governor's performance in highly critical terms.

He has made a shambles of responsible procedures. His political rhetoric is as careless and irresponsible as a drunken driver. His enemies, by definition, are any persons who don't exactly agree with him on something, and he feels free to label them as Communists or traitors or worse. If he doesn't care for a project . . . it becomes in his public pronouncements an evil and sinister Socialist scheme.

Georgia survived four years of Lester Maddox as governor. We will certainly survive three more years of Lester Maddox as lieutenant governor and presiding officer of the State Senate. But there's no use pretending he's doing a good job.[9]

Senator Lamar Plunkett's resignation as chairman of the powerful Senate Appropriations Committee inspired the *Constitution*'s editorial. A competent, mild-mannered lawmaker who had earned the respect and confidence of his fellow senators, Plunkett had been voted "Outstanding Senator of 1971" by the capitol press corps. He resigned after Maddox refused to appoint him to a House-Senate conference committee on the budget. Traditionally, the Appropriations Committee chairman headed the Senate conferees, but Plunkett's support of too many administration measures had offended Senate leaders, and they set out to embarrass him.[10] Carter immediately took advantage of the situation and asked the popular senator to manage the controversial Human Resources Department-State Board of Health bill in the Senate. The martyred Plunkett proceeded to corral enough votes to push the Governor's proposal through the upper chamber, handing the Senate leadership one of its most severe and unexpected defeats.[11]

Carter often managed to turn the tactics of his Senate foes to his own advantage. Through a constant flow of press releases, public statements, and press conferences he kept his antagonists on the defensive, exposing their obstructionism, and, at times, their hypocrisy. Such leading reorganization critics as Stanley Smith, Lester Maddox, and Sam Caldwell, for example, had made a major issue of the constitutionality of HB 1. For months they had reiterated their opposition to the "illegal manner" employed to effect the plan rather than reorganization as such. Carter's decision to resubmit approved sections of the reorganization plan as affirmative legislation, of course, eliminated all such constitutional questions, but it did not lessen the opposition of those who had created the issue. Instead, they attempted to bottle up the affirmative bills in the Senate EREG Committee and prevent a vote on the measures.

Putting aside all arguments concerning the merits or demerits of reorganization and the manner in which it was to be accomplished, Carter confronted the hard-core opposition of some twenty-five lawmakers in the Senate who consistently voted against reorganization. The anti-administration bloc thus needed only four additional votes to place the Governor completely at its mercy on the issue. Given this tenuous position, Carter needed to retain the support of normally pro-administration senators and add enough votes from undecided or uncommitted senators to secure approval of the plan. Through effective floor management, timely compromises, and the exercise of gubernatorial power to reward and punish legislators, the Governor contained the opposition and secured the votes necessary to push the reorganization plan through the upper chamber.

During the legislative session the administration developed detailed procedures for following legislation introduced in either house of the General Assembly. A Legislative Control Team consisting of selected staff members, legislators, and department heads assumed supervisory responsibility in assigned areas. State Budget Officer J. Battle Hall, for example, monitored all budgetary matters, Jody Powell handled press coverage, Frank Sutton supervised legislative liaison, and Hamilton Jordan assumed responsibility for department head activities. In all, the administration identified ten areas of responsibility along with the person or persons assigned supervisory duties in each area.[12]

The staff also maintained a Summary Bill Book containing legislative summary sheets reflecting the status of each bill and resolution introduced in the General Assembly. The summary sheets contained comments by affected department heads, staff members, concerned legislators, and others interested or involved in particular legislation. The sheets included a listing of significant amendments along with the administration's position on the proposed changes. Legislation in the Summary Bill Book was filed by bill number, and to facilitate reference and analysis, several related lists were constructed to provide easy cross referencing. These lists included:

List showing bills assigned to each legislator for monitoring purposes

List showing bills assigned to each department head for monitoring purposes

List showing bills authored by each legislator

List showing bills assigned to each legislative committee

List showing bills to be monitored by the administration. This list will also show the legislator in each house and the department head responsible for monitoring.[13]

Each evening during the session, Carter prepared a brief analysis of his position on bills likely to be considered the following day. Pertinent members of the Legislative Control Team received a copy of the analysis the following morning. The daily schedule included numerous meetings that provided the Governor with an opportunity to discuss his position on matters arising during the day and an opportunity to facilitate communications between administration spokesmen. In a memorandum to the Legislative Control Team, Carter outlined the schedule of daily meetings.

7:15 A.M. *Governor's Staff Meeting*

> This meeting will be held each morning in my office with the 11 people who have been assigned specific areas of responsibility. I will discuss my position on key issues and make task assignments.

8:00 A.M. *Meeting with Department Heads*

> Hamilton Jordan will hold this meeting with department heads each morning in the Conference Room to review task assignments. The legislative leaders, other members of my personal staff and I will attend when it is necessary to provide additional information.

8:30 A.M. *Meeting with Legislators*

> Al Holloway, Hugh Carter, Al Burruss, and Frank Sutton will bring together all legislators who will be involved in the key issues during the day so I can explain my position and let the legislators explain how they plan to approach the problem and what action the other legislators and I need to take.

12:00 Noon *Status Meeting*

> Each day an informal status meeting will be held from 12 noon to 1:00 P.M. in the Information Center. Everyone should stop by for a few minutes to convey any information he thinks might be pertinent during the afternoon.

5:00 P.M. *Progress Meeting*

> In order that I may be aware of all pertinent facts each night when I plan the activities for the next day, we will have a progress meeting each afternoon at 5:00 P.M. The meeting will be attended by the core staff (the 11 persons assigned specific responsibilities) plus any legislator or department head who is specifically involved in one of the issues to be discussed.[14]

These meetings, supplemented by a series of daily reports, were designed "to get the right information to the right persons on a timely basis."[15] On occasion, other procedures were utilized when appropriate. During legislative debates on reorganization, for example, Carter ordered two members of his legal staff to be available at all times to draft amendments accommodating particular lawmakers or the changing votes and attitudes of General Assembly members.[16]

A well-coordinated legislative lobbying effort directed from the Governor's office complemented the daily monitoring and management of administration measures in the General Assembly. Newspapermen gave Carter-appointees Bert Lance, Ellis Mac-Dougall, and Jim Parham especially high marks for lobbying effectiveness. With a trace of awe in his voice, Maddox noted that some department heads and Democratic party officials "just moved in over here and lobbied for bills."[17] The Governor himself, however, by all accounts most effectively lobbied administration measures through the state legislature. Carter's ability to sit down with a reluctant legislator and later emerge with a key vote on a particular measure continually amazed his associates.[18]

After the surprising Senate vote on the human resources proposal, Carter-critic Hugh Gillis concluded that the Governor had effectively used, as he said, "P & P" (Patronage and Punishment) to assure his victory in the Senate.[19] Certainly, Carter did not hesitate to use gubernatorial powers to convince reluctant legislators of the wisdom of supporting administration measures. The threat to veto a pet bill proved an especially effective way of disciplining recalcitrant legislators. Along similar lines, money from the Governor's contingency fund flowed into the districts of congenial legislators in the form of such politically visible improvements as new library buildings, road paving and repairs, or Little League ball parks.[20] Bert Lance's threat to move a Highway Department maintenance shop out of one senator's district changed a critical vote on the Human Resources Department proposal.[21] Rumors of primary opposition in upcoming legislative elections also suddenly began circulating in the districts of key legislators.[22] While it is difficult to measure the effects of these activities on legislative voting behavior, the Governor had more power to give and to take away than any other official in state government, and he did not hesitate to exercise that power. Consequently, many uncommitted senators and representatives and those facing reelection contests found supporting the administration the most prudent course of action.

The final and, in many ways, most important ingredient in Carter's legislative success was his ability to negotiate acceptable compromises at critical junctures during the General Assembly reorganization debate. Compromises assured the continued support of House leaders, undermined the arguments of critics, and facilitated the building of the necessary coalition of support that secured General Assembly approval of the reorganization plan. Furthermore, the compromises did not greatly alter the basic elements of the proposal. If political leadership is practicing the art of the possible, Carter played the game with consummate skill.

To identify more precisely the sources of administration support and opposition and the composition of the crucial swing vote, Senate roll-call voting behavior was analyzed through several quantitative measures. The following analysis is largely confined to the Senate. The key to House voting on reorganization revolved around the Governor's ability to reach agreements with Speaker Smith and other House leaders. Once an agreement was struck— and Carter rarely failed to do so—the proposals received overwhelming House approval. The situation in the Senate was significantly different. Not only was roll-call voting much closer, but the Senate leadership usually opposed the Governor on the issue.

Guttman scalogram analysis of appropriate roll-call votes taken during each legislative session permitted a comparison of Senate voting behavior on roll calls pertaining to the passage of authorization legislation (HB 1) in the 1971 legislative session and votes on the various reorganization bills considered during the 1972 session.[23] The scalograms provide a clear picture of the group of senators who usually either supported or opposed the administration as well as those swinging from one position to the other on particular roll calls. A longitudinal analysis of the positive, swing, and negative positions identified in Figures 7 and 8 confirms Carter's observation that those senators opposing the reorganization plan during the 1972 session were essentially the same ones who had attempted to sabotage HB 1 during the preceding session.[24] Although the Governor never made an issue of it, the reverse also held true; those who had most consistently supported the authorization bill also tended to approve the provisions of the reorganization bill Carter presented to the General Assembly in 1972. The only significant change in voting alignments between the two sessions occurred among the swing voters. Only two of the swing voters of the 1971 session remained in that category a year later.

Five of the 1971 swing voters dropped down to the negative position in 1972, while four moved to the positive category. Significantly, all the senators moving to the negative position were Democrats and all those switching to the positive category were Republicans. This GOP support was of crucial importance to Carter in gaining approval of the reorganization plan in the Senate.

Figure 8 also reveals that the anti-reorganization senators voted much more consistently against reorganization (−415, +21) than pro-reorganization senators voted for it (+336, −76). Divisions between swing voters were, of course, much closer (+99, −129), and swing voters cast many more "error" votes (thirty-eight) than either the pro- or anti-reorganization senators. (Error votes are those failing to conform to otherwise consistent voting patterns. On Figures 7 and 8, such votes are indicated by an asterisk.) Taken as a whole, senators cast many more votes against the administration on scaled reorganization votes than for it (−620, +456). Yet, Carter secured approval of almost all of the reorganization plan, a dramatic reflection of the significance of the reverse veto procedure used in many of these votes, the Governor's ability to win on the most crucial votes, and his success in reversing earlier losses through affirmative legislation or in House-Senate conference committees.

Pro- and anti-reorganization coalitions also can be identified through cluster bloc analysis which provides an effective way of identifying distinct voting blocs in a legislative chamber.[25] Using a .70 level of agreement, that is, the percentage of times two legislators voted identically on a series of roll-call votes, the thirty-one contested votes on various aspects of the reorganization plan recorded in the *Senate Journal* were tested for clusters. The result, illustrated in Figure 9, revealed four distinct voting blocs on reorganization issues. The largest bloc—identified for purposes of analysis as the Maddox bloc—consisted of twenty-two senators who regularly voted against reorganization. Five additional senators on the fringe of the Maddox bloc also generally opposed the administration on reorganization. Thus the Maddox forces needed only two additional votes to exercise a virtual veto over all reorganization proposals.

Figure 7. Reorganization Georgia Senate 1971

```
Senator              123123

Broun                DDD
Brown                DDD
Carter               DDD
Chapman              DDD
Cleland              DDD
Dean                 DDD
Doss                 DDD
Fincher, W.          DDD
Garrard              DDD          ⌐
Hamilton             DDD          (1)
Henderson            DDD        e
Hill                 DDD        v
Holloway             DDD        i
Johnson              DDD        t
McDuffie             DDD        i
Parker               DDD        s
Plunkett             DDD        o
Scott                DDD        P
Smalley              DDD
Stephens             DDD
Walling              DDD
Ward                 DDD
Webb                 DDD
Adams                 DDD
Ballard               DDD
Bateman               RRR
Coverdell             RRR         (2)
Patton                RRR
Tysinger              RRR       g
Rilley                D D *     n
Searcey               D D *     i
Hudgins             *  D D      w
Jackson             *  D D      S
Overby              *  D D
Coggin                DDD
Cox                   DDD
Eldridge              DDD
Fincher, J.           DDD
Gillis                DDD
Herndon               DDD
Higginbotham          RRR         (3)
Kennedy               DDD       e
Kidd                  DDD       v
Lester                DDD       i
London                DDD       t
McGill                DDD       a
Reynolds              DDD       g
Rowan                 DDD       e
Smith, W.             RRR       N
Starr                 DDD
Young                 DDD
Zipperer              DDD
Holley                 DDD
Smith, S.              DDD
```

Not Listed:
    Summers (absences)
    Sutton (absences)

Coefficient of Reproducibility = .97

Marginal Frequencies	*Classes*	
1 = .50	Positive	= 23
2 = .53	Swing	= 11
3 = .96	Negative	= 20

Figure 8. Reorganization Georgia Senate 1972

```
                    111111111122          111111111122
Senator      1234567890123456789011234567890123456789011234567890
Cleland      DDDDDDDDDDDDDDDDDDDDDD
Walling      DDDDDDDDDDDDDDDDDDDDDD
Carter       DDDDDDDDDDDDDDDDDDDDDD
Smalley      DDDDDDDDDDDDDDDDDDDDDD
Webb         DDDDDDDDDDDDDDDDDDDDDD
Plunkett     DDDDDDDDDDDDDAADDDDAAA
Parker       DD DDDDDDDDDDDDDDDDDD     *
Dean         DDDDDDDDDD  DDDDDDDDDD              **
Stephens     DDDDDDD DAA   DDDDADDD          *    **        ─┐
Ward         DDDDDDDDDDDDDDDDDDDDDDD                          │
Garrard      DDDDDDD DDDDDDDDDDDDDD          *                │
Patton       RRRRRRRRR  RRRRR RRRR               **     *     │
Hamilton     DDDDDDDDDDDDDDDDDDDDDD                           │ Positive (1)
Holloway     DDDDDDDDDDDDDDDDDDDDDD                           │
Doss         DDDDDDD  DDDDDDDDDDDD                **          │
Tysinger     RRRRRRRR  RRRRRRRRRRR              **            │
Scott        DDDDDDDDDDDDDDDDDDDDDD                           │
Coverdell    RRRRRRRRRRRRRRRRRRRRRR                           │
Bateman      RRRRRRR RRR RRRRRRRRR         *    *           ─┘
Chapman      ** DD  D DDDDDDDD DDD  D    ** *           *
Herndon        DDDDDDDDDDDDDDDDDDDDDD                         ─┐
Broun          D D D DDDDDDDDDDDDDDD * * *                     │
Fincher, W.    DADADAAA AA AADDDDADD              *   *        │
Adams          DDDDDD   ADADDDAADA               ****         │
Reynolds     *  DDD DAA  DDDADDDDD DD      *   **             │ Swing (2)
Eldridge       *   DADDDDAD DDADDDD DDDD               *       │
Henderson    *  *  D DDDADDDDDDDD DA DDD *                     │
Hill            D DDDD  DDDADDDDDDDD *     **                  │
Ballard         DDDD AADDDDDDDDDDADDA    *                     │
Smith, W.      *   * RRRR  RRRRRRRRR RRR R      **             │
Young             DD  D  DDDDDDDDDDDDDD     ** **              │
Johnson      **      *   DDDDD DDDAD  DDDDD DD     *           │
Rowan        * *       *    * DD DDD D DDDAD DDDD D *        ─┘
Searcey              DDDDDDDDDDDDDDDDDDDDD                    ─┐
Summers              D DDDDDDDDDDDDDDDDDDDD *                  │
Jackson      *       *    **  DDDDDDDDD DDD DDD  DD            │
Sutton               DDDDDDDDDDDDDDDDDDDDD                     │
Rilley               DDDDDDDDDDDDDDDDDDDDD                     │
Zipperer             ADDDDDDDDDDDDDDDDDDAADD                   │
Cox          **       *     DDDDDDDD  DDD DDDDDDD             │
Lester              *    **  ADDDDDDDDDDD DDD  DDDD           │
Brown                  *    DDADDDDDDDDDDDDD DDDD             │ Negative (3)
Hudgins              DDDDDDDDDDDDDDDDDDDDDADD                  │
McDuffie             ADDDDDDDDDDDDDDDDDDDDD                    │
McGill               *   DDDDDDDDDDDDDDDD DDDD                 │
Fincher, J.        *    DDDDDDDDDDDDD DDDDDDD                 │
Coggin               DDDDDDDDDDDDDDDDDDDDD                     │
Gillis               DDDDDDDDDDDDDDDDDDDDD                     │
Higginbotham         RRRRRRRRRRRRRRRRRRRRRR                   │
Kennedy              DDDDDDDDDDDDDDDDDDDDD                     │
Overby               DDDDDDDDDDDDDDDDDDDDD                     │
Holley               ADDDDDDDDDDDDDDDDDDDD                     │
London               ADDDDDDDDDDDDDDDDDDDDD                    │
Smith, S.            ADDDDDDDDDDDDDDDDDDDD                     │
Kidd                 DDDDDDDDDDDDDDDDDDDDDD                   ─┘
```

Not Listed:
Starr (absences)

Coefficient of Reproducibility = .96

Marginal Frequencies

			Classes	
1 = .02	8 = .45	15 = .50	Positive	= 20
2 = .03	9 = .45	16 = .52	Swing	= 13
3 = .19	10 = .46	17 = .54	Negative	= 22
4 = .25	11 = .46	18 = .54		
5 = .31	12 = .47	19 = .56		
6 = .41	13 = .48	20 = .59		
7 = .45	14 = .48	21 = .98		

Figure 9. Cluster Blocs—Reorganization Georgia Senate 1972

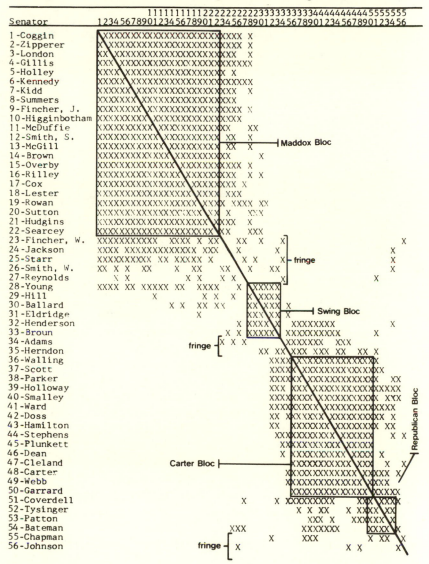

The Carter bloc, consisting of fourteen senators, comprised the second largest bloc in the upper house. A small satellite cluster of five Republicans and four fringe senators bolstered the administration's consistent support to a total of twenty-three votes, six votes short of a majority. The final cluster, a swing bloc of six senators, did not vote consistently with either the Maddox or Carter blocs, although three leaned toward the anti-reorganization position and the other three toward the administration. These six senators acted as the pivotal force and, in effect, determined the fate of reorganization.

The cluster blocs dramatically affirm the vital role Republican senators played in Carter's reorganization success. When the Republicans defected, the relatively small Carter bloc, consisting of only fourteen of the fifty-six senators, usually lost. Moreover, Maddox bloc senators were more fervently committed than administration supporters, a conclusion attested to by the extraordinarily high agreement scores among opposition senators. Consequently, compromises, patronage, promises of rewards, and threats of punishment—all played vitally important roles in firming up the support of fringe senators, obtaining Republican allegiance, and winning the votes of swing bloc senators.

Not surprisingly the members of the swing bloc usually found themselves on the winning side of roll-call votes on reorganization issues. Collective success scores computed for each of the four Senate blocs reveal that the swing bloc had a collective score of .79, followed in order by the Maddox bloc (.69), the Republican bloc (.60), and the Carter bloc (.53). Senator Paul Broun, a swing bloc member, had the highest success score (.86) and was closely followed by another swing bloc senator, Jack Henderson, who registered an .84. Max Cleland, the only senator to support reorganization on all scaled reorganization votes, had a success score of .38, the lowest score registered by any of the fifty-six senators. Lamar Plunkett, another faithful Carter ally, followed Cleland in this dubious distinction with a .41. Meanwhile, the eleven senators who voted negatively on all scaled reorganization votes had a collective success score of .68. The success score is calculated by dividing the number of times a particular legislator voted with the majority on a roll call by the total number of times he voted (see Table 3).[26]

Table 3. Success Scores—Reorganization Georgia Senate 1972

MADDOX BLOC		CARTER BLOC		SWING BLOC		REPUBLICAN BLOC	
Brown	.80	Johnson*	.80	Broun	.86	Bateman	.62
Summers	.78	Chapman*	.71	Henderson	.84	Tysinger	.57
McDuffie	.76	Scott	.62	Ballard	.82	Coverdell	.57
Rowan	.76	Doss	.62	Hill	.80	Garrard	.57
Searcey	.76	Holloway	.62	Eldridge	.72	Patton	.48
Jackson*	.76	Parker	.57	Young	.71		
Sutton	.72	Ward	.57				
Overby	.71	Hamilton	.57				
Smith, W.*	.71	Herndon*	.57				
Hudgins	.71	Smalley	.52				
Lester	.71	Carter	.52				
McGill	.70	Dean	.52				
Rilley	.67	Stephens	.48				
Zipperer	.67	Walling	.48				
Coggin	.67	Webb	.48				
Fincher, J.	.67	Adams*	.47				
Fincher, W.*	.67	Plunkett	.41				
Gillis	.67	Cleland	.38				
Higginbotham	.67						
Kennedy	.67						
Kidd	.67						
London	.67						
Smith, S.*	.62						
Holley	.62						
Reynolds*	.57						
Starr*	.57						
Cox	.57						

*Fringe members.

In order to compare voting behavior on reorganization roll calls to that on other issues considered during the legislative session, the 115 contested Senate votes recorded during the 1971 General Assembly session were subjected to cluster bloc analysis.[27] Although the general voting alignments that appeared on reorganization votes generally held on other issues, significant changes in the configuration of voting blocs did occur (see Figure 10). The cohesive swing bloc disappeared, but the number of uncommitted senators grew. An interlocking bloc of pro-administration and urban senators increased the Governor's consistent support to nineteen, while the Maddox bloc shrunk by one to twenty-two. A comparison of success scores on reorganization to overall voting reveals that Carter bloc senators' success scores rose substantially and would have gone even higher if the reorganization votes had been eliminated from the calculation. In other words, supporters had greater success on issues other than reorganization (see Table 4).

Table 4. *Comparative Success Scores Georgia Senate 1972*

BLOCS	ALL ISSUES	REORGANIZATION
Swing	.710	.792
Maddox	.683	.693
Carter	.667	.526
Republican	.645	.603
Urban	.650	—

Discriminate analysis provides a method of identifying more precisely the sources of support and opposition that existed on reorganization roll calls.[28] Six biographical and four district variables were identified for each senator. (The biographical variables were: party affiliation, occupation, length of service, years in public service, education, and age. District variables were: geographical area, district wealth, Atlanta *v.* out-state, and urban-rural district character.) The preceding analysis also permitted the construction of two derivative variables: a measure of factional affiliation developed from the cluster bloc analysis of Senate voting on all contested issues during the session (Figure 10), and a measure

Figure 10. *Cluster Blocs—All Issues Georgia Senate 1972*

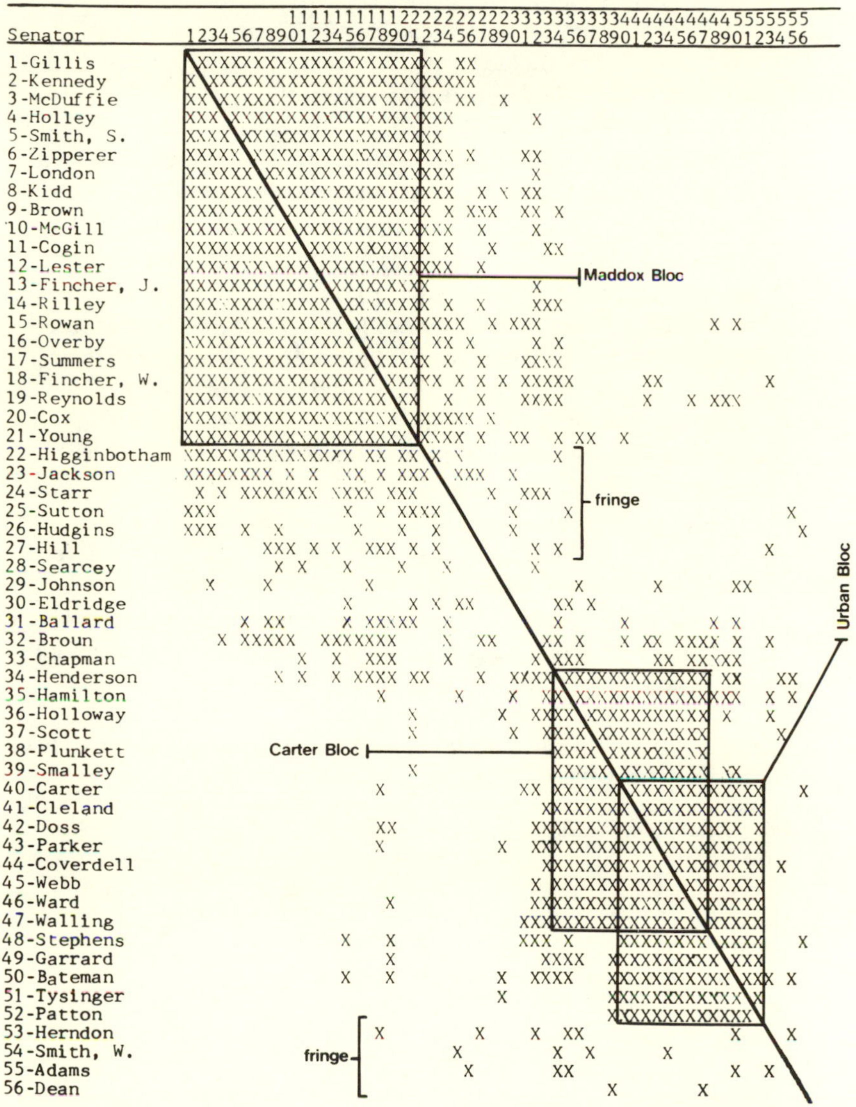

of the relative significance of ideological influences on voting behavior. The latter was derived from a dimensional analysis of twelve issue areas that emerged from the 115 contested Senate votes during the 1972 General Assembly session.[29]

A two-group discriminate analysis comparing those in the positive and negative scale positions on reorganization roll-call votes revealed that of the twelve variables tested, factional affiliation outweighed all others in predicting scale position. Ideological convictions and biographical variables as noted correlated at low but relatively insignificant levels when compared to factional voting (see Table 5). The inclusion of swing voters in the analysis simply emphasized further the seminal importance of factional identification in explaining reorganization voting behavior.

The discriminate analysis indicated that those supporting the administration on reorganization tended to be younger, less entrenched in office, better educated, more urban, and more ideologically liberal than those opposing reorganization. These differences, however, pale in significance when compared to the pervasive influence of factional identification. Clearly, the critical issue in predicting voting behavior on reorganization roll calls revolved around each senator's allegiance in the factional divisions existing within the Georgia Senate.

Table 5. *Two-Group Discriminate Analysis Georgia Senate 1972*

VARIABLE	F-SCORE	CHANGES IN RAO'S V
Factional identification	1677.08	1677.08
Ideology	141.89	141.89
Occupation	3.10	136.28
Education	2.16	105.53
District wealth	1.94	97.18
Atlanta *v.* out-state	1.94	111.00
Length of service	1.89	117.27
Years in public service	———	90.69

In summary, against almost insurmountable odds, Jimmy Carter won his congressional victories in the classic tradition of effective political leadership. He did so by adding enough senators to a relatively small cadre of faithful supporters to win the most vital reorganization votes. To a considerable extent, the issue bifactional-ized the traditional multifactional Georgia Senate. The opposition, which coalesced around Lester Maddox, was effectively stopped just a few votes short of drastically altering or killing the reorga-nization program. Carter's allies on the issue represented an im-probable coalition of Democrats and Republicans, urban and rural senators, liberals and conservatives, and representatives of virtually every other distinguishable biographical or district type. Carter ultimately put together a coalition of senators, some enlisting in the cause by choice and the remainder finding it expedient, for vari-ous reasons, to go along with the administration, albeit with little enthusiasm. It was an impressive performance by the Governor.

CONCLUSION

JIMMY CARTER'S
LEGISLATIVE STYLE

> Jimmy's his own worst enemy as far as getting
> something done is concerned. He feels he's right
> and he's got a lot of integrity, but he just doesn't
> communicate.
>
> *Disgruntled State Legislator*

A study of Jimmy Carter's efforts to reorganize state government
and a perusal of his gubernatorial papers provide valuable insights
into the manner in which the Governor developed his legislative
priorities and the methods used to secure their enactment. Carter's
unorthodox and often confusing style of legislative leadership
derived primarily from the political environment in which he
functioned, his own personality, his political philosophy, and the
unusually comprehensive reform agenda he outlined when taking
office.

Events occurring prior to his election greatly influenced legislative relations during Carter's gubernatorial term. Carter inherited
an executive office much weakened by his predecessor. The Georgia General Assembly had elected Lester Maddox, and it dominated
state government during his governorship. By the end of Maddox's
term, the power and influence of particular legislative leaders had
grown tremendously, and they jealously guarded their new-found
independence. Lester Maddox became a willing ally in this endeavor. After his stunning triumph in the lieutenant governor's
race, most political observers assumed Maddox would recapture
the governorship four years later. Carter, then, confronted in the

lieutenant governor a legislative leader who was not only a popular former chief executive but a likely future governor. Much to the detriment of his own future political career, by siding with those legislators seeking to frustrate the new governor Maddox precipitated an acrimonious four-year conflict with the incumbent and created a political environment more conducive to wild, reckless rhetoric than the sober consideration of the people's business. During Senate debates on Carter's reorganization bill, Maddox exhibited his gift for excessive language while commenting on his own style of legislative relations.

Rather than twisting arms, I held your hands. Thus I am more than grieved when, at this very moment, a brazen, unbelievable and illegal attempt is being made to set up a dictatorship in state government designed to wreck constitutional and representative government.[1]

But if Lester Maddox practiced an unusual style of political leadership, it quickly became apparent that his successor led in an even more unorthodox manner. After observing Carter's executive leadership for a year, the editors of the *Atlanta Constitution* assessed his character and political style.

The new session of the General Assembly will be interesting. It should be a battleground between a new sort of politician, Gov. Jimmy Carter, and more traditional types. . . . Gov. Carter is not one for the smoke filled rooms, the hearty slap on the back and fervent friendships formed instantaneously. A touch of the quarterdeck manner remains from his USN days. . . .

For better or for worse the governor believes the people are on his side. But since when has the General Assembly been notably receptive to the people? And since when have the people really bothered to make themselves felt? Virtue is on the governor's side, certainly, but how many votes has virtue?[2]

Criticism of Carter's style began before his inauguration and continued virtually unabated during the four years of his term. Before taking the oath of office, Carter had warned legislators that he would endeavor not only to reorganize state government but also to initiate programs in such politically volatile areas as welfare reform, tax policy, conservation, education, judicial reform, and consumer protection. Legislators groaned under the anticipated weight of the legislative burden and chided the Governor for subjecting them to an impossible workload. Nevertheless, few critics denied the need for reform. The legislative priorities enumerated by the Governor had been the subject of numerous studies and investigations by private and public agencies, and the overwhelming conclusion of those inquiries supported the argument for reform. Thus while recognizing the need for change, the comprehensiveness of the Carter program and the urgency with which he pressed it upon them dismayed the lawmakers. Substantial reform in any one of the areas would have constituted a significant accomplishment in the notoriously inefficient Georgia legislature, but to take action on the entire reform package seemed inconceivable to most state legislators.

In assessing his governorship near the end of his first year in office, Carter conceded at least one point to his legislative critics. "If I have made one mistake," he declared, "it has been in undertaking too many things simultaneously."[3] This statement, however, appears designed to pacify state legislators more than to reflect accurately upon the Governor's true convictions. Carter's experience in the Georgia General Assembly undoubtedly influenced his legislative strategy. Having sat in the state Senate for four years and observed firsthand the manner in which it conducted its business, he realized state legislators seldom took bold initiatives in the reform areas that concerned him. Consequently the executive branch would have to provide strong leadership to get anything done.[4] He also recognized that enactment of the types of reforms he proposed would only be accomplished after an extended period of debate and discussion inside and outside legislative chambers. Therefore, the proposals had to be made early. Carter had a four year, nonrenewable lease on the governor's mansion. The legislative agenda he outlined during the early days of his governorship constituted a four-year plan, different elements of which he would concentrate upon during each legislative session. Thus Carter's successes and failures could not be measured accurately at the end of a single General Assembly session or by an arbitrary standard such as Franklin Roosevelt's famous "100 days" or John Kennedy's less famous "1,000 days." Rather Carter measured success by assessing the degree to which he accomplished the legislative agenda he had set for himself by the end of his term.

The Governor's leadership style and legislative strategy easily could have dissolved into a war of attrition with legislators. When defeated on a particular proposal, Carter viewed it as a temporary setback that could be reversed later. During the reorganization struggle, he repeatedly stated that if the General Assembly failed to enact the plan in substantially the form presented, it would be resubmitted in subsequent sessions until it became law. In view of the controversial nature of and the potential political liabilities imbedded in many of his proposals, such a threat could not be taken lightly. The Governor also used the veto threat to protect the substance of reforms already enacted and to short-circuit proposals conflicting with reforms he sought to institute. And he exercised the veto often enough to give substance to the threat.[5]

More than anything else, the combination of Jimmy Carter's reform psychology and, closely related, his fundamental abhorrence to the uniquely American practice of legislative logrolling produced his unorthodox legislative style and, in turn, provoked his volatile relationship with the more traditional politicians in the Georgia General Assembly.[6] The planner-engineer mentality Carter brought into government bred an organic view of reform. He envisioned a major reform program as an interrelated, mutually dependent series of proposals. A significant alteration in one area would have repercussions in other areas that could ultimately convert a logically developed reform program into an irrational patchwork of unrelated or even contradictory changes. That is not to say that Carter lacked flexibility or a willingness to compromise but rather that his conception of the nature of reform restricted the areas in which he found it possible to compromise. When a proposed change threatened the logical construct of a program or violated established policy, his resistance to change grew along with his reputation for stubbornness and obstinacy.

Many of the criticisms of Carter's intransigence, emanating from friends and foes alike, derived from his obdurate resistance to the endemic political trade-offs so common (and perhaps necessary) in the American political system. Carter's hostility to this practice sprang from the heart of his philosophy of government. To a considerable extent his commitment to reform resulted from a profound hostility to waste, inefficiency, and disorder. The reforms Carter sponsored during his governorship did not encompass bold, new, innovative programs but rather sought to make existing programs operate more efficiently, economically, and justly. While essentially conservative in character, many of these reforms carried with them the possibilities for far-reaching social change. Many Georgians, for example, viewed zero-based budgeting as a unique opportunity to re-slice the economic pie represented by the state's billion dollar annual budget.[7]

The consequences for Carter's style of legislative relations was also great. Much of the waste and inefficiency Carter sought to eliminate was the by-product of legislative logrolling; he could hardly attack the symptoms of the disease and ignore the causes of the malady. More orthodox in his approach to legislative relations, Hamilton Jordan frequently suggested trades to the Governor hoping to give Carter added leverage in securing General Assembly support for his proposals. Early in his administration, Carter established a policy that the state would not absorb cost overruns on state-financed local projects. When such a cost overrun occurred on the West Georgia Airport Authority near Carrollton, legislators from the area contacted the Governor's office seeking financial assistance. Jordan saw in this situation an opportunity to build legislative support in the upcoming General Assembly session and recommended that the Governor strike a bargain with the legislators. Reminding his young executive secretary that to do so would violate a necessary policy, Carter rejected the suggestion.[8] In another instance Jordan wanted to use an appropriation sought by the Central Savannah River Area Planning and Development Commission to discipline legislators from the area who had opposed administration programs. Deeply committed to the concept of regional planning, however, Carter would have none of it.[9]

The Governor realized his commitments in this respect sometimes worked to the disadvantage of his political friends and supporters. Before vetoing a bill creating an additional judgeship in the district of Senator Jimmy Parker, a loyal administration supporter, Carter wrote to him explaining his action.

One of the more difficult aspects of being Governor is having to make a decision contrary to the wishes of a close and valued friend. Because of a personal belief and often expressed commitment to back the Judicial Council's decision if they disapproved a judgeship, I will veto the Douglas Circuit.

Recognizing that this may cause you some undeserved political problems, I hope that you will let me try to overcome them in other ways.[10]

Obviously, the Carter legislative style worked a great hardship on those staff members responsible for legislative liaison, particularly Hamilton Jordan and Frank Moore. At times, Jordan actively lobbied with the Governor on behalf of a loyal legislative supporter seeking a special favor. On other occasions, he counseled legislators on how best to approach Carter with a particular proposition.[11] Nevertheless, criticism abounded of Carter's "young and inexperienced staff" which "didn't react quickly enough when a legislator wanted something." Shortly before the convening of the 1972 General Assembly session, Carter relieved Jordan of the executive secretary's traditional legislative liaison responsibilities. Bill Shipp of the *Atlanta Constitution* correctly assessed the situation "Hamilton Jordan has been made a goat of the administration's shortcomings in dealing with the General Assembly," the columnist wrote. "If he did not react quickly enough to the wants of individual legislators it was usually because his boss wouldn't let him." Shipp than gave his readers an example of the problems Jordan encountered in this respect.

Carter badly needed votes in the Senate on a recent issue. One senator said he would vote with the governor if Jordan would make one phone call assuring the senator's father (a state employee) of a slight promotion to an existing vacancy. The senator appeared at the time to hold the deciding vote. Jordan wanted to make the call. Carter said no. And the governor lost.[12]

The Governor's obstinacy in this regard constantly irritated and frustrated state legislators who considered him out-of-touch with political reality and, more particularly, insensitive to their immediate constituency interests. "Jimmy's his own worst enemy as far as getting something done is concerned," reported one garrulous House leader. "He feels he's right and he's got a lot of integrity, but he just doesn't communicate."[13]

Nevertheless, complaints about breakdowns in communication and criticism of the Governor's youthful staff often were little more than the creations of unhappy legislators to vent their frustration with the Governor for his unwillingness to participate in traditional logrolling activities. These critics could hardly condemn Carter for refusing to wheel and deal in traditional political fashion, so they contrived other complaints to give voice to their dissatisfaction. All this contributed to Carter's unenviable standing among Georgia lawmakers as one of the least popular governors in the state's recent history. When asked by a newspaper reporter to identify the Governor's faithful House supporters, Al Burrus, a Carter House floor manager, quipped, "It's not going to be a long article is it?"[14] Another veteran legislator concurred, "Your [sic] not gonna find too many in the House you could classify as his friends. Even Lester [Maddox] could boast more friends."[15]

The nature of the reforms Carter advocated increased his unpopularity not only among legislators but among government bureaucrats as well. Constructive managerial reforms contribute significantly to the collective well-being, but they provide few if any immediate and tangible benefits to specific individuals or groups of individuals. Thus while most people approve such reforms in principle, they seldom rank high on anyone's list of priorities; consequently there is little or no natural constituency that will mobilize automatically to support these reforms. Conversely, such reforms encounter numerous points of resistance. Well-established programs and procedures inevitably create among particular legislators, bureaucrats, and private interest groups a perceived vested interest in maintaining the status quo, and they fiercely resist any change that appears to threaten that interest.

Carter's effort to reorganize the Georgia state government provided numerous illustrations of this resistance to reform. Constitutional officers hotly resented changes in their departments that did not add to the power and prestige of their offices. Doctors fought to maintain the Board of Health they controlled, teachers resisted changes in the education department, farmers angrily denounced proposals to consolidate agricultural agencies, veterans organized to preserve the Department of Veterans Service, and so it went.

For legislators, then, managerial reforms contained potential political liabilities but little promise of political reward. Lawmakers could not realistically anticipate any great outpouring of public gratitude because they supported such reforms, and they even might arouse the hostility of a powerful political broker or the antagonism of an influential interest group. State legislators were unlikely to bestow their love and affection upon a governor who continually placed them on the threshold of such a potentially hazardous political quagmire.

In the absence of party responsibility or regularity, proponents of management reforms must of necessity build coalitions of support behind their programs. This requirement confronted Carter with one of the more perplexing dilemmas of his governorship. The type of political trade-offs associated with legislative logrolling constitutes the most common and generally effective method of creating such coalitions on specific issues. With this tactic foreclosed to him, Carter had to build enough public support behind his programs to pressure legislators into supporting reform measures they might otherwise oppose or, more likely, let die for want of attention. Building public support behind rather abstract, intangible governmental reforms, however, was no easy task. It required a massive educational and public relations campaign. Carter initiated these efforts very early. He used his gubernatorial campaign to draw public attention to the reforms he planned to introduce after assuming office. During the 1970 campaign he advocated almost all the major reforms with which he later confronted the General Assembly. Another vital part of Carter's effort to build public support for his program involved a plan to promote active citizen involvement and participation in public affairs. Taking advantage of an existing state planning program,

Carter launched the Goals for Georgia program shortly after assuming office. Through this program, he sought to involve Georgia citizens in the construction of a priority list for programmatic and procedural changes beneficial to the entire state. The Governor correctly assumed that the results of this citizen survey would correspond closely to his own list of reform priorities. He hoped those activist and concerned citizens who participated in establishing the Goals for Georgia would develop an interest in the results of the program and express that concern to legislators in their areas.[16] Similarly, Carter used the "taking the government to the people" program discussed earlier to build support for his reforms and to create at least the appearance of citizen input in governmental decision making.

The Public Awareness Program designed to sell government reorganization to the people of Georgia provides the clearest illustration of how Carter attempted to build public support for major reform initiatives. The program included a variety of tactics for getting the reform message to the public and for building citizen support. The administration utilized endorsements from popular public and private figures as well as Republican leaders, employed the broadcast and print media extensively, dispatched administration personnel to plug the proposal in every conceivable forum, and endeavored to mobilize private interest groups and public service organizations in support of reorganization.

The Public Awareness Program worked effectively to generate public support for the reorganization effort, but the strategy had obvious limitations and potential hazards. The effort was too expensive and time-consuming to be used with any regularity. Moreover, overuse of the tactic would erode its effectiveness. The success of the program could be seriously compromised at any point. An uncooperative or hostile press easily could confuse the issues and counteract the educational propaganda disseminated by the administration. Similarly, the administration needed bipartisan support to avoid the stigma of "politics as usual" and to isolate and dramatize the obstructive character of the opposition. Finally, the success of the program required active citizen involvement at all levels. When these conditions existed, public support could be mobilized and pressures placed on legislators.

In his search for legislative support, the Governor actively cultivated Republicans in the General Assembly. Even though the
Georgia Republican party was weak and its legislative delegation
relatively small, Carter vitally needed GOP support not only for
creating the aura of consensus approval of his major programs but
also because the Republicans often held the balance of power in
the factionalized General Assembly. Although vigorously partisan
in national politics, Carter appeared almost oblivious to party differences on the local and state level, especially between elections.
He apparently viewed the Republican legislative delegation as
simply another cohesive faction in the General Assembly that
might support his policies if properly approached and courted.
The Governor's harsh criticism of Richard Nixon and the Water-
gate affair sometimes strained his relationship with state Republican leaders, but nevertheless he managed to maintain a close, even
cordial, relationship with the minority leadership in both houses
of the legislature. For the important legislative successes during his
governorship, Carter owed much to these Georgia Republicans.[17]

As in his ability to win bipartisan support, Carter's effectiveness
in creating workable compromises contributed significantly to his
success in gaining legislative approval of his major programs. If,
as Theodore Roosevelt suggested, politics is the art of the possible,
Carter diligently sought to extend the possible to the maximum.
Throughout his governorship, state legislators, government officials, and, indeed, the general public perceived Carter as an in-
ordinately stubborn and unbending chief executive. Yet time after
time on specific measures, press reports emphasized the timely
compromises that had insured a gubernatorial victory. To some
extent, Carter appears to have fostered this paradoxical view of his
executive leadership; certainly it served his political purposes.
Enough a political realist to recognize that compromises would
be necessary to get major programs through the General Assembly,
he nevertheless tried to limit and to some extent control the nature
of the compromises. In discussing their endeavors with members
of the study teams that wrote the reorganization plan, Carter told
them to draft the most perfect plan possible without regard to
politics. He said he would make the necessary compromises to
get the bill through.[18]

While recognizing that changes would have to be made, the Governor inevitably exhibited a hardline attitude when introducing a measure, arguing that the legislation should be adopted without change. Thereafter, he essentially maintained that posture even while "reluctantly" accepting changes, some of which he quietly had proposed and urged legislators to support. Because he rarely admitted publicly the wisdom or necessity for any changes in proposed reforms, those he accepted, or at times instigated, usually served a specific political purpose—pacifying a powerful legislative leader whose support he needed, undermining the opposition of a particularly influential interest group, eliminating an unfavorable public perception, or securing key votes on particular measures.

Carter made numerous such compromises during the reorganization struggle. Many of the changes in the original plan permitted the Governor to secure and maintain the critically important support of Speaker George L. Smith and other House leaders. The decision to exempt University System computers from the consolidation of data processing services pacified Paul Broun, a key swing bloc senator whose district encompassed the University of Georgia. Another compromise placated religious fundamentalists who fought to retain the inactive and ineffective Children's Literature Commission, the abolition of which, they contended, would open the floodgates of pornography. For similar reasons, Carter dropped plans to abolish the independent Department of Veterans Services. Other changes served to counter two of the most vigorously discussed issues in the reorganization debate: the argument that HB 1 contained an unconstitutional delegation of legislative power to the executive branch; and that, if implemented as proposed, the plan would substantially increase gubernatorial power.

On proposed changes affecting the vital substance of reforms, Carter deserved his reputation for intransigence. Despite considerable pressure and at some risk to the entire reorganization proposal, he did not waiver in his determination to abolish the State Board of Health although he was willing to compromise on the composition of the governing board of the Department of Human Resources. He frankly accepted as a major defeat the Senate's refusal to incorporate the Forestry Department in the new Department of Natural Resources, and until the final hours of the legislative session, he fought against the exclusion of the Labor Department's data processing equipment from the consolidation of computer services.

Compromise, then, was an integral part of Carter's legislative style. While using compromises effectively, however, the manner in which he made concessions distorted their significance. Carter inevitably characterized a reform proposal as a comprehensive package, implicitly denying any interest in incremental reform. Yet over and over again he ultimately accepted less than the whole loaf while at the same time, attempting to add as many slices to the traditional half-a-loaf as possible. By adopting a resolute, uncompromising posture even in areas in which he was quite willing to accept changes, he gained a degree of leverage and control over the types of changes made. As a result, he could better protect the vital elements of a program while conceding a number of sometimes substantive but at other times largely Pyrrhic victories in areas that did not threaten the essentials of his proposals. The strategy did push government reorganization through the legislature with relatively few substantive changes, but the tactic did little for Carter's public image. When after vigorously resisting change, the Governor supinely compromised, commenting that the change did not seriously alter the substance of his proposal, he created the public impression of a confused, indecisive executive afflicted with more than a touch of sophistry.

Although obviously preferring compromise and conciliation to confrontation, when given little choice as he was with the Senate leadership during the reorganization struggle Carter could turn hostile and aggressive. His four-year feud with Lester Maddox attracted the most attention, but the Governor had an equally volatile if less publicized relationship with a number of other legislative leaders and government officials. As the state's chief executive officer, Carter had an access to the press, which he diligently used to berate his antagonists. Invariably, he associated their opposition with pressure group politics, and the charges contained enough truth to create considerable discomfiture for the targets of his rhetorical barbs. Moreover, the administration carefully analyzed the voting record of at least one hostile senator in an effort to document charges of consistent support of particular interest groups.[19] At times the Governor could be absolutely ruthless. More than one Georgia legislator primly escorted influential constituents into the Governor's office only to be bitterly chastized for opposing administration measures in their presence.[20] In similar fashion, Carter used his veto power to emphasize his unhappiness with particular legislators. Rather than routinely signing the many local bills passed during a legislative session, the Governor scrutinized each one carefully and vetoed a number of them. Such vetoes could be very painful for legislators attempting to build local political capital. In one case, Carter pointedly raised "constitutional questions" when vetoing the local bill of a state legislator who had continually questioned the constitutionality of the reorganization proposal.[21] The "pet bills" of such antagonists as Maylon London, Culver Kidd, and Sam Caldwell received similar treatment.[22] Carter also used his gubernatorial appointment power to punish adversaries. His refusal to reappoint Jim Gillis, Jr., the brother of Senate President Pro Tem Hugh Gillis, to the Soil and Water Conservation Committee provides a vivid illustration. Gillis had served on the committee for twenty years.[23]

These examples to the contrary, Carter was neither an unusually petty person nor one likely to carry and act upon a long-term grudge. More often than not, he initiated efforts to reconcile differences and consciously strived to avoid pettiness.[24] When he felt he had been betrayed or deceived, however, he often reacted spontaneously, denouncing the offender in unqualified terms. The unscheduled news conference during which the Governor publicly ripped opponents became rather commonplace during Carter's governorship. In many ways, Carter tended to take the obligations and responsibilities of public office much more seriously than many of the lawmakers for whom politics represented a somewhat ritualistic game in which the antagonists quickly forgot the bitter denunciations expressed on the chamber floor once the bell sounded ending the day's proceedings. The Governor believed that public officials had a moral obligation to act in the public interest, and he had little more than contempt for those obstructionist or demagogic lawmakers who, he felt, repeatedly sacrificed the common good for personal aggrandizement or to satisfy the demands of special interests.

In these cases, Carter's hostility went well beyond verbal denunciation. Within the realm of political practicality, he used all the leverage he possessed as the state's chief executive officer to undermine and discredit such legislators. He funneled gubernatorial patronage to opposing factions in their districts and quietly encouraged candidates to enter primary races against them. The Carter 1970 campaign organization, which had been revived during the reorganization struggle, came to life once again during the 1972 elections. Ed Barker, a middle-Georgia campaign manager during Carter's two gubernatorial campaigns, successfully retired the Governor's archenemy, Stanley Smith, to his Perry, Georgia business interests. Beverly Langford, father-in-law of Carter's son, Jack, successfully challenged Jack Fincher, a reorganization opponent who had helped to organize opposition to the Human Resources Department proposal. Another former Carter county campaign manager, Cecil Passmore, entered the primary race against Hugh Gillis, who had not faced primary opposition in the previous ten years. Although Gillis survived the challenge, Passmore pushed him into a runoff and made a close race of it.[25]

Carter publicly denied any involvement in these efforts to defeat hostile legislators, but four of his most persistent Senate foes found their service in the General Assembly terminated. Meanwhile, most of the Governor's loyal supporters survived the election relatively unscathed even though many of their districts had been disadvantageously altered by the Smith-Kidd forces during the 1971 redistricting. Led by Culver Kidd, Carter's antagonists developed their own "kill list" and organized a "Political Action Committee" to solicit funds facilitating challenges to lawmakers loyal to the administration.[26] Of the ten senators on Kidd's list, however, all easily won reelection, and only one, in an especially mutilated district, was forced into a runoff.[27] The results of the 1972 legislative elections clearly suggested that opposition to the Governor's programs could be dangerous to one's political career, while support had its own rewards.[28]

To some extent, Carter's basic personality resulted in a style of legislative relations that created problems. He often neglected such traditional political courtesies as consulting with legislators about appointments in their districts or permitting them to make the public announcement of the allocation of state or federal funds to their district, the initiation of a state project in the area, or the appointment of a local figure to state office. Too often, legislators learned about such matters from newspaper reporters. Since friendly as well as antagonistic senators complained about these violations of political etiquette, Carter's conduct appears to have been primarily the product of unthinking neglect.[29]

personality profile:
HUGH ALTON CARTER, SR.

Born in Plains, Georgia, on August 13, 1920, Hugh Carter graduated from Plains High School in 1937. Thereafter, he matriculated at Georgia Southwestern College in nearby Americus before enrolling at the University of Georgia, where he received a BS in commerce in 1941. He served in the United States Army during World War II, eventually becoming an infantry platoon leader. After the war he remained in the active reserve, rising to the rank of lieutenant colonel before retiring in 1964.

While working in his father's general merchandise store, which he eventually converted into an antique shop, the future Georgia senator began a small fish bait business. He started by selling crickets and eventually expanded into red worms. He later wrote several books on how to raise crickets and worms and began to sell breeder stock to other prospective worm farmers. The business grew spectacularly and Hugh Carter eventually proclaimed himself the "Worm King of America."

After Jimmy Carter decided to run for governor in 1966, Hugh announced his candidacy for his cousin's state Senate seat. He won the nomination and election as well as the chairmanship of the Senate Education Committee. Hugh and Hamilton Jordan managed Jimmy Carter's 1970 gubernatorial campaign. After the election, he became the Governor's assistant floor leader in the Senate.[30]

Carter's inability to participate in the customary glad-handing camaraderie with legislators that could have defused opposition and generated support also marked his legislative style. He also failed, consistently or effusively enough, to express his gratitude to loyal legislators who had supported administration measures, often at some political risk. Hugh Carter, who served as the Governor's assistant Senate floor leader, believed that in this area he had made an especially important contribution to the administration's successful legislative record. More gregarious than his cousin, Senator Carter had many friends in the legislature and even managed to maintain a good rapport with Lieutenant Governor Maddox. After a Senate vote on an administration measure, Hugh made the rounds of his colleagues, thanking those who had supported the administration and, in hopes of developing support for some future roll call, soothing those in opposition. Senator Carter concluded that his ability to sit down and quietly reason with wavering senators had been largely responsible for many of his cousin's legislative victories. Although recognizing the important role Hugh Carter played, other administration leaders concluded that friendly persuasion was ultimately less important in the administration's legislative victories than the Governor's adroit use of political patronage.[31]

Of the patronage weapons at his disposal, Carter most effectively used his $2 million emergency (or contingency) fund and his control over state highway building projects. Although grants from the emergency fund were seldom large, they did provide recipient legislators with timely appropriations to renovate athletic facilities, improve a small town's water supply or sewage disposal system, send a local high school band to the Rose Bowl Parade, or for a variety of other purposes. Similarly, sympathetic legislators usually found Transportation Commissioner Bert Lance receptive to their requests for local highway improvements and other services offered by the Department of Transportation.[32]

Indeed, good things seemed to happen to those who had supported the Governor. Four of the small corps of Carter's consistent Senate supporters received judicial appointments before he left office, including Horace Ward, the first Georgian of African descent to sit on the state bench since Reconstruction. Other loyal legislators received appointments to state office or later the federal bureaucracy.[33] Unfortunately for Carter, such rewards came after the fact and probably, if anything, had a negative impact on his legislative program as faithful administration supporters left the General Assembly to assume other offices.

Carter also freely dispensed gubernatorial honors and recognition. Rather than the usual colonels, Carter appointed honorary admirals in the Georgia navy. LeRoy Johnson, a black Atlanta senator whose support Carter desperately needed, received one such appointment. Surprised and a bit bemused, Johnson thanked the Governor for the recognition.

Being too young to serve our country in World War II and being a pre-Korean War father, thus being robbed of the opportunity to serve in defense of our country in the Korean conflict; and being too old to be drafted in defense of democracy in Viet Nam, I naturally assumed that I would never be accorded a title of honor relative to the forces that make up the military defense of our country.

You have accorded me a great honor by bestowing upon me the title of Admiral of the Georgia Navy. Governor, "You are the Greatest."[34]

Other prerogatives of his office also helped the Governor. He often dispensed his complimentary tickets to athletic events, especially University of Georgia and Georgia Tech football games, with a political purpose in mind. Similarly, Carter's recognition of the state's physical attractions pleased environmentalists and outdoor enthusiasts. Whether canoeing on the state's rivers, fishing on the sea islands, or making gubernatorial appearances at symphony concerts and other cultural events, he attracted the favorable attention of an influential segment of the Georgia population.

Perhaps more than any other accouterment of office, Carter used the stately Georgia governor's mansion to the best possible political advantage. Lawmakers, government officials, media personnel, and a great variety of citizen activists dined at the mansion or spent a quiet evening with the Governor and his family. The recognition and ego satisfaction derived from an invitation to the governor's mansion undoubtedly left the recipients more receptive to their host's views. The Carter family, especially Rosalynn, Hugh,

Lillian, and, in her own way, Amy, contributed in important ways to the Governor's efforts to build support for his policies.

Just as he used the governor's mansion, Carter skillfully used the symbols and heritage of his office. Georgians had traditionally held their governors in high esteem, and Carter actively, if selectively, sought to identify with the gubernatorial tradition. He repeatedly associated his administration with that of Richard B. Russell, one of the state's most popular and respected public figures. Given the status of the office, Carter's handwritten notes on office stationery assumed even greater significance. His gubernatorial papers contain numerous notes thanking constituents for their suggestions or support, congratulating others for their accomplishments, or simply continuing an exchange of essentially nonpolitical views on a great variety of subjects.

Although less tangible than his use of the prerogatives of the gubernatorial office, Carter's continual emphasis on the positive aspects of the state's historical heritage helped him. A decade of fierce resistance to civil rights demands and the national scorn it inspired had severely wounded the morale, pride, and self-image of many Georgians, especially white Georgians. Carter refused to repudiate the past but at the same time emphasized the necessity of adjustment and change, thus making the adjustment less painful and humiliating. In many ways the Governor came to symbolize Georgia's accommodation with twentieth-century realities. As a consequence, while never a particularly popular governor, Carter became for many Georgians a very necessary one.[35]

EPILOGUE

On December 12, 1974, shortly before leaving the governor's office, Jimmy Carter formally announced his candidacy for the office of president of the United States. During the subsequent two-year campaign, Carter's record as Governor of Georgia became an important issue. He used it in establishing his qualifications to hold the presidential office. In attempting to document his credentials, the candidate pointed especially to his reorganization of state government in Georgia and promised, if elected, to initiate a similar reorganization of the federal bureaucracy. As could be expected, Carter's opponents attempted to minimize his accomplishments in office and especially attacked reorganization, identifying real or imagined shortcomings.

While the ultimate success of reorganization is an important question, there has been no effort in this monograph to assess its effectiveness. At this time, such an assessment would still be premature. Nevertheless, a few general observations can be made. T. McNeil Simpson, a University of Tennessee political scientist who analyzed the reorganization plan from the perspective of structural reform and management improvements, gave it a generally favorable assessment. He concluded that while the degree of change brought about through reorganization had been exaggerated by both proponents and opponents, it was nevertheless a significant reorganization of state government. He concluded:

Modification of governmental structure is an important if often unattended, phase of public administration, and it is to Governor Carter's credit that he did not take the structure he acquired as already perfect to its tasks.[1]

The establishment of the huge Department of Human Resources was and remains the most controversial feature of the reorganization plan. The effort to consolidate the 21,000 state employees involved in the administration of health, welfare, and related services into a single agency created severe administrative problems. One critic suggested that "trying to get a hold of DHR was like wrestling a hippopotamus in a swimming pool of glue."[2] In 1975 the General Assembly gave Governor George Busbee blanket authority to make changes in the department. Busbee's subsequent changes, however, were relatively modest. The most significant change involved the removal of the corruption-riddled Medicaid program from the department's supervision.

Not unexpectedly, those involved in the formulation of the reorganization plan remain very positive about the product of their labors. State employees are somewhat less enthusiastic. Almost everyone, it seems, has a specific complaint about some feature of reorganization such as centralized purchasing or the consolidation of computer and printing services. Conversely, few are critical of the plan as a whole, and after six years of experience with it, there are no obvious movements on the horizon to make major structural or management changes in the program. The fact that so little of it has been altered in subsequent years is perhaps ultimately the best measure of the overall effectiveness of the reorganization effort. Meanwhile, of course, state officials and their employees are slowly developing a vested interest in the current state of the bureaucracy that eventually will make it as resistant to change as the governmental structure it replaced.

In the years since the reorganization plan was developed and approved by the Georgia General Assembly, the lives and careers of many of those involved in the reorganization struggle have undergone significant change. An update follows.

Banks, Peter. After practicing law in Barnseville, Banks ran unsuccessfully for the Democratic nomination for Congress from Georgia's Sixth Congressional District.

Burson, William H. Burson, adopting the tactic that Lawton

Childs had successfully parlayed into a Democratic senatorial nomination in Florida, vowed to walk through Georgia in quest of the United States senatorial nomination. When he lost the Democratic primary, Burson wryly concluded that he had walked when he should have been running. He then attempted to retain the state treasurer's office which had been abolished through reorganization. He later accepted a position as administrative aide to Lieutenant Governor Zell Miller.

Busbee, George D. Busbee succeeded Jimmy Carter in the governorship and, after a constitutional amendment passed in 1972, easily won renomination and reelection for a second four-year term in 1978.

Caldwell, Johnnie L. Caldwell successfully won renomination and reelection as comptroller general in the general elections of 1974 and 1978.

Caldwell, S. Sam. After surviving a federal investigation of his administration of federal Department of Labor programs in Georgia, Sam Caldwell easily won renomination and reelection as Commissioner of Labor in the general elections of 1974 and 1978.

Carter, Hugh A., Sr. At the same time he was reelected to the Georgia Senate from the fourteenth senatorial district in 1978, Hugh Carter published an autobiographical account of his association with Jimmy Carter entitled *Cousin Beedie and Cousin Hot.*

Carter, James Earl, Jr. James Earl Carter, Jr. was inaugurated thirty-eighth president of the United States on January 20, 1977.

Cleland, Joseph Maxwell. Although Cleland ran unsuccessfully for the Democratic nomination for lieutenant governor in 1974, he was appointed administrator of Veterans Affairs after Carter's election.

Davis, Ernest B. Davis was reappointed state auditor in 1975 by Governor Busbee, but he resigned the position in 1976 to take the position of director of the World Congress Center in Atlanta.

Egan, Michael J. Egan remained minority leader in the Georgia House of Representatives until Carter's election. Shortly thereafter, he accepted appointment as associate attorney general of the United States.

Eizenstat, Stuart E. Eizenstat served as issues and policy director in Carter's 1976 presidential campaign organization. After the election, he became assistant to the president for Democratic Affairs and Policy.

Fortson, Benjamin Wynn, Jr. Fortson successfully won renomination and reelection as secretary of state in the general elections of 1974 and 1978. Fortson died on May 19, 1979.

Gambrell, David H. After losing the Democratic nomination for the United States Senate seat to which he had been appointed, Gambrell returned to the private practice of law.

Gillis, Hugh M., Sr. Although consistently winning reelection to the Georgia Senate, Hugh M. Gillis lost the position of president pro tem of the Senate to Senator A. W. Holloway prior to the 1975 session of the General Assembly.

Hall, Cloyd K. At the conclusion of Carter's gubernatorial term, Hall accepted appointment as vice president for Medical School Development, Mercer University School of Medicine.

Hall, J. Battle. Hall became temporary commissioner of the Department of Human Resources in 1972 and, after a permanent commissioner was named, accepted appointment as assistant commissioner. He retired in 1973 after his position was abolished.

Harden, Richard. Harden served as commissioner of the Department of Administrative Services between April and September 1972. Thereafter, he served as commissioner of the Department of Human Resources through the remainder of Carter's term in office. He then worked in the Carter campaign organization, and after Carter's election to the presidency, became special assistant to the president for Information Management and director of the Office of Administration.

Holley, Rudolph Eugene. Beset by numerous financial problems, Holley did not seek reelection in 1976. As a result of the Arab oil embargo of 1973, a series of fortuitous Texas oil investments returned unexpectedly high profits which Holley parlayed into a worldwide financial empire. Unfortunately, much of it was financed on credit through largely unsecured loans from Georgia banks. The recession of the mid-1970s along with speculative real estate and Persian Gulf oil investments that did not return anticipated profits placed great strains on Holley's financial resources and confronted him with potential losses in excess of $100 million.

As a result of a religious conversion experience during the 1975 Christmas season, the former Georgia senator had a thirty-seven-foot illuminated cross mounted on the roof of the ultra-modern glass penthouse he had constructed atop the Southern Finance Building in downtown Augusta. In the 1976 presidential campaign, he supported his erstwhile foe, Jimmy Carter.

Holloway, Albert Weston. With the election of his friend, George Busbee, to the governorship in 1974, Holloway successfully challenged Hugh Gillis for election to the position of president pro tem of the Georgia Senate and continues to serve in that position after easily withstanding a challenge from Senator Beverly Langford prior to the 1979 session of the General Assembly.

Irvin, Thomas I. Irvin successfully won renomination and reelection to the post of commissioner of agriculture in the elections of 1974 and 1978.

Jordan, William Hamilton McWhorter. Jordan successfully managed Jimmy Carter's 1976 presidential campaign. After the election, he was appointed assistant to the president.

Kidd, Edwards Culver, Jr. Kidd survived two separate federal indictments charging him with accepting a bribe, conspiring to obstruct the enforcement of state gambling laws, and lying to a grand jury. Despite his legal difficulties, he has easily won renomination and reelection from his senatorial district every two years and remains one of the most powerful and influential legislators in the Georgia General Assembly.

Lance, Thomas Bertram. Lance ran unsuccessfully for the Democratic nomination for governor of Georgia in 1974. Thereafter, he returned to his private banking career before joining Carter's presidential campaign organization. After the election, he was appointed director of the Office of Management and Budget. The exposure of a series of irregular banking practices in Georgia forced his resignation in September 1977.

Levitas, Elliott H. Levitas won the Democratic nomination and was elected to Congress from Georgia's Fourth Congressional District in 1974. He won renomination and reelection in 1976 and 1978.

Linder, Tom M., Jr. After completion of the reorganization of state government, Linder became director of the Office of Planning and Budget. As a result of a minor controversy that arose when it was discovered that during the reorganization struggle Linder's secretary had for a short time driven his five-year-old son to school, Linder submitted his resignation on October 2, 1972. Governor Carter, describing it as a "small and insignificant problem," believed Linder had overreacted but Linder refused to withdraw his resignation. After leaving office, Linder accepted the position of vice president of the International City Corporation, a newly formed organization directing its efforts at urban redevelopment projects. In 1975 Linder started his own food brokerage firm, Linder International and Associates, which arranges food produce sales overseas, especially the exportation of southern agricultural products.

Lipshutz, Robert J. After serving as chief fund raiser and national treasurer of Carter's 1976 presidential campaign, Lipshutz was appointed counsel to the president. He resigned that position in August 1979 to work in Carter's reelection campaign.

MacDougall, Ellis. MacDougall left the Carter administration in 1973 to accept a position on the faculty of the University of South Carolina as a professor of criminal justice.

McIntyre, James T., Jr. After Carter's election, McIntyre was appointed assistant director of the Office of Management and Budget and was elevated to the directorship after Bert Lance's resignation in September 1977.

Maddox, Lester Garfield. Maddox ran unsuccessfully for the Democratic gubernatorial nomination in 1974, running far behind George Busbee in the primary runoff election. The campaign left him heavily in debt. Attempting to regain financial solvency, he opened two new Pickrick restaurants both of which eventually failed. In 1976 he won the presidential nomination of an independent conservative party which only served to increase his money woes. With Bobby Lee Fears, a former employee of one of his eating establishments, he formed a night club act entitled, "The Governor and the Dishwasher." Like most of his other ventures after 1974, the act failed and ultimately cost Maddox money. A severe heart attack in the fall of 1977 further complicated his personal financial difficulties. Thereafter, he opened a real estate office which did very little business. In 1978 a group of Democratic politicians and Atlanta businessmen formed a "Get Well Lester Maddox Committee" to solicit funds to pay the former governor's campaign debts.

Moore, Frank B. Moore became executive secretary to the Governor in late 1973 and later joined the Carter presidential campaign organization. After the election, he was appointed assistant to the president for congressional liaison.

Nix, Jack P. Nix successfully won renomination and reelection as state superintendent of schools in 1974 and 1978.

Nunn, Samuel. Nunn won the Democratic nomination for the United States Senate seat to which Carter had appointed David Gambrell. Nunn easily won reelection in 1978.

Plunkett, Lamar R. Although voted "Outstanding Senator of

1971" by the capitol press corps, Plunkett did not seek reelection to the Senate after the expiration of his term in 1973. On February 16, 1974, Carter appointed him to the State Board of Regents.

Powell, Joseph L., Jr. Powell served as news director for Jimmy Carter's 1976 presidential campaign. After the election he was appointed press secretary to the president.

Rafshoon, Gerald M. Having served as media consultant during Carter's presidential campaign Rafshoon accepted appointment to the White House staff as assistant to the president for communications in 1978.

Rainwater, Peggy E. Rainwater worked in Carter's 1976 presidential campaign and after the election was appointed associate director of the Presidential Personnel Office.

Sanders, Carl. Although retaining an interest in political affairs, Sanders became a partner in a large Atlanta law firm after losing the 1970 gubernatorial nomination. He has exhibited no interest in again becoming involved in electoral politics.

Smith, George Leon, II. George Leon Smith II died on December 9, 1973.

Smith, Stanley Eugene, Jr. Stanley Eugene Smith, Jr. returned to his Perry business enterprises after losing his bid for reelection in the 1972 Democratic primary elections. On August 9, 1973, the former legislator died from a heart attack at the age of fifty-three.

Tanner, Joseph D. Tanner was reappointed commissioner of the Department of Natural Resources by Governor George Busbee in 1975.

NOTES

PREFACE

1. Edwin Bridges and D'Arcy Jones, archivists at the Georgia Department of Archives and History related this information to the author during several conversations. Before the collection was opened, two files—a legislative review file and a judicial appointments file—were closed by order of the Georgia attorney general. According to the terms agreed to by the Archives and the Governor, the attorney general would review files containing sensitive personal information and rule on whether or not they would be closed. Other than this, there is no evidence that the collection has been edited or screened in any way. In an unpublished paper read at the Fifth Annual Meeting of the Georgia Association of Historians, April 22, 1978, the author discussed the Carter gubernatorial papers at greater length.

2. For a discussion of the more useful books in this literature, see the Bibliographical Essay.

3. Carter provides an account of these early years in his autobiography, *Why Not the Best?* (Nashville: Boardman Press, 1975). The best secondary source is Leslie Wheeler, *Jimmy Who? An Examination of Presidential Candidate Jimmy Carter: The Man, His Career, His Stands on the Issues* (New York: Barron's, 1976). Hugh Carter, *Cousin Beedie and Cousin Hot: My Life with the Carter Family of Plains, Georgia* (Englewood Cliffs, N.J.: Prentice Hall, 1978) adds interesting details to Jimmy Carter's account of those years.

4. *The Atlanta Journal*, September 13, 1966.

5. In describing his relationship with Callaway, Carter regrets the pettiness on his part. *Why Not the Best?*, pp. 130, 131.

INTRODUCTION: THE TEMPERAMENTAL PRAGMATISM OF JIMMY CARTER

1. *The Atlanta Constitution*, June 14, 1966. Newspaper reporters and political writers covering the 1976 presidential campaign who

sought to classify Carter into traditional ideological categories found the candidate's ambiguity especially perplexing. Carter, however, saw some merit in his ideological flexibility. "Why should a candidate be liberal or conservative down the line, he argued, when most of the American people are not?" Jules Witcover, *Marathon: The Pursuit of the Presidency, 1972-1976* (New York: Viking, 1977), p. 207.

2. On the first page of his autobiography, Carter inserted quotes from Neibuhr, Dylan, and Dylan Thomas. On the second page, he evidences his admiration of Admiral Rickover. *Why Not the Best?* (Nashville: Boardman Press, 1975), pp. 9, 10.

3. Ibid., pp. 11, 12.

4. See Jimmy Carter, *A Government as Good as Its People* (New York: Simon & Schuster, 1977); Frank Daniel, comp., *Addresses of Jimmy Carter: Governor of Georgia, 1971-1975* (Atlanta: Georgia Department of Archives and History, 1975); Bill Adler, *The Wit and Wisdom of Jimmy Carter* (New York: Citadel Press, 1977); Robert W. Turner, ed., *"I'll Never Lie to You": Jimmy Carter in His Own Words* (New York: Ballatine, 1976). See also Record Group 1, Subgroup 1, Series 5, of the Jimmy Carter Gubernatorial Papers (hereafter cited as the Carter Papers) located in the Georgia Department of Archives and History, Atlanta.

5. Paul Conkin has caustically criticized the careless use of such terms as "liberal," "conservative," and "pragmatic." See, for example, Conkin's *The New Deal* (New York: Crowell, 1965). Conkin, however, defines these words in such puristic philosophical terms that they have little relationship to the manner in which either political historians or politicians traditionally have used them. In his study of American conservatism, Clinton Rossiter developed several classifications of conservatism. This provides a much more useful and ultimately more sensible solution to the problem than the word "genocide" proposed by Conkin. Clinton Rossiter, *Conservatism in America: The Thankless Persuasion*. 2d ed. (New York: Knopf, 1962), pp. 5-15.

6. Rossiter, *Conservatism*, pp. 65, 66.

7. David Kucharsky, *The Man from Plains: The Mind and Spirit of Jimmy Carter* (New York: Harper & Row, 1976), p. 19.

8. Several writers have discussed Neibuhr's influence on Carter. See, for example, William L. Miller, *Yankee from Georgia: The Emergence of Jimmy Carter* (New York: Harper & Row, 1978), chap. 12 passim; Kucharsky, *Man from Plains*, pp. 16-22; Leslie Wheeler, *Jimmy Who? An Examination of Presidential Candidate Jimmy Carter: The Man, His Career, His Stands on the Issues* (New York: Barron's, 1976),

pp. 27, 28, 48, 147, 152; and Niels Nielsen, Jr., *The Religion of Jimmy Carter* (Nashville: T. Nelson, 1977).

9. Carter, for example, used this quote on the frontispiece of his autobiography. The Carter Papers contain numerous letters reflecting the social dimension of the Governor's religious attitudes. See Record Group 1, Subgroup 1, Series 5. *Why Not the Best?* and Carter's notorious *Playboy Magazine* interview with Robert Scheer (November 1976) also provide evidence of his religious convictions.

10. At a news conference, Carter was asked whether he literally believed everything in the Bible to be true. Although the question was patently hostile and reflected an ignorance of the evangelical view of the Bible, Carter patiently explained, "I don't believe everything in the Bible to be literally true. I don't think the earth was created in seven days as we know days now and I reserve the right to make my own interpretation." Kucharsky, *Man from Plains*, p. 23.

11. Carter's religious convictions have attracted considerable attention. In addition to scattered comment in previously cited works, see especially Nielsen, *Religion of President Carter*; James Hefley and Marti Hefley, *The Church that Produced a President: The Remarkable Spiritual Roots of Jimmy Carter* (New York: Wyden Books, 1977); Jessyca Gaver, The Faith of Jimmy Carter (New York: Manor Books, 1977); M. B. Abram, "Governor Carter's Religion," *Nation* 223 (1976); E. Brooks Holifield, "The Three Strands of Jimmy Carter's Religion," *New Republic*, June 5, 1976.

12. Carter to Pierre Howard, September 7, 1973, Record Group 1, Subgroup 1, Series 5, Carter Papers.

13. Carter to F. N. Boney, June 18, 1974, ibid.

14. See, for example, Tom Linder's memorandum to Carter, December 10, 1971, Record Group 1, Subgroup 15, Series 64, ibid.; *The Atlanta Journal and Constitution*, September 3, 1978.

15. Carter, *Why Not the Best?*, pp. 118, 119; *The Atlanta Constitution*, January 21, 1966.

16. *The Atlanta Constitution*, March 16, 1966.

17. Carter, *Why Not the Best?*, pp. 118, 119; Carter to George Smith, February 1, 1972, Record Group 1, Subgroup 1, Series 5, Carter Papers.

18. Wheeler, *Jimmy Who?*, p. 55; *The Atlanta Constitution*, January 16, 1974.

19. Carter, *Why Not the Best?*, chap. 12.

20. Carter to Senator Scott Hudgens, March 13, 1973, Record Group 1, Subgroup 1, Series 5, Carter Papers.

21. Carter, *Why Not the Best?*, pp. 131, 132; *The Atlanta Journal*,

October 30, 1963; *The Atlanta Constitution*, August 10, 1964, December 30, 1965, May 28, 1968.

22. Mattie S. Anderson, "Governor Jimmy Carter's Goals for Georgia: A Study of Carter's Commitment to Planning and Citizen Participation," seminar paper, Georgia State University, 1978. See also Carter, *Why Not the Best*, p. 149.

23. The DeKalb County boxes in Record Group 1, Subgroup 1, Series 5, Carter Papers, contain a great deal of correspondence on this subject. See, for example, Bert Lance to T. Foley Treadway, January 18, 1973.

24. Carter, *Why Not the Best?*, pp. 155, 156. Extensive correspondence on this issue is located in Record Group 1, Subgroup 1, Series 5, Carter Papers.

25. Carter, *Why Not the Best?*, chap. 6; Wheeler, *Jimmy Who?*, chap. 3; Miller, *Yankee from Georgia*, chap. 3.

26. Carter to Maynard Jackson, March 12, 1974. Record Group 1, Subgroup 1, Series 5, Carter Papers.

27. Carter, *A Government as Good as Its People*, p. 23.

28. Carter to George L. Smith, February 27, 1973, Record Group 1, Subgroup 1, Series 5, Carter Papers.

29. Carter to Pat Chapman, August 5, 1974, ibid.

30. Carter to Rev. J. E. Lowery et al., February 20, 1973, ibid. During his term in office, Carter increased the number of blacks serving on major state boards and agencies from three to fifty-three. He also increased the number of black state employees from 4,850 to 6,684. He appointed the first black to the state bench and the State Board of Regents since Reconstruction. Wheeler, *Jimmy Who?*. p. 80.

31. Carter, *Why Not the Best?*, pp. 123, 124.

32. During the 1970 gubernatorial campaign, Carter effectively associated his Democratic opponent, Carl Sanders, with Georgia Power, Fuqua Industries, and the "Atlanta establishment." Thereafter, Carter's advisors sought to avoid any such identification on the part of their man. Stuart E. Eizenstat to Carter, July 15, 1971, Record Group 1, Subgroup 1, Series 5, Carter Papers. See also *The Atlanta Constitution*, July 10 and August 27, 1970; Robert Shogan, *Promises to Keep: Carter's First 100 Days* (New York: Crowell, 1977), p. 30; Wheeler, *Jimmy Who?*, chap. 4; and Reg Murphy and Hal Guillver, *The Southern Strategy* (New York: Charles Scribner's Sons, 1971), chap. 8.

33. Kucharsky, *Man from Plains*, p. 19.

34. Carter to Harold McKenzie, August 26, 1973, Record Group 1, Subgroup 1, Series 5, Carter Papers.

35. Carter, *Why Not the Best?*, p. 123. During his governorship,

Carter successfully pushed a state sunshine bill through the Georgia General Assembly.

36. Stuart Eizenstat to Carter, July 19, 1971; Jody Powell to Eizenstat, July 19, 1971, Record Group 1, Subgroup 1, Series 5, Carter Papers.

37. Carter to Rafshoon, August 30, 1973, ibid.

38. Carter to Mr. and Mrs. Dobbins, December 14, 1972, ibid. Numerous other examples can be found in the Carter Papers.

39. Carter to John Woolfolk, May 16, 1971, ibid.

40. Carter to Carl Mahoney, February 23, 1973 (emphasis added), ibid.

41. Rossiter, *Conservatism*, p. 13.

42. Harold Lasswell, *Politics: Who Gets What, When, How* (New York: Knopf, 1936).

CHAPTER 1: HOUSE BILL No. 1: THE BEGINNINGS OF THE CARTER-MADDOX FEUD

1. *The Atlanta Journal and Constitution*, November 1, 1970.

2. *The Atlanta Journal*, November 16, 1970; *The Atlanta Constitution*, November 18, 1970.

3. Carl Sanders had been the latest to express an interest in executive reorganization. During his administration, he appointed a commission for efficiency and improvement which made several recommendations for administrative reform but nothing came of the suggestions.

4. *The Atlanta Constitution*, December 18, 1970; Leslie Wheeler, *Jimmy Who? An Examination of Presidential Candidate Jimmy Carter: The Man, His Career, His Stands on the Issues* (New York: Barron's, 1976), p. 69; Bruce Galphin, *The Riddle of Lester Maddox* (Atlanta: Camelot, 1968), chap. 12.

5. Galphin, *Lester Maddox*, pp. 11, 139, 176; Lester G. Maddox, *Speaking Out: The Autobiography of Lester Garfield Maddox* (New York: Doubleday, 1975), pp. 29, 73, 138, 139.

6. Maddox, *Speaking Out*, 138, 139.

7. *The Atlanta Constitution*, January 19, 1971.

8. Ibid., November 5, 1966; *The Atlanta Journal*, October 4, 1966.

9. Jimmy Carter, *Why Not the Best?* (Nashville: Boardman Press, 1975), pp. 77-81; Wheeler, *Jimmy Who?*, pp. 30-34; William L. Miller, *Yankee from Georgia: The Emergence of Jimmy Carter* (New York: Harper & Row, 1978), chap. 3.

10. Miller, *Yankee from Georgia*, pp. 105, 106; Carter, *Why Not Best?*, pp. 127-130; *The Atlanta Constitution*, September 2, 1966.

11. Galphin, *Lester Maddox*; Maddox, *Speaking Out*; *The Atlanta Journal and Constitution*, May 7, 1978.

12. *The Atlanta Constitution*, September 15, 1970.

13. Ibid., September 24, 1970. Twice a month during his governorship, Maddox threw open the door of the governor's office to permit "little people" to personally advise the governor of their problems. Galphin, *Lester Maddox*, pp. 178, 179.

14. *The Atlanta Journal*, October 21, 1970; *The Atlanta Journal and Constitution*, February 7, 1971.

15. *The Atlanta Constitution*, October 8, 1970.

16. *The Atlanta Journal*, October 7, 1970.

17. Ibid., October 21, 1970.

18. Maddox, *Speaking Out*, pp. 136-138.

19. Ibid., chap. 11.

20. Ibid., pp. 135, 136.

21. Ibid., p. 138.

22. Ibid., pp. 136, 137.

23. *The Atlanta Constitution*, December 15, 1970.

24. Ibid., September 26, 1970.

25. Ibid., November 6, 1970.

26. *The Atlanta Journal and Constitution*, November 8, 1970.

27. *The Atlanta Constitution*, November 18, 1970.

28. *The Atlanta Journal*, February 8, 1971.

29. Maddox, *Speaking Out*, pp. 142, 143.

30. *The Atlanta Constitution*, January 9, 1972; Galphin, *Lester Maddox*; Maddox, *Speaking Out*. Maddox apparently told his executive secretary, Zell Miller, a different version of his meeting with Carter. Dan Carter related the Miller version during a session on "Carter in the Classroom," at the Georgia Studies Symposium, Atlanta, February 4, 1978.

31. *The Atlanta Constitution*, August 25, 1971; *Macon News*, November 23, 1971 .

32. *Macon News*, November 23, 1971.

33. Carter to Dilworth, March 1, 1972, Record Group 1, Subgroup 1, Series 5, Carter Papers.

34. *The Atlanta Constitution*, February 26, 1971.

35. Carter to Thomas, June 6, 1972, Record Group 1, Subgroup 1, Series 5, Carter Papers.

36. *The Atlanta Constitution*, November 18, 1970.

37. Ibid., January 15, 1971; author's interview with Senator A. W. Holloway, November 1, 1978 (referred to hereafter as the Holloway Interview).

38. State of Georgia, *Georgia Official and Statistical Register, 1971-1972* (Atlanta: Georgia Department of Archives and History, n.d.) p. 408 (referred to hereafter as the *Georgia Statistical Register*); *The Atlanta Journal and Constitution*, April 15, 1977 .

39. *The Atlanta Constitution*, November 18 and December 30, 1970; *The Atlanta Journal*, January 15, 1971.

40. *The Atlanta Constitution*, January 7, 1971.

41. Ibid., January 8, 1971.

42. Ibid., January 11, 14, 1971; *The Atlanta Journal and Constitution*, February 7, 1971.

43. *The Atlanta Constitution*, January 13, 20, 1971.

44. Ibid., January 14, 15, 1971.

45. *The Atlanta Journal*, January 14, 1971.

46. *Georgia Statistical Register, 1971-1972*, p. 448; *The Atlanta Constitution*, December 10, 1973; *The Atlanta Journal*, December 10, 1973; Holloway Interview.

47. *The Atlanta Constitution*, February 6, 1972.

48. Ibid., January 21, 1971.

49. *The Atlanta Constitution*, January 21, 28, 1971.

50. Ibid., February 7, 8, 9, 1971.

51. Ibid., January 27, 1972.

52. Ibid., February 7, 1971.

53. Ibid., February 10, 11, 1971.

54. See the analysis of legislative voting behavior in chap. 7.

55. *The Atlanta Constitution*, February 8, 1971; *The Atlanta Journal*, February 8, 1971; Maddox, *Speaking Out*, pp. 143-146.

56. *The Atlanta Constitution*, February 10, 1971.

57. Ibid., February 8, 1971.

58. Ibid., February 9, 1971.

59. Ibid., February 10, 1971.

60. Ibid., February 11, 1971.

61. Ibid.

62. *The Atlanta Journal*, February 11, 1971.

63. Ibid.

64. *The Atlanta Constitution*, February 11, 1971.

65. Ibid.

66. Ibid., February 16, 1971.

67. Ibid.

68. Ibid., February 12, 1971.

CHAPTER 2. THE REORGANIZATION AND MANAGEMENT IMPROVEMENT STUDY

1. Minutes, Executive Committee, Reorganization and Management Improvement Study (n.d.), Record Group 1, Subgroup 15, Series 67, Carter Papers; "Progress Report," September 30, 1971, Record Group 1, Subgroup 15, Series 65, ibid.

2. Author's interview with Tom M. Linder, Jr., November 8, 1978 (referred to hereafter as Linder Interview); "Revised Biographical Sketch—Tom M. Linder, Jr.," Record Group 1, Subgroup 15, Series 65, Carter Papers.

3. State of Georgia, *Reorganization and Management Improvement Study*, November 1971 (referred to hereafter as RAMIS), p. 4; *The Atlanta Journal and Constitution*, December 26, 1971.

4. Carter to Patrick J. Lucey, July 23, 1971, Record Group 1, Subgroup 15, Series 66, Carter Papers.

5. Carter to Christopher Bond, Governor of Missouri, September 25, 1973, Record Group 93, Subgroup 8, Series 15, ibid; Carter to C. E. Walker, December 23, 1971, Record Group 1, Subgroup 15, Series 66, ibid. In these two long, substantive letters, Carter discusses the reorganization effort in considerable detail. Numerous other letters contained the same general themes. See also, RAMIS, pp. 5, 6.

6. "Evaluation of Consultant Proposals and Qualifications," Record Group 1, Subgroup 15, Series 64, Carter Papers. This eight-page document provides an insight to the administration's priorities and predispositions in the reorganization effort.

7. Ibid.

8. Ibid. Ultimately, the administration was very pleased with its selection and especially with George Kaiser whose experience in state government reorganization was invaluable. Linder Interview.

9. *The Atlanta Journal*, June 4, 1971.

10. Carter to Moore, Record Group 1, Subgroup 1, Series 5, Carter Papers.

11. *The Atlanta Journal*, April 2, 1971.

12. Carter to Linder, August 23, 1971, Record Group 1, Subgroup 15, Series 65, Carter Papers.

13. Carter to Walker, December 23, 1971; "Reorganization: A Program to Save Georgia's Taxpayers Millions of Dollars and Improve Services" (Pamphlet produced by the Public Awareness Program, RAMIS); *The Atlanta Journal and Constitution*, December 26, 1971. The measure of thirty-four man-years was based on a 40-hour week and a 240 work-day year. Thus 1,920 man-hours equals 1 man-year.

14. "Reorganization, Summary of Reported Hours by Project Personnel through August, 1971," Record Group 1, Subgroup 15, Series 65, Carter Papers.

15. Carter to Governor Bond, September 25, 1973, ibid.

16. RAMIS, p. 8.

17. *The Atlanta Journal*, May 4, 1971; Linder to A. W. Holloway, July 13, 1971, Record Group 1, Subgroup 15, Series 15, Carter Papers; Tom M. Linder, Jr., "Reorganization" (a memorandum describing the reorganization effort), Record Group 93, Subgroup 8, Series 14, ibid.

18. Linder, "Reorganization," Record Group 93, Subgroup 8, Series 14, ibid.; Linder Interview; author's interview with James L. Maddex, Jr., December 7, 1978 (referred to hereafter as the Maddex Interview); Carter to Governor Bond, September 25, 1973, Record Group 93, Subgroup 8, Series 15, Carter Papers; Leslie Wheeler, *Jimmy Who? An Examination of Presidential Candidate Jimmy Carter: The Man, His Career, His Stands on the Issues* (New York: Barron's, 1976), p. 83.

19. *Gainesville Daily Times*, October 27, 1971; *The Atlanta Constitution*, July 1, 15, 1971; Minutes, Executive Committee, Reorganization and Management Improvement Study, June 30, 1971, Record Group 1, Subgroup 15, Series 67, Carter Papers.

20. Linder, "Reorganization;" Linder Interview; Maddex Interview; *The Atlanta Journal*, September 23, 1971.

21. *The Atlanta Journal*, September 23, 1971.

22. Ibid.; Carter to Governor Bond, September 25, 1971; RAMIS, pp. 5-7; "Reorganization: A Program to Save Georgia's Taxpayers Millions of Dollars and Improve Services," Record Group 1, Subgroup 15, Series 77, Carter Papers.

23. RAMIS, p. 97.

24. Ibid., p. 51.

25. Linder Interview.

26. RAMIS, pp. 201-203.

27. Linder Interview; Maddex Interview; Holloway Interview. Those involved in the reorganization study were greatly impressed with Kaiser. His experience and expertise proved invaluable to the success of the reorganization effort.

CHAPTER 3. SELLING REORGANIZATION TO THE PEOPLE

1. "Public Awareness Program," Reorganization and Management Improvement Study, Record Group 1, Subgroup 15, Series 75, Carter Papers.

2. Minutes, Advisory Committee of the Public Awareness Program, May 27, 1971, ibid.

3. "Progress Report," Reorganization and Management Improvement Study, April 30, 1971, Record Group 1, Subgroup 15, Series 68, ibid.; "Work Program," Public Awareness Program, Record Group 1, Subgroup 15, Series 77, ibid.

4. Rafshoon to Public Awareness Advisory Committee on State Reorganization, May 13, 1971, Record Group 1, Subgroup 15, Series 75, ibid.

5. Ibid.

6. Minutes, Advisory Committee of the Public Awareness Program, May 27, 1971, ibid.

7. "Public Awareness Program," ibid.

8. Linder to Carter, May 24, 1971 and June 14, 1971; "Progress Report," Reorganization and Management Improvement Study, June 30, 1971, Record Group 1, Subgroup 15, Series 68, ibid.

9. Kandy Stroud, *How Jimmy Won: The Victory Campaign from Plains to the White House* (New York: Morrow, 1977), pp. 206-208; *The Atlanta Journal and Constitution*, October 16, 1977; *The Atlanta Constitution*, November 8, 1977.

10. *The Atlanta Constitution*, May 29, 1971; Rafshoon to Public Awareness Advisory Committee on State Reorganization, May 13, 1971, Record Group 1, Subgroup 15, Series 75, Carter Papers.

11. Rafshoon to Public Awareness Advisory Committee on State Reorganization, May 13, 1971.

12. Minutes, Advisory Committee on the Public Awareness Program, May 27, 1971, ibid.

13. See Record Group 1, Subgroup 15, Series 75, ibid.

14. "Status Summary," Public Awareness Program, August 1971, Record Group 1, Subgroup 15, Series 77, ibid. Evidence of this activity is scattered throughout Record Group 1, Subgroup 15, Series 75-80, ibid.

15. See, for example, Peter Banks to Linder, July 8, 1971, Record Group 1, Subgroup 15, Series 75, ibid., and "Public Awareness Schedule," Reorganization and Management Improvement Study, Record Group 1, Subgroup 15, Series 80, ibid.

16. Minutes, Advisory Committee of the Public Awareness Program, May 27, 1971, Record Group 1, Subgroup 15, Series 75, ibid.; Larry Levitan to Cloyd Hall, June 9, 1971, ibid.

17. Maddox to Hall, July 2, 1971, ibid.

18. Information on the construction and distribution of the brochures can be found in ibid.

19. *The Atlanta Constitution*, December 28, 1971; *Savannah Morning News*, December 31, 1971.

20. Copies of the newsletter can be found in Record Group 1, Subgroup 7, Series 67, Carter Papers.

21. *The Atlanta Constitution*, December 28, 1971.

22. *Columbus Enquirer*, December 16, 1971.

23. "Memo to the Files," JoAnn DiBella Hawkins, September 1, 1971, Record Group 1, Subgroup 15, Series 77, Carter Papers.

24. *The Atlanta Journal and Constitution*, December 26, 1971.

25. Leah Janus to Carter, July 21, 1971, Record Group 1, Subgroup 1, Series 5, Carter Papers; Hawkins to Linder, October 27, 1971, Record Group 1, Subgroup 15, Series 75, ibid.; Hawkins to Linder, October 4, 1971, Record Group 1, Subgroup 15, Series 77, ibid.

26. Hawkins to Linder, October 14, 1971, Record Group 1, Subgroup 15, Series 77, ibid.

27. Sidney Q. Janus to Linder and Hawkins, December 8, 1971, Record Group 1, Subgroup 15, Series 77, ibid.; William J. Cirone to Linder, January 10, 1972, Record Group 1, Subgroup 15, Series 65, ibid.

28. Janus to Carter, July 21, 1971, Record Group 1, Subgroup 1, Series 5, ibid.

29. Ibid.

30. Carter to Janus, December 6, 1971, ibid.

31. *The Atlanta Journal*, November 11, 1971; Mrs. George Hahn to Linder, November 19, 1971, Record Group 1, Subgroup 15, Series 65, Carter Papers; Mrs. Bob Sideman to Carter, January 13, 1972, Record Group 1, Subgroup 1, Series 5, ibid.

32. See "Status Reports," Public Awareness Program, Record Group 1, Subgroup 15, Series 77, ibid.

33. Linder to Larry Colet, June 15, 1971, and Linder to Sam Roberts, June 15, 1971, Record Group 1, Subgroup 15, Series 65, ibid.

34. Bryant to Linder, September 22, 1971, ibid.

35. Ernie O'Neal to Jaycee Local Presidents, n.d., Record Group 1, Subgroup 15, Series 64, ibid.

36. See Record Group 1, Subgroup 15, Series 77, ibid.

37. Linder to Carter, November 19, 1971, Record Group 1, Subgroup 15, Series 65, ibid.

38. Ibid., November 18, 1971.

39. Linder Interview.

40. "Weekly Progress Report," Public Awareness Program, June 21, 1971, Record Group 1, Subgroup 15, Series 77, Carter Papers.

41. "Status Report," Public Awareness Program, July 12, 1971, ibid.

42. See Record Group 1, Subgroup 15, Series 79, ibid.

43. Linder to Abit Massey, July 1, 1971, Record Group 1, Subgroup 15, Series 65, ibid.; "Weekly Progress Report," Public Awareness Pro-

gram, Record Group 1, Subgroup 15, Series 77, ibid.; Linder to Carter, December 17, 30, 1971, and January 14, 1972, Record Group 1, Subgroup 15, Series 64, ibid.

44. Linder to Carter, December 17, 30, 1971, and January 14, 1972, Record Group 1, Subgroup 15, Series 64, ibid.; *The Atlanta Journal*, October 5, 1971, and December 5, 1971.

45. *The Atlanta Constitution*, June 14, 1971.

46. Shipp covered the legislature and the capitol and conducted periodic interviews with political figures that were published in *The Atlanta Constitution.*

47. Linder to Ray Moore, December 7, 28, 1971, and January 13, 1972, Record Group 1, Subgroup 15, Series 65, Carter Papers.

48. Carter to Elmo Ellis, n.d., Record Group 1, Subgroup 1, Series 5, ibid.

49. *The Atlanta Constitution*, January 6, 1972.

50. See, for example, *Camilla Enterprise*, July 7, 1971.

51. *The Atlanta Constitution*, June 15, 1971.

52. Ibid., October 28, 1971, and November 11-13, 1971; *The Atlanta Journal and Constitution*, November 14, 1971.

53. *Albany Journal*, November 18, 25, 1971.

54. Ibid., November 25, 1971.

55. Ibid.

56. "Status Report," Public Awareness Program, August 9, 1971, Record Group 1, Subgroup 15, Series 77, Carter Papers; *Athens Banner-Herald*, December 19, 1971.

57. *The Atlanta Constitution*, December 31, 1971. The inspiration for regional press conferences and the plan to move the capital temporarily to various cities came from Stuart E. Eizenstat who saw this as a means of building Carter's strength in south Georgia, avoiding the appearance of being a "creature of the Atlanta establishment," and diminishing the influence of the often hostile capitol press corps. Eizenstat to Carter, July 15, 1971, Record Group 1, Subgroup 1, Series 5, Carter Papers.

58. Linder Interview.

59. *The Atlanta Journal and Constitution*, December 19, 1971.

CHAPTER 4. SELLING REORGANIZATION TO THE BUREAUCRACY

1. "Public Awareness Program," Reorganization and Management Improvement Study, Record Group 1, Subgroup 15, Series 75, Carter Papers.

2. *The Atlanta Constitution*, April 2, 1971.

3. Linder to "All Group Leaders," August 23, 1971, Record Group 1, Subgroup 15, Series 65, Carter Papers; Linder Interview.

4. *The Atlanta Journal*, July 28, 29, 1971; *The Atlanta Constitution*, July 29, 1971.

5. *The Atlanta Journal*, July 5, 1971.

6. Ibid., July 29, 1971; *The Atlanta Constitution*, July 29, 1971.

7. *The Atlanta Constitution*, July 29, 1971.

8. Ibid., August 6, 1971.

9. *Georgia Statistical Register, 1971-1972*, p. 52.

10. *The Atlanta Constitution*, August 6, 1971; Linder Interview; Maddex Interview.

11. *The Atlanta Constitution*, August 6, 1971.

12. Ibid.

13. Linder to Carter, September 7, 1971, Record Group 1, Subgroup 15, Series 65, Carter Papers; *South Fulton Recorder*, September 20, 1971.

14. Harden to Carter, October 28, 1971, Record Group 1, Subgroup 1, Series 5, Carter Papers.

15. *The Atlanta Journal*, September 9, 1971; Harden to Carter, October 21, 1971, Record Group 1, Subgroup 1, Series 5, Carter Papers.

16. *The Atlanta Journal*, September 9, 1971.

17. Ibid., July 7, 1971; Irvin to Carter, October 22, 1971, Record Group 1, Subgroup 15, Series 65, Carter Papers.

18. *Columbus Ledger*, December 2, 1971. Nix released the letter to the press at the same time he forwarded it to the Governor, reflecting the political nature of the communication.

19. *Georgia Statistical Register, 1971-1972*, p. 148; *The Atlanta Journal and Constitution*, December 24, 1978; *The Atlanta Constitution*, August 5, 1973.

20. *Camilla Enterprise*, July 7, 1971.

21. *Savannah Morning News*, December 18, 1971; *The Atlanta Journal*, November 20 and December 2, 1971; *Macon Telegraph*, December 5, 20, 1971.

22. *The Atlanta Journal*, December 2, 1971; *The Atlanta Constitution*, December 3, 1971.

23. Caldwell's top assistant was a close political ally and advisor to Talmadge. Moreover, Talmadge's political friends in the Georgia Senate ranked among Carter's most implacable foes.

24. *The Atlanta Journal*, December 3, 1971.

25. Ibid., December 2, 1971.

26. Burson to Carter, n.d., Carter to Burson, June 29, 1971, Record Group 1, Subgroup 15, Series 65, Carter Papers; *LaGrange Daily News*, December 16, 1971; *Macon Telegraph*, December 5, 1971.

27. Record Group 1, Subgroup 15, Series 75, Carter Papers, contains numerous copies of resolutions passed by veterans' groups opposing movement of the Department of Veterans Service.

28. *The Atlanta Journal*, November 10, 16, 1971; *The Atlanta Constitution*, November 16, 1971.

29. *The Atlanta Constitution*, November 18, 19, 1971; *The Atlanta Journal*, November 18, 1971.

29. *The Atlanta Constitution*, November 18, 19, 1971; *The Atlanta Journal*, November 19, 1971.

30. Carter to Bob Young, April 24, 1972, Record Group 1, Subgroup 1, Series 5, Carter Papers.

31. *The Atlanta Constitution*, November 22, December 17, 1971; *The Atlanta Journal*, November 17, 1971; Linder to Carter, November 18, 1971, Record Group 1, Subgroup 15, Series 65, Carter Papers.

32. Linder to Paul C. Pritchard, April 29, 1971, Record Group 1, Subgroup 15, Series 65, Carter Papers; *Atlanta Constitution*, December 17, 1971.

33. *The Atlanta Constitution*, January 5, 1972; Carter to Richardson, January 5, 19, 1972, and Richardson to Carter, January 12, 1972, Record Group 1, Subgroup 1, Series 5, Carter Papers.

34. *The Atlanta Constitution*, December 13, 1971; *The Atlanta Journal*, December 29, 1971. See Record Group 1, Subgroup 15, Series 66, Carter Papers, for examples of this correspondence.

35. *Macon Telegraph*, December 5, 1971; Linder Interview; Maddex Interview.

36. Carter to Beattie, November 23, 1971, Record Group 1, Subgroup 1. Series 5, Carter Papers.

37. *The Atlanta Constitution*, December 23, 1971; *The Atlanta Journal*, December 23, 1971; *Augusta Chronicle*, December 23, 1971.

38. *Macon Telegraph*, December 31, 1971.

39. *The Newnan Times-Herald*, December 16, 1971.

40. Ibid.; *The Atlanta Journal*, December 14, 1971; *The Atlanta Constitution*, December 14, 1971.

41. *Waycross Journal-Herald*, December 20, 1971.

42. Those involved in the reorganization effort concluded that opposition from constitutional officers could not have been avoided. Linder Interview, Maddex Interview; Holloway Interview.

CHAPTER 5. SELLING REORGANIZATION TO THE LEGISLATURE

1. Minutes, Executive Committee, Reorganization and Management Improvement Study, March 31 and April 16, 1971, Record Group 1, Subgroup 15, Series 67, Carter Papers.

2. Work Program, Reorganization and Management Improvement Study, Record Group 1, Subgroup 15, Series 77, ibid.

3. Status Summary, Public Awareness Program, Record Group 1, Subgroup 15, Series 77, ibid.; Linder to Al Holloway, July 13, 1971, and Linder to "All Group Leaders," August 23, 1971, Record Group 1, Subgroup 15, Series 65, ibid.; Minutes, Executive Committee, Reorganization and Management Improvement Study, Record Group 1, Subgroup 15, Series 67, ibid.; Progress Report, Reorganization and Management Improvement Study, May 31, 1971, Record Group 1, Subgroup 15, Series 68, ibid.; Carter to Holley, December 28, 1971, Record Group 1, Subgroup 1, Series 5, ibid.

4. Carter to George Busbee, July 21, 1971, Carter to Al Holloway, July 20, 1971, and Carter to George L. Smith, July 20, 1971, ibid.

5. Paul C. Broun to Carter, August 5, 1971, Carter to Jack Fincher, August 16, 1971, Hamilton Jordan to Carter, n.d., Carter to Ronald Adams, July 11, 1971, and Carter to Jimmy Lester, October 7, 1971, ibid.

6. See, for example, Eugene Holley to Carter, September 13, 1971, ibid.

7. This correspondence is scattered throughout Record Group 1, Subgroup 1, Series 5, ibid.

8. *The Atlanta Constitution*, March 13, 1971.

9. Ibid.

10. Ibid., October 27, 1971.

11. Cloyd Hall to Carter, July 20, 1971, and Carter to Holley, December 28, 1971, Record Group 1, Subgroup 1, Series 5, Carter Papers; G. C. Kaiser to Cloyd Hall, April 21, 1971, Record Group 1, Subgroup 15, Series 75, ibid. Nunn headed the Goals for Georgia program, Levitas managed Carter's consumer legislation in the House, and Burrus served as the administration's floor leader in the House of Representatives.

12. *The Atlanta Journal*, July 22, 1971.

13. Holloway to Carter, July 27, 1971, and Carter to Max Cleland, August 20, 1971, Record Group 1, Subgroup 1, Series 5, Carter Papers; *The Atlanta Constitution*, July 28, 1971.

14. Holley to Democratic state senators, August 20, 1971, Record Group 1, Subgroup 1, Series 5, Carter Papers.

15. *The Atlanta Journal and Constitution*, June 26, 1977; *Georgia Statistical Register*, p. 413.

16. *The Atlanta Journal*, July 22, 1971.

17. Holley to Democratic state senators, August 20, 1971, Record Group 1, Subgroup 1, Series 5, Carter Papers.

18. *The Atlanta Constitution*, August 20, 1971.

19. Ibid., August 25, 26, 1971.

20. Ibid.

21. Ibid., August 27, 1971; Carter to Rex Woods, August 30, 1971, Record Group 1, Subgroup 1, Series 5, Carter Papers.

22. Carter to Holley, September 2, 8, 1971, and Holley to Carter, September 13, 1971, Record Group 1, Subgroup 1, Series 5, Carter Papers.

23. Carter to George L. Smith, August 9, 1971, ibid.; *The Atlanta Constitution*, September 23, 24, 28, 29, 1971; *The Atlanta Journal*, September 29, 1971.

24. *The Atlanta Constitution*, September 23, 1971.

25. Ibid., December 11, 1971; *Gainesville Daily Times*, December 13, 1971; *The Atlanta Journal*, December 11, 1971.

26. *The Atlanta Constitution*, December 11, 1971.

27. Charles Moritz, ed., *Current Biography Yearbook, 1977* (New York: H. W. Wilson Co., 1977), pp. 262-64.

28. *The Atlanta Constitution*, August 5, 1971.

29. Carter to Marvin Griffin, August 30, 1971, Record Group 1, Subgroup 1, Series 5, Carter Papers.

30. *Augusta Chronicle*, December 1, 1971; *The Atlanta Constitution*, December 10, 1971; *Gainesville Daily Times*, December 20, 1971.

31. *The Atlanta Constitution*, December 18, 1971; *The Atlanta Journal*, January 11, 1972; Suit to Carter, February 26, 1971, and Carter to Suit, March 6, 1971, Record Group 1, Subgroup 1, Series 5, Carter Papers.

32. Mike Egan to Carter, September 1, 1971, Carter to Egan, September 2, 1971, and Carter to Stan Collins, September 1, 1971, Record Group 1, Subgroup 1, Series 5, Carter Papers.

33. For example, Hamilton Jordan to Senator Jim Tysinger, n.d., ibid.; Linder to Paul Coverdell, August 6, 1971, Record Group 1, Subgroup 15, Series 65; Oliver Bateman to Carter, January 29, and November 22, 1971, Record Group 1, Subgroup 1, Series 5, ibid.

34. *The Atlanta Constitution*, November 25, 1971.

35. *Macon News*, November 25, 1971.

36. *The Atlanta Constitution*, December 14-16, 1971.

37. Ibid.

38. Ibid., December 16, 1971.

39. Ibid., February 6, 1972, August 10, 1973; *Georgia Statistical Register, 1971-1972*, p. 411.

40. *The Atlanta Constitution*, December 14, 1971; Peggy Rainwater to Carter, n.d., Record Group 1, Subgroup 7, Series 67, Carter Papers.

41. *The Atlanta Journal*, December 17, 1971; *Waycross Journal-*

Herald, December 18, 1971; *Savannah Morning News*, December 18, 1971.

42. *Athens Banner-Herald*, December 19, 1971; *Columbus Enquirer*, November 26, 1971.

43. *Macon News*, November 25, 1971.

44. *Waycross Journal-Herald*, December 18, 1971.

45. *Savannah Morning News*, December 23, 1971.

46. *Statesboro Herald*, December 14, 1971.

47. *Marietta Daily Journal*, December 14, 1971.

48. *Macon News*, November 25, 1971.

49. Ibid.

50. *The Atlanta Journal*, December 11, 1971; *The Atlanta Constitution*, December 11, 1971.

51. *Gainesville Daily Times*, December 13, 1971.

52. Ibid.; *The Atlanta Journal*, December 11, 1971; *The Atlanta Constitution*, December 11, 1971.

53. *The Atlanta Journal and Constitution*, December 26, 1971.

54. Ibid., December 19, 1971.

55. *Savannah Morning News*, December 23, 1971; *Gwinnett Daily News*. December 21, 1971; Lester G. Maddox, *Speaking Out: The Autobiography of Lester Garfield Maddox* (New York: Doubleday, 1975), pp. 141, 142.

56. See Record Group 1, Subgroup 7, Series 67, Carter Papers, for precedents and legal briefs supporting the constitutionality of HB 1.

57. Chaps. 4 and 5 contain numerous examples of such charges.

58. *Savannah Morning News*, December 23, 1971; *News of Gwinnett*, December 24, 1971; Carter to Senator Steve Reynolds, December 28, 1971, Record Group 1, Subgroup 1, Series 5, Carter Papers.

59. *The Atlanta Constitution*, November 12, 17, 1971.

60. Ibid.

CHAPTER 6. THE FRUITS OF PLANNING: LEGISLATORS DEBATE THE REORGANIZATION PLAN

1. *Early County News*, December 16, 1971.

2. *The Atlanta Constitution*, January 5, 1972.

3. Ibid., January 9, 1972.

4. Memorandum, Tom Linder to Carter, January 6, 1972, Record Group 1, Subgroup 15, Series 65, Carter Papers.

5. *The Atlanta Constitution*, January 6, 1972.

6. Ibid., January 7, 1972.

7. Ibid., January 8, 1972.
8. *The Atlanta Journal,* January 6, 1972.
9. Ibid., January 8, 1972; *The Atlanta Constitution,* January 8, 1972.
10. *The Atlanta Constitution,* January 9, 1972.
11. Ibid.
12. Ibid., January 10, 1972.
13. Ibid.
14. Ibid., January 11, 1972.
15. Ibid.
16. *Journal of the Senate,* January 11, 1972.
17. *The Atlanta Constitution,* January 12, 1972.
18. Ibid.
19. Ibid.
20. Ibid.
21. Ibid.
22. Ibid.
23. Ibid.
24. Ibid.; *The Atlanta Journal,* January 12, 1972.
25. *The Atlanta Constitution,* January 13, 1972.
26. Ibid.
27. Ibid.
28. Ibid.
29. Ibid., January 14, 1972; *Journal of the House of Representatives,* January 13, 1972.
30. *Journal of the House of Representatives,* January 14, 1972; *The Atlanta Journal,* January 14, 1972; *The Atlanta Constitution,* January 15, 1972.
31. *The Atlanta Constitution,* January 15, 17, 1972.
32. *Journal of the House of Representatives,* January 17, 1972; *The Atlanta Constitution,* January 18, 1972.
33. *The Atlanta Constitution,* January 18, 1972.
34. Carter to George L. Smith, January 18, 1972, Record Group 1, Subgroup 1, Series 5, Carter Papers.
35. *Journal of House of Representatives,* January 18, 1972.
36. *The Atlanta Constitution,* January 19, 1972; *The Atlanta Journal,* January 19, 1972.
37. *The Atlanta Constitution,* January 15, 1972.
38. *Journal of the Senate,* January 18-20, 1972; *The Atlanta Constitution,* January 21, 1972.
39. *The Atlanta Constitution,* January 22, 1972.
40. *The Atlanta Journal,* January 24, 1972.

41. Ibid.; *The Atlanta Constitution*, January 24, 1972.

42. *The Atlanta Constitution*, January 24, 1972.

43. Ibid., January 26, 1972.

44. Ibid., January 31, 1972, and February 1, 1972.

45. Ibid., February 3, 1972.

46. Ibid.

47. Ibid., February 4, 1972.

48. Ibid., February 5, 1972; *The Atlanta Journal and Constitution*, February 6, 1972.

49. *The Atlanta Journal*, March 27, 31, 1978, and April 20, 1978; *The Atlanta Constitution*, March 25, 1978; *The Atlanta Journal and Constitution*, March 19, 26, 1978.

50. *Georgia Statistical Register, 1971-1972*, p. 415; *The Atlanta Constitution*, November 20, 1976, and March 19, 27, 1978.

51. *The Atlanta Constitution*, February 21, 1972.

52. *Journal of the House of Representatives*, February 21, 1972; *The Atlanta Constitution*, February 23, 1972.

53. *The Atlanta Constitution*, February 24, 1972.

54. *The Atlanta Journal*, February 25, 1972.

55. *Journal of the Senate*, March 1, 1972.

56. *The Atlanta Constitution*, March 3, 1972.

57. Ibid., March 5, 1972.

58. *The Atlanta Journal*, March 9, 1972.

59. *The Atlanta Constitution*, March 10, 1972.

60. Ibid.; *The Atlanta Journal*, March 10, 1972.

61. *The Atlanta Constitution*, March 10, 11, 1972.

CHAPTER 7. HOW CARTER DID IT: AN ANALYSIS OF LEGISLATIVE VOTING BEHAVIOR IN THE GEORGIA SENATE

1. Carter to Smith, March 15, 1972, Record Group 1, Subgroup 1, Series 5, Carter Papers.

2. See, for example, *The Atlanta Constitution*, February 2-4, 24, 1972.

3. Ibid., January 11, 1972.

4. Ibid., February 6, 1972.

5. Ibid., February 3, 1971.

6. Ibid., January 9, 1972.

7. Ibid., February 6, 1972.

8. Bruce Galphin, *The Riddle of Lester Maddox* (Atlanta: Camelot, 1968); *The Atlanta Journal and Constitution*, May 7, 1978.

9. *The Atlanta Constitution*, February 24, 1972.

10. Ibid.

11. Ibid., March 2, 1972.

12. Carter to Legislative Control Team, February 8, 1972, Record Group 1, Subgroup 1, Series 5, Carter Papers.

13. Ibid.

14. Ibid.

15. *The Atlanta Journal and Constitution*, March 12, 1972.

16. Ibid.

17. Ibid., May 5, 1972.

18. Interviews with those involved in the reorganization effort provided much of the documentation concerning Carter's personal lobbying. Almost all those interviewed testified to Carter's effectiveness in such endeavors. Holloway Interview; Linder Interview; Hugh Carter to the author, n.d.

19. *The Atlanta Constitution*, March 5, 1972.

20. Record Group 1, Subgroup 1, Series 5, Carter Papers, contains numerous examples of the way in which gubernatorial patronage was used to reward and penalize legislators.

21. *The Atlanta Constitution*, March 2, 1972.

22. Ibid., April 4, 1972; *The Atlanta Journal and Constitution*, June 4, 1972.

23. The Statistical Package for the Social Sciences (SPSS), Version 6, was used for all statistical procedures in this chapter. For a description and analysis of the various programs available, see *SPSS*, 2d ed. (New York: McGraw Hill, 1972). For a discussion of Guttman scaling, see Lee F. Anderson et al., *Legislative Roll-Call Analysis* (Evanston, Ill.: Northwestern University Press, 1966); Duncan MacRae, Jr., *Issues and Parties in Legislative Voting: Methods of Statistical Analysis* (New York: Harper & Row, 1970).

24. See Aage Clausen, "Measurement Identity in the Longitudinal Analysis of Legislative Voting," *The American Political Science Review* 61 (1967): 1020-1035.

25. For a discussion of cluster bloc analysis, see Anderson, *Legislative Roll-Call Analysis*, chap. 4. David B. Truman, *The Congressional Party: A Case Study* (New York: Wiley, 1959), provides an example of the use of cluster bloc analysis.

26. Robert Dahl, "The Concept of Power," *Behavioral Science* 2 (1957): 201-215; Richard Jensen, "Power and Success Scores," *Historical Methods Newsletter* 1 (1968): 1-6.

27. For this analysis a .66 agreement score was used.

28. Discriminate analysis is a statistical procedure whereby a col-

lection of discriminating variables are used to identify and measure the characteristics on which two or more groups differ. The step method of selecting independent variables for entry into the analysis was used to discover the relative discriminating power of each variable. Two criteria were used to measure differences between groups: The overall multivariate F ratio which measures the discriminating power of a particular variable after controlling for the discrimination achieved by other selected variables; and Rao's V, a measure indicating which variable, when added to other discriminating variables, provides the most overall separation of the groups. The higher the F-score, or the greater the increase in Rao's V, the more discriminating power a particular variable had.

29. Twelve issue area scales were constructed as a result. Senators were then placed into high, medium, and low categories depending on their scale position. Approximately one-third of the Senators were located in each category. Values were then assigned to the various categories—high (1), medium (2), and low (3)—and mean scale scores computed. Based on those scale scores, the senators were then placed in one of three groups—liberal, swing, and conservative.

CHAPTER 8. CONCLUSION: JIMMY CARTER'S LEGISLATIVE STYLE

1. *The Atlanta Journal*, January 12, 1972.

2. *The Atlanta Constitution*, January 9, 1972.

3. Ibid., October 2, 1971.

4. In his autobiography, *Why Not the Best?* (Nashville: Boardman Press, 1975), Carter provides an account of his experiences in the Georgia General Assembly, see chap. 8. (It is also interesting to note that Carter did much the same thing during the early months of his presidency.)

5. Carter vetoed 150 bills and resolutions during his governorship.

6. Legislative logrolling refers to the practice among legislators of voting for each other's bills, especially on pork-barrel legislation.

7. Robert Holmes, a political scientist and state legislator representing a predominantly black Atlanta constituency, expressed this view most pointedly. "A Georgian in the White House: Reflections on the First Year of the Carter Presidency," Georgia Studies Symposium, February 3, 1978.

8. Dudley Crosson to Lamar Plunkett, December 13, 1972; Plunkett to Jordan, December 27, 1972; Jordan to Crosson, January 12, 1973, Record Group 1, Subgroup 1, Series 5, Carter Papers.

9. Tim F. Mauch to Carter, February 14, 1972, ibid.

10. Carter to Parker, March 22, 1974, ibid.

11. Among the examples in Record Group 1, Subgroup 1, Series 5, Carter Papers, see Jordan to Carter, March 7, 1973; Jordan to David Tysinger, February 7, 1972, ibid.

12. *The Atlanta Constitution*, November 27, 1971; *The Atlanta Journal*, November 28, 1971.

13. *The Atlanta Journal and Constitution*, January 9, 1972.

14. Ibid.

15. Ibid.

16. Mattie S. Anderson, "Governor Jimmy Carter's Goals for Georgia: A Study of Carter's Commitment to Planning and Citizen Participation," seminar paper, Georgia State University, 1978; Jimmy Carter, *Why Not the Best?* (Nashville: Boardman Press, 1975), p. 149; Maddex Interview; Linder Interview.

17. For examples of Carter's relationship with influential Republican leaders in the state, see his correspondence with Michael Egan, Hal Suit, Paul Coverdell, Harry Geisinger, John W. Savage, Jr., and Oliver Bateman, Record Group 1, Subgroup 1, Series 5, Carter Papers.

18. Maddex Interview; *The Atlanta Constitution*, June 15, 1971.

19. Johnny Martin to Frank Moore, October 9, 1973, Record Group 1, Subgroup 1, Series 5, Carter Papers.

20. *The Atlanta Constitution*, February 19, 1971.

21. Ibid.

22. *The Atlanta Journal*, April 12 and June 1, 1972.

23. Ibid., May 18, 1973.

24. The Carter Papers contain numerous examples of his efforts to reconcile differences with antagonistic legislators. See, for example, his extensive correspondence with Culver Kidd and Eugene Holley, Record Group 1, Subgroup 1, Series 5, Carter Papers.

25. *The Atlanta Journal and Constitution*, June 4, 1972; *The Atlanta Journal*, August 9, 1972; *The Atlanta Constitution*, April 6 and August 11, 1972.

26. *The Atlanta Constitution*, August 3, 10, 1972; Carter to Dick Pettys, August 2, 1972, Record Group 1, Subgroup 1, Series 5, Carter Papers.

27. *The Atlanta Constitution*, August 10, 1972.

28. Recognizing the needs of senators affected by redistricting to build political support in the new counties added to their senatorial districts, Carter used contingency fund monies, gubernatorial appointments, and Bert Lance's State Highway Department to this end. For an especially good example of this activity, see the Governor's corre-

spondence with Hugh Carter in Record Group 1, Subgroup 1, Series 5, Carter Papers.

29. *The Atlanta Journal and Constitution*, January 9, 1972; Holloway Interview; Linder Interview; Hugh Carter to the author, n.d. By the end of his term the Governor had become somewhat more sensitive to such political niceties; see, for example, Carter to Frank Eldridge and others, February 28, 1974, Record Group 1, Subgroup 1, Series 5, Carter Papers.

30. *Georgia Statistical Register, 1972-1978*, p. 582; Hugh Carter, *Cousin Beedie and Cousin Hot: My Life with the Carter Family of Plains, Georgia* (Englewood Cliffs, N.J.: Prentice Hall, 1978).

31. Holloway Interview; Linder Interview.

32. Record Group 1, Subgroup 1, Series 5, Carter Papers, contains numerous examples of such patronage activities.

33. See the Epilogue. Interestingly, Ward had been denied admission to the University of Georgia Law School because of race and had successfully sued for admission.

34. Johnson to Carter, July 12, 1971, Record Group 1, Subgroup 1, Series 5, Carter Papers.

35. A good account of Georgia's political response to the civil rights movement is contained in Numan V. Bartley, *From Thurmond to Wallace: Political Tendencies in Georgia, 1948-1968* (Baltimore: Johns Hopkins University Press, 1970). See also Bartley's *The Rise of Massive Resistance: Race and Politics in the South during the 1950's* (Baton Rouge: Louisiana State University Press, 1969), and his contribution to Kenneth Coleman et al., *A History of Georgia* (Athens: University of Georgia Press, 1977).

EPILOGUE

1. Quoted in Leslie Wheeler, *Jimmy Who? An Examination of Presidential Candidate Jimmy Carter: The Man, His Career, His Stands on the Issues* (New York: Barron's, 1976), p. 76.

2. Ibid., p. 74.

BIBLIOGRAPHICAL ESSAY____

For over a quarter century, virtually every analysis of politics in the modern South has begun, as it should, with V. O. Key's *Southern Politics in State and Nation* (New York: Knopf, 1949). As Jimmy Carter's election to the presidency so vividly illustrates, however, much has changed in the South since Key published his classic study at mid-century. As a consequence, efforts have been made to bring Key's analysis up-to-date. By far the most successful is Jack Bass and Walter DeVries, *The Transformation of Southern Politics: Social Change and Political Consequences Since 1945* (New York: Basic Books, 1976). Less useful but still valuable is Neal R. Pierce, *The Deep South States of America: People, Politics, and Power in the Seven Deep South States* (New York: W. W. Norton, 1974). Other valuable analyses of southern politics, less closely tied to Key's methodological structure, include Monroe Lee Billington, *The Political South in the Twentieth Century* (New York: Scribner's, 1975); William C. Havard, ed., *The Changing Politics of the South* (Baton Rouge: Louisiana State University Press, 1972); Numan V. Bartley, *The Rise of Massive Resistance: Race and Politics in the South during the 1950s* (Baton Rouge: Louisiana State University Press, 1969), and Bartley and Hugh Davis Graham, *Southern Politics and the Second Reconstruction* (Baltimore: Johns Hopkins University Press, 1975); Reese Cleghorn, *Climbing Jacob's Ladder: The Arrival of Negroes in Southern Politics* (New York: Harcourt, Brace, Jovanovich, 1967); Stephen F. Lawson, *Black Ballots: Voting Rights in the South, 1944-1969* (New York: Columbia University Press, 1976); and Charles P. Roland, *The Improbable Era: The South Since World War II* (Lexington, Kentucky: University of Kentucky Press, 1975).

Numan V. Bartley has firmly established himself as the leading authority on modern Georgia politics. His contribution to Kenneth C. Coleman et al., *A History of Georgia* (Athens: University of Georgia Press, 1975), contains the best available survey of modern Georgia politics. In *From Thurmond to Wallace: Political Tendencies in Georgia, 1948-1968* (Baltimore: Johns Hopkins University Press, 1970), Bartley employed a quantitatively based analysis to examine voting trends and political behavior in Georgia, and his "Jimmy Carter and the Politics of the New South," *The Forum Series* (St. Louis: Forum Press, 1979), provides a survey of the Carter family history which attempts to place Jimmy Carter in the perspective of modern southern politics. The books by Key, Bass and DeVries, and Pierce also contain interesting chapters on Georgia. Useful background information can be found in Joseph L. Bernd, *Grass Roots Politics in Georgia: The County Unit System and the Importance of the Individual Voting Community in Bifactional Elections, 1942-1954* (Ann Arbor: University Microfilms, 1960), and Bernd, "Georgia: Static and Dynamic," *The Changing Politics of the South*, ed. William C. Harvard (Baton Rouge: Louisiana State University Press, 1972). Reg Murphy and Hal Gulliver, past and present editors of *The Atlanta Constitution*, also provide an analysis of the state of Georgia politics in *The Southern Strategy* (New York: Schribner's, 1971). Matt W. Williamson, "Contemporary Tendencies toward a Two-Party System in Georgia" (Ph.D. dissertation, University of Virginia, 1969), contains a useful analysis of party divisions. The Georgia General Assembly and the relationship between the governor and the legislature is examined in Val B. Mixon, "The Growth of the Legislative Powers of the Governor of Georgia: A Survey of the Legislative Program of Governor Herman Talmadge, 1949-1954" (M.A. thesis, Emory University, 1959); Hugh M. Thomason, "The Legislative Process in Georgia" (Ph.D. dissertation, Emory University, 1961); and Jane W. Gurganus, "A Study of the Composition of the General Assembly of Georgia, 1959-1966" (M.A. thesis, Emory University, 1966). In "Governor Jimmy Carter: Idealist or Realist, A Study of Carter's Commitment to Citizen Participation and Planning in the Goals for Georgia Program" (M.A. thesis, Georgia State University, 1979), Mattie S. Anderson used the Carter Papers extensively to produce a provocative study of Carter's philosophy of government.

Of the numerous books that have appeared on Jimmy Carter since his nomination and subsequent election to the presidency, none can be classified as truly scholarly, and few include more than passing references to his governorship. Theodore H. White's announcement that he would not write a book on the 1976 presidential campaign brought several pretenders to the fore, all seeking to lay claim to

White's undisputed title as the master of campaign trivia. The best of these studies is Jules Witcover's *Marathon: The Pursuit of the Presidency, 1972-1976* (New York: Viking, 1977). Witcover, however, has only scattered references to Carter's governorship, and these are more incidental than substantive. James T. Wooten, because of his familiarity with the Georgia scene before 1976, might have been expected to produce a more concrete and tangible account, but the result, *Dasher: The Roots and the Rising of Jimmy Carter* (New York: Summit Books, 1978), is highly impressionistic and generally disappointing, although well written. Bartley's treatment of these years in *A History of Georgia* and Leslie Wheeler's *Jimmy Who? An Examination of Presidential Candidate Jimmy Carter: The Man, His Career, His Stands on the Issues* (New York: Barron's, 1976), provide the best available accounts of the gubernatorial years. Although his analysis does not include an account of Maddox's years as Georgia's lieutenant governor, Bruce Galphin's *The Riddle of Lester Maddox: An Unauthorized Biography* (Atlanta: Camelot, 1968), includes good background information on Georgia politics and personalities, and, of course, provides insights into the character of Carter's major antagonist during his governorship.

A number of popular biographies of Carter have appeared in print since 1976. Among the more substantive are David Kucharsky, *The Man from Plains: The Mind and Spirit of Jimmy Carter* (New York: Harper and Row, 1976), and William L. Miller, *Yankee from Georgia: The Emergence of Jimmy Carter* (New York: Harper and Row, 1978). Those readers interested in reinforcing existing hostile assumptions about Carter will enjoy Victor Lasky's *Jimmy Carter: The Man and the Myth* (New York: R. Marek, 1979). The master of the scurrilous biography, Lasky manages to portray Carter as both a shrewd Machiavellian and a hopeless incompetent, depending, of course, upon the point he is seeking to make.

As is their wont, the psychohistorians struck early while the market was still hot. Bruce Mazlish and Edwin Diamond wrote "Thrice Born: A Psychohistory of Jimmy Carter's 'Rebirth'," *New York Magazine* (August 30, 1976), and a short time later Lloyd deMause and Henry Ebel edited an anthology entitled *Jimmy Carter and American Fantasy: Psychohistorical Explorations* (New York: Two Continents, 1977). Characterized by inadequate research and highly impressionistic generalizations, these early analyses must be used with extreme caution. Presently, at least two major psychohistories of Carter are under way; and it is hoped they will prove more worthy examples of the psychohistorical art.

Although little attention was paid to Carter's religious convictions during his governorship, the national media seized on this subject during the 1976 presidential campaign and made it a major issue. Since then, it has attracted the attention of several students of religious theology. Nevertheless, in many ways, E. Brooks Holifield's short essay, "The Three Strands of Jimmy Carter's Religion," *New Republic* (June 5, 1976), remains one of the most perceptive accounts. Also useful are James T. Baker, *A Southern Baptist in the White House* (Philadelphia: Westminister Press, 1977); James C. Hefley and Marti Hefley, *The Church that Produced a President: The Remarkable Spiritual Roots of Jimmy Carter* (New York: Wyden Books, 1977); Jessyca Graver, *The Faith of Jimmy Carter* (New York: Manor Books, 1977); and Neils D. Neilsen, Jr., *The Religion of Jimmy Carter* (Nashville: T. Nelson, 1977).

The Carter gubernatorial papers deposited at the Georgia Department of Archives and History constitute by far the most valuable primary source for a study of Carter's term as Georgia's chief executive. An extensive and unusually substantive collection, these papers provide valuable insights into Carter's political character, his leadership and administrative style, and his policy commitments. Unfortunately, none of the other principals involved in Carter's governorship has as yet released his papers, although many are willing to discuss their activities and experiences. Among the published primary sources, Frank Daniel, comp., *Addresses of Jimmy Carter: Governor of Georgia, 1971-1975* (Atlanta: Georgia Department of History and Archives, 1975), is the best. Also worth consulting are Jimmy Carter, *A Government as Good as its People* (New York: Simon and Shuster, 1977), Robert W. Turner, ed., *"I'll Never Lie to You": Jimmy Carter in His Own Words* (New York: Ballantine, 1976), and Bill Adler, *The Wit and Wisdom of Jimmy Carter* (New York: Citadel Press, 1977).

For obvious reasons, few autobiographical accounts have yet appeared that illuminate aspects of Carter's governorship. *Why Not The Best?* (Nashville: Boardman Press, 1975), Carter's own memoir, contains numerous references to the Georgia political scene and his role in it. Although somewhat sophomoric in style and composition, this is one of the more interesting and revealing memoirs to appear from the pen of an active political figure in recent years, especially in this age of ghost-written accounts. *Speaking Out: The Autobiography of Lester Maddox* (New York: Doubleday, 1975) also contains valuable information reflecting Maddox's relationship with Carter and the four-year struggle they waged for control of state government in Georgia. Hugh Carter's *Cousin Beedie and Cousin Hot: My Life with the Carter Family of Plains, Georgia* (Englewood Cliffs, N.J.: Prentice Hall, 1978), besides providing an invaluable description of the worm and cricket culture, contains useful information on Jimmy Carter's early life and some material on his governorship. Hugh Carter helped manage his cousin's 1970 gubernatorial campaign and served as an administration floor leader in the Georgia Senate during Jimmy Carter's governorship.

INDEX

ABOUT THE AUTHOR_____

GARY M FINK is Professor of History at Georgia State University. His earlier books include *Labor's Search for Political Order*, *Biographical Dictionary of American Labor Leaders* (ed.) (Greenwood Press, 1974), *Labor Unions* (ed.) (Greenwood Press, 1977), and *Essays in Southern Labor History* (ed.) (Greenwood Press, 1977).